Thinking How to Live

Thinking How to Live

ALLAN GIBBARD

HARVARD UNIVERSITY PRESS
Cambridge, Massachusetts
London, England   2003

The lyrics on p. 48, Chapter 3, are from *Trial by Jury*, by W. S. Gilbert

Library of Congress Cataloging-in-Publication Data
Gibbard, Allan.
   Thinking how to live / Allan Gilbert.
      p. cm.
Includes bibliographical references and index.
ISBN 0-674-01167-8
1. Expressivism (Ethics)   2. Normativity (Ethics)   I. Title.
BJ1500.E94G53 2003
170'.42—dc21   2003047801

To Beth with love

Contents

Preface

A family, a house, a book, or a career emerges from decisions by the thousands. It is the upshot of answers to a multitude of questions: whether to wed her, what flooring to use, what to explore next. The aim of this book is to ask about these questions. I can ask myself how to spend the next few minutes, whether to attend a conference, or how to spend next year. I can ask myself too what to believe: Experts debate the extent to which differences in genes from person to person make for contrasting personalities, and I can investigate and ask myself what to believe on this score, given the evidence. And I can ask myself how to feel about a friend's divorce or rivalry with a friend for a job.

These don't strike us as questions of fact alone; in asking what to do, I don't seem to be seeking a *fact* of what to do. Facts, to be sure, do bear on what to do: many facts bear, say, on whether to marry one's love. But is there a fact of *whether to marry her?* That might sound bizarre. Still, closely related questions do have more the ring of fact. *Ought* I to wed her? Does it *make most sense* to wed her? Is wedding her *the thing to do?* And if it is, is that a fact? Talk of fact here might sound tendentious, but a claim to facthood for *ought*s is one that philosophers do make; whole branches of philosophy deal in such purported facts. Some philosophical theories of fact leave no doubt of facts like these—while others leave no doubt that there are no such facts.

The hypothesis of this book is easy to state: *Thinking what I ought to do is thinking what to do.* The concept of ought, I propose, is to be explained on this pattern—not for every sense of the term, but for a crucial sense that figures in a wide array of concepts. These are *normative* concepts, concepts "fraught with ought", as Wilfrid Sellars put it: moral concepts, concepts of rationality, concepts of the shameful or the enviable, of meriting credence or meriting aesthetic admiration, and other concepts. Thinking what's admirable, for instance, is thinking what to admire—this is another instance of the hypothesis. There is no special mystery, then, in normative concepts, even though they behave in ways that have led some philosophers to speak mysteriously of "non-natural qualities". If we understand concluding what to do, then we understand concluding what a person ought to do.

Does this mean that there are no facts of what I ought to do, no truths and falsehoods? Previously I thought so, but other philosophers challenged me to say what this denial could mean. In this book, I withdraw the denial and turn non-commital. In one sense there clearly are "facts" of what a person ought to do, and in a sense of the word 'true' there is a truth of the matter. That's a minimalist sense, in which "It's *true* that pain is to be avoided" just amounts to saying that pain is to be avoided—and likewise for "It's a fact that". Perhaps, as I used to think, there are senses too in which we can sensibly debate whether *ought* conclusions are true or false. Nothing in this book, though, depends on whether there is any such sense.

What I hope to show is this: in a sense in which there *are* facts of what to do, these facts act in many ways much like familiar, uncontentious facts; they act much like the fact, say, that the moon circles the earth. Indeed in a way, normative facts will turn out to be plain old natural facts. In another way, indeed, normative facts turn out to be non-natural facts—though believing such facts, I claim, is no mystery; it consists just in settling on what to do.

But all this is to get ahead of myself. Is there a *fact* of whether marrying her is the thing to do? Is it a natural fact? Straight yes-or-no answers would tell us little, but these questions point to more precise ones that do have clear answers, if I am right. They point as well to questions that are harder to formulate and to answer, questions that greatly matter in life. What basis can there be for answers to questions of how to live? Do we discover how best to live, or is it a matter of arbitrary choice—or what? I promise no straight answers to these deeper questions, but they are the kinds of questions that spur my inquiries.

Years ago I published a book, *Wise Choices, Apt Feelings*, which advocates a set of answers to these metaquestions, to these questions about our normative questions. Moral questions, I argued, are at base questions of how to feel about things people do or might do. Questions of rational action, questions of what it makes sense to do, are at base questions of what to do. Answers to these questions, I maintained in that book, are not answers of fact; they are not, strictly speaking, true or false. The book was wide-ranging: I ventured a loose psychological theory of moral judgments and judgments of rationality, placing these judgments within a naturalistic picture of humanity and human activities. We are a complex species because of billions of years of natural selection, including millions of years adapting us genetically to an ecology of intense social interaction. I speculated on peculiarly human emotions, and on a "normative control system" that in some measure governs our emotions. Philosophical discussion of ethics I painted as a refinement of an adaptive human activity, of "normative discussion", as I called it, discussion that serves to coordinate our feelings and our actions in "evolutionary bargaining situations". I talked of the ways in which our moral and other normative judgments might count as objective, and explored, in broad terms, how to conduct moral inquiry in light of the kind of metatheory I had developed.

Why, then, another book? The scope of this new work is much narrower than the previous one; in this book I extend just one of the lines I ventured in *Wise Choices, Apt Feelings*. Its central thesis I retain, that normative questions are, at base, questions of what to do, what to believe, and how to feel about things. I treat this as a hypothesis, asking mostly not whether it is correct, but what the consequences would be if it were. These consequences are far-reaching, more so than I managed to discover in *Wise Choices, Apt Feelings*. These further consequences are a main theme of this book. I start simply from us as planners, able to think what to do now and in future contingencies, and conducting thought experiments on what to do in plights that are merely hypothetical. From this starting point, familiar normative phenomena emerge: We see how *ought*s "supervene" on natural *is*s, the ways that what a person ought to do supervenes on the natural facts of her situation. A kind of naturalism is a further consequence: there is a broadly natural property, I argue, that *constitutes* being the thing to do. The system that results mimics most closely the "non-naturalism" of G. E. Moore, Henry Sidgwick, A. C. Ewing, and others. I begin, then, as a naturalist about humanity, about human thinking and planning, but in a sense I end up a non-naturalist about *oughts*. Much of what non-naturalists say is right, I conclude—but this needn't be mysterious to any naturalist.

Simon Blackburn calls the program we share *quasi-realism:* from a basis that excludes normative facts and treats humanity as part of the natural world, I explain why we would have normative concepts that act much as normative realists proclaim. This book I think of as realizing Blackburn's program—though not, perhaps, in a way he would entirely accept. The force of all this, if it works, is to confirm the hypothesis I'm exploring. Suppose that (i) normative realists are right about how normative concepts act, and (ii) my hypothesis has as a consequence that normative concepts act this way. Then the hypothesis explains the phenomena—and no normative realism that extends beyond the hypothesis is needed.

The questions I ask in this book are not directly questions of how to live, and they are not questions of how we ought to live. They are questions *about* these questions. I work toward ways of viewing our lives and our plans for what to do, to think, and to feel; I ask how we can live as thinkers and planners who know that our thinking and planning are a part of the natural order. Any book is delimited, but this one is delimited highly. It isn't a general book on moral or normative philosophy, and I certainly don't put forth its style of inquiry as demonstrating the chief way to do the philosophy of the normative. The problems here are not the ones I would most love to solve. Rather, I choose problems on which I may have found something new to tell philosophical readers. That's a part of my excuse for claiming your attention.

Of course I have fears for this book as well as hopes. One of my fears is that I'll be depending on things that you *have* heard before and that you reject. I'll try to argue for the cogency of what I'm doing, responding to critiques and displaying my account of normative concepts as natural and inevitable. Clearly, though, I can't cover all the grounds you might have for dissent. A greater fear is that the problems that engage me here won't engage you. The book is hard work in many places, and even if it succeeded entirely in its aims, it would tell you only about the *structure* of thought—perhaps more than you want to know. At the outset I'll work to convince you that my structural questions matter, that they tie to concerns that we all must share. From then on, though, I'll go about my business, without trying at every point to persuade you of its moment. My focus will mostly be on trying to get matters right if I can. The book, I recognize, traces a long path from the initial concerns that motivate my inquiry. We must all keep asking whether the path is leading somewhere it's worth great effort to go. Mostly, though, I'll work on constructing the path.

~ THIS BOOK has been long in the writing. I was supported over the years by the University of Michigan as a Nelson Fellow in the Department of Philosophy, by a sabbatical, and in other ways. For my sabbatical year 1998–1999, I was kindly hosted as a visitor at the Centre for Philosophy of Natural and Social Science, London School of Economics, supported by an ACLS Fellowship from the American Council of Learned Societies and by a National Endowment for the Humanities Fellowship for University Teachers. I am immensely grateful for all this support.

The book includes passages that have appeared elsewhere. I am grateful for publishers' permission to adapt and include passages from the following: "Reply to Blackburn" and "Reply to Railton," *Philosophical Issues* 4, E. Villanueva, ed., *Naturalism and Normativity* (Atascadero, Calif.: Ridgeview, 1993), pp. 52–59, 67–73; "Reply to Blackburn, Carson, Hill, and Railton," *Philosophy and Phenomenological Research* 52 (1992): 969–980; "Preference and Preferability," in C. Fehige, G. Meggle, and U. Wessels, eds., *Preferences* (Berlin: de Gruyter, 1998), pp. 239–259. After I began work on the book itself in 1996, I adapted material from the developing manuscript for part of the article "Knowing What to Do, Seeing What to Do," in Philip Stratton-Lake, ed., *Ethical Intuitionism* (Oxford: Oxford University Press, 2002), and for most of "Normative and Recognitional Concepts," *Philosophy and Phenomenological Research* 64:1 (2002): 151–167. I thank the publishers for permission to use this material.

Over the years I have presented drafts and predecessors of various parts of the book in numerous venues, and benefited from many discussions. Before I started organizing a book, I presented material that later went into it at the Sociedad Filosofica Ibero-Americana, at the Joint Session of the Aristotelian Society and Mind Association, and to philosophy departments, conferences, and colloquia at Indiana University, Bloomington; University of Michigan, Ann Arbor; Universität des Saarlandes; University of Florida, Gainesville; University of North

Carolina, Chapel Hill; University of California, San Diego; Harvard University; New York University Law School; University of Chicago; Rutgers University; and University of Nebraska, Lincoln. After I began the book itself, I presented adaptations of drafts and other material that eventually was adapted into the book at the Pacific Division of the American Philosophical Association, in Paris at Centre de Recherche en Epistémologie Appliquée, in Italy at the Summer School on Analytic Philosophy in Parma and at a conference on "Justification and Meaning" in Siena, and also to philosophy departments, conferences, and colloquia at the University of Connecticut, Storrs; Bowling Green State University of Ohio; University of Sydney; Australia National University Research School in the Social Sciences; University of Sheffield; University of Leeds; University of Stirling; University of Keele; University of North Carolina, Chapel Hill; Brown University; and Università di Roma–la Sapienza. Discussion on these occasions contributed much to shaping the book. Two of my seminars at the University of Michigan scrutinized draft chapters of the book, and among the people I must thank are Steven Daskal, John Doris, Charles Goodman, Thomas Hofweber, Nadeem Hussain, Robin Kar, Amit Kurlekar, Robert Mabrito, Karen Sam, François Schroeter, Nishiten Shah, Jason Stanley, and Kevin Toh. Among those who in earlier seminars discussed work that was adapted into the book were John Devlin, Craig Duncan, Manyul Im, Samuel Ruhmkopf, Stephen Schulz, and James Woodbridge.

The philosophical influences on the book are far too numerous to mention. Both readers for Harvard University Press provided comments that were very helpful for making final revisions; indeed David Copp gave me thirty remarkable pages of detailed commentary. Among the people who have delivered formal commentaries on material destined for the book are Carla Bagnoli, Simon Blackburn, Roger Crisp, James Dreier, John Hawthorne, Thomas Nagel, Julian Nida-Rümelin, Peter Railton, and Michael Smith. Simon Blackburn has been a major influence on my thinking ever since we discovered in 1984 how similar were the lines on which we had been thinking independently. Many acknowledgments I leave to footnotes, but I should add that I have taken over more ways of thinking from R. M. Hare than the footnotes might indicate. I owe immense thanks to many colleagues, and especially to the "ethics lunch" long anchored by my late colleagues Richard Brandt and William Frankena and continued with Stephen Darwall and Peter Railton; our discussions at these lunches have been a major influence on my thinking. Jason Stanley has worked to set me straight on questions pertaining to linguistics and philosophy. These lists no doubt omit many people who should be included, and I apologize for my lapses and profoundly thank those I should have included. I have mostly not even attempted to acknowledge individually significant conversations, e-mail exchanges, and the like for which I owe thanks.

My family graciously tolerated—encouraged even—the strange life of a philosopher, as I sat with my laptop in the kitchen or in the morning shade on the back deck struggling to get my thoughts into some kind of coherent order. I have watched with love and delight as my sons grew into adults pursuing each his own goals and enthusiasms, Stephen with his technical prowess, his active life, and his watchful eye on how the world works, and George with his fine abilities and accomplishments with languages and linguistics. My wife, Beth, has been the loving mainstay of my life over the whole period of work on this book, from first seeds to completion; she opens new vistas for me with her pursuits and passions, her insight and clear thinking. Who knows if I could have done anything much without the three of them—but for sure I would have found it far less rewarding.

Thinking How to Live

∼ I
Preliminaries

~ 1

Introduction: A Possibility Proof

*H*OLMES IS STALKED by Moriarty. He plans to escape by train, packing as late as possible to conceal his intentions. But by now it may be too late to catch the train, in which case packing is useless. If he has enough time, on the other hand, he might take a hansom cab and stop on the way by the river to investigate. Thinking through the considerations, he decides to start packing.

What kind of thought is his decision to pack? What kind of utterance would express it—"express," that is, in the way a statement of fact expresses a belief in that fact? What kinds of reasoning can figure in his decision? Will his reasonings be confined to the facts, or are there special kinds of reasoning that enter into deciding?

Some of Holmes's thoughts I'll pass over as pretty straightforward: his thoughts, for instance, about when the train is scheduled to leave. Likewise for his thoughts as to how likely he would be to catch the train if he packed quickly and sent for a cab: conditionals like these and their probabilities do raise problems, but they aren't the problems that concern me now. I want instead to focus on thoughts that don't seem just straightforwardly to describe Holmes's circumstances with greater or lesser certainty. Holmes will end his thinking about when to start packing with a decision: he can tell himself, "So start packing now!" He thus can express his decision as an imperative. What reasoning could lead to such an imperatival conclusion? It is hard to see how it could follow from straight facts alone—at least if these are ordinary facts

3

about train schedules, traffic, and the like. What sorts of premises, then, can he reason from?

One possible answer is this: not only is his conclusion imperatival, but so are some of his premises. His premises, rendered fully explicit, include not only descriptive ones like "the cab will take at least half an hour," but also imperatives. He tells himself, "Escape Moriarty!" Imperative out requires imperative in.

Alternatively, there seem to be straight assertions that will do the job. "I must escape Moriarty," Holmes can begin his thinking. His decision too, it seems, he could express with a statement: "I must pack now," or "It's now time to pack," or "Packing is now the thing to do." Perhaps what he needs if he is to come to a decision is just more facts—facts, though, of a special kind, facts of what he *must do* and the like. In his current predicament, he can begin with the fact that he must escape Moriarty. Indeed his decision itself, we might try claiming, consists in recognizing a fact of a special kind: that the time has come to pack, that he now *must* pack. These facts are special in that they seem laden with an importunate "to-be-doneness". Perhaps that's their glory—or perhaps it makes such putative facts "queer" enough to worry about, as Mackie would put it (Mackie, *Ethics*, 1977).

These alternatives are reminiscent of perennially opposing views in moral theory, in metaethics. There is an advantage, though, to facing the problem in the context of practical reasoning, of thinking what to do. Deciding what to do seems not just straightforwardly to be deciding on some matter of fact. Perhaps the same could be said for moral conclusions: to conclude that something is wrong, we may want to claim, is *ipso facto* to be in some way against doing it. But this claim about morals is controversial; leading moral philosophers declare themselves to be "externalists" with regard to morals. A "sensible knave" like Moriarty, they say, can conclude that fraud is a grievous wrong, and treat that as in no way bearing on questions of whether to commit fraud. This knave may be making no mistake in reasoning; he just doesn't care in the right way about moral facts he fully recognizes. Moral findings have direct import for what to do, such externalists tell us, only if one cares about morality.[1] Now I myself think that moral thought, if it is coherent, can only be an outgrowth of moral concern. But to say how I

1. For externalist arguments, see, for instance, Boyd, "How to Be a Moral Realist" (1988) and Brink, *Moral Realism* (1989).

think such thought works, I don't need initially to wade into the issues of internalism versus externalism for morals. Start instead, I propose, with something that might be less controversial: that conclusions on *what to do* have an automatic bearing on what to do. I put this as a tautology, but what I really want us to agree on at the outset is this: that deciding it's time to start packing, that packing is now the thing to do, is not best explained as just coming to a belief in some special kind of fact.

Suppose, though, someone really were a "practical realist": to decide what now to do, this philosopher thinks, is to conclude that one of the acts open to me has a special property—the property of "conclusive *to-be-done*ness". Such a practical realist can't be a practical externalist. He can't claim that my conclusion "packing my bags now has conclusive *to-be-done*ness" leaves open one's decision what to do. For if it does, then this wasn't a full conclusion in my reasoning to a decision. True, you might decide what to do and still not act on your decision, through fear, or through laziness and inertia, or through a cozy absorption in the morning paper. But then your problem is beyond anything that reasoning what to do can settle by itself. If, then, there's a real property conclusive *to-be-done*ness, it will have to be a "queer" property: trivially, it is laden with *to-be-done*ness.

Could there, then, be *facts* like these of what to do—facts we recognize in coming to any correct decision? And if there are, is it just a brute feature of the metaphysical universe that there are such familiar but strange-seeming facts? What I claim in this book is, first, that *what to do* is remarkably fact-like in its behavior. Second, this is not a brute truth of metaphysics, but an intelligible consequence of the nature of planning and deciding. We are *agents*, in philosophers' lingo, beings who can reason our ways to decisions. Anyone who reasons what to do, I argue, is committed to something very much like *facts* of what to do. Reasoning what to do commits us to thinking in terms of conclusive *to-be-done*ness. It commits us to this thinking's being very much like thinking of properties. In our reasoning to decisions, we must think very much as if there were properties that include, in some queer way, this conclusive *to-be-done*ness.

Metaethical Expressivism

In Chapter 3 I return to Holmes and Moriarty. There I begin a long possibility proof: whether or not our actual language fits the account I offer, I start to argue, a language that does is at least possible. It's a language that we need, moreover, if we are to state all the issues that arise on the way to decision. Later in the book, I ask how this possible language bears on the language we already speak (Chapter 7).

The theory I develop is a form of "metaethical expressivism". Metaethics asks what ethical questions are: what does it *mean* to call an act wise or foolish, admirable or reprehensible? This is a metaquestion about ethics, a second-order question of what ethical questions could really be—and to this question, philosophers have offered a bewildering variety of answers. I myself offered a set of answers in *Wise Choices, Apt Feelings* (1990). In this successor book I explore aspects of the *style* of answer I gave in that earlier work.

The expressivists' strategy is to change the question. Don't ask directly how to define 'good', for no correct definition can break out of a normative circle, a circle of ought-like terms. On that point, nonnaturalists like Moore, Prichard, Ross, and Ewing were right. The word 'good' might indeed mean, say, desirable, or *fittingly desired*—but that just shifts the burden to the normative term 'fittingly'. Any other straight definition will either fail or likewise shift the burden. Instead of seeking a straight definition, expressivists propose, seek a characterization of a different form. Ask what *states of mind* ethical statements *express*. Emotivists like Ayer, for instance, said that ethical statements express feelings or attitudes; to say "Compassion is good" might be to express one's *approval* of compassion (Ayer, *Language, Truth and Logic*, 1936, 1946, chap. 6). Equivalently, shift the question to focus on judgments: ask, say, what *judging* that compassion is good consists in. It consists, according to Ayer, in a mental state of approval or the like. Other versions of expressivism differ in their accounts of the states of mind expressed; not all expressivists are emotivists.[2] Here, for example,

2. Hare, as I read him, thinks that moral statements express preferences all told that don't depend on who's who in a situation; see, for instance, Hare, *Moral Thinking* (1981) and Gibbard, "Hare's Analysis" (1988). Korsgaard, as I read her, thinks that moral claims express one's reflective endorsement of policies for living. Moral reflection, she says, "is practical and not theoretical: it is reflection about what to do, not reflection about what is to be found in the normative part of the world." Korsgaard, *Sources of Normativity* (1996), p. 116; see my "Morality as Consistency" (1999) for this reading of Korsgaard. Stevenson was an emotivist though at first not a pure expressivist in my sense: in "The Emotive Theory" (1937) and *Ethics and Language* (1944), he did not explain moral meanings in terms of states of

is my own view to a first approximation: to think that compassion is good is to *accept a norm* that says to desire compassion. The term 'expressivism' I mean to cover any account of meanings that follows this indirect path: to explain the meaning of a term, explain what states of mind the term can be used to express.

This book explores just one aspect of expressivism and normative concepts, what we might call the logical "workings" of these concepts. A central thesis is of a partial convergence: that expressivists, intuitionists, and naturalists converge, to a large degree, in what we say about normative concepts. Put as oracular dicta, some of my conclusions run as follows: There is indeed a property that constitutes being good—perhaps a natural property. There are no specially queer properties laden with *to-be-done*ness; there are just plain old properties and relations. Or at least, we don't *need* queer properties to explain reasoning what to do. There are, though, special *concepts* that figure in planning and decision—such as the concept of *being the thing to do*. Being the thing to do might be the same property as being pleasure-tending, for anything I'll be arguing, but the concepts are different. The concept of being pleasure-tending is "descriptive" and requires no special style of explanation, whereas the concept of being the thing to do is *plan-laden:* it is to be explained in the kind of way I explore. Plan-laden concepts, though, act in many ways very much like descriptive concepts, and I explore why.

My ultimate aim is to study the workings of familiar *ought*-laden or "normative" concepts, like *good* and *admirable* and *reprehensible*, and offer an expressivistic theory of them. To do this, though, I start out considering just one particular kind of judgment, a kind for which expressivism *must* be right. These are judgments of *what to do*. For these judgments, I conduct a thought experiment and fashion my possibility proof: it is possible to have concepts that work as expressivists say our normative concepts work. To establish this, I appropriate the phrase 'the thing to do' to serve as an expressive term—ignoring all question of what this phrase means in normal English. Suppose, let me stipulate, the phrase works like this: to conclude, say, that fleeing

---

mind expressed by moral assertions. Later he did; see essay 11, "Retrospective Comments" in *Facts and Values* (1963), pp. 210–214. I thank Kevin Toh for pointing me to this change in Stevenson's analyses.

the building is *the thing to do* just *is* to conclude what to do, to settle
on fleeing the building. By sheer stipulation, then, the meaning of
this phrase 'the thing to do' is explained expressivistically: if I assert
"Fleeing is the thing to do", I thereby express a state of mind, deciding
to flee. I then proceed to ask how language like this *would* work. In the
back of my mind, of course, is the hypothesis that important parts of
our actual language do work this way. Mostly, though, I don't argue for
this hypothesis; rather I ask whether the hypothesis is coherent and
what its upshots would be. Only much later in the book do I turn to our
actual everyday thoughts and ask if the shoe fits.[3]

This stipulation will take effect not now but in Chapter 3. For the
moment, return to familiar ethical concepts and other normative concepts. About these, why not just be descriptivists? Why bear the philosophical costs of expressivism? But also, why think that expressivism, as
a strategy for explaining these concepts, has such high philosophical
costs? Many philosophers agree that descriptivism in every form leads
to puzzles, but they find expressivism even less acceptable. Why?

Properties and Choice

G. E. Moore examined "naturalistic" definitions of *good* and other ethical concepts, chiefly definitions in terms of such psychological and sociological notions as happiness, pleasure, belief, and desire. He concluded that no such definition captures what the word 'good' means.
Good, he concluded, is a property of a special kind, not a natural property that could figure in empirical sciences, and not a supernatural or a
metaphysical property either. We know of this property not by ordinary empirical investigation, but by insight or intuition. Non-naturalism and intuitionism may by now seem quaint and dated, but many
current philosophers accept the core of intuitionists' doctrines: they
are "realists" about oughts and reasons to do things, they hold that eth-

3. Some current writers use as their basic normative notion not an *ought* or being
the thing to do, but being a *reason* or counting in something's favor. See, for instance, Scanlon, *What We Owe* (1998); see also Baier, *Moral Point of View* (1958).
The English term 'reason' has many senses, and careful writers like Scanlon take
pains to make clear which sense they intend. I agree that Scanlon's sense of the
term 'reason', as a reason to do something, can serve as a basic normative term, and
I might have developed my account to fit being a reason in this sense. See my *Wise
Choices* (1990), pp. 160–164.

ical and other normative properties don't figure in the natural and the psycho-social sciences, they maintain that we can have knowledge of these properties, and accept that knowing what I ought to do (or what I have most reason to do) leaves no further question of what to do.[4]

What good, though, is a *sui generis*, non-natural property? Settling what's good settles what to go for, or so it's meant to do. We are to further the good and oppose the bad. Why, though, further one non-natural property and oppose another? Is it apparent by some further intuition that good is the quality to promote? Perhaps, but that's not usually said; what intuition tells us, according to the usual presentation of the theory, is what sorts of things *are* good.

Non-naturalism, if it is meant to offer an explanation, takes the crucial questions of living—what to promote and pursue, what to do and why—and substitutes metaphysical questions about the layout of non-natural properties in a special realm. Why leave the burning building? Because to stay risks quick and painful death, whereas to leave offers normal prospects for life. That seems the full answer, but strictly speaking, I agree, it leaves implicit an obvious step. Intuitionism itself, though, is in danger of attributing one implicit step too many. To choose to get out, it seems, I must accept two items: (i) the claim that normal prospects for life are *better* than quick and painful death, and (ii) the injunction to *choose* what is better. Is it intuition, then, that delivers the second finding, so that we need an intuition for (ii) as well as for (i)? That's one more obvious finding than we need; what's obvious is to choose life over death.

Expressivism takes this line of thought seriously. As I put my own version of the doctrine, *ought* questions and *reason* questions are by their very nature questions of what to do. Understanding this is the way to understand what *ought* assertions mean. I the chooser don't face two clear, distinct questions, the question what to do and the question what I ought to do. *Descriptivism*, in contrast, is the doctrine that *ought*

4. See Scanlon, *What We Owe* (1998), pp. 17–78; Dworkin, "Objectivity and Truth" (1996); Nagel, *View from Nowhere* (1986). But these views perhaps should not be classified with Moore's non-naturalism. These authors would not use the term 'non-naturalism' to label their views. They are, though, "realists" who reject naturalism for moral concepts. Nagel vehemently rejects "Platonism" as a familiar philosopical excess; he isn't claiming "an extra set of properties of things and events in the world" (pp. 139–140). For recent discussions, see Stratton-Lake, *Ethical Intuitionism* (2002). I touch on these views in Chapter 9.

claims describe rather than prescribe, that an *ought* claim describes an act as having a certain special property. This gives the wrong picture, we expressivists say: *ought* claims instead are claims about what to do.

A non-naturalist—or even a naturalist—might accept this last, that *ought* claims are claims of what to do, but object that I am reversing the true order of explanation. *Ought* claims amount to claims of what to do, true enough—and so yes, we don't need separate groundings for the two kinds of claims, in intuition or otherwise. But the explanation for the equivalence is this: when I ask myself what to do, my question just *is* what I ought to do. We all understand *ought* questions, and talk of "what to do" is mere elegant syntactic variation on talk of "ought", not something to understand independently, on its own. Settling what to do just *means* settling what one ought to do.[5]

Well, to be sure, I do think that what to do and what one ought to do are the same question. That's what I have been proclaiming. But we cannot explain this single question by identifying a property, natural or non-natural, that the term 'ought' picks out. Rather, say I, we *live* our conclusions on what to do. Asking what to do right now eventuates in decision and action. Imagine a person for whom conclusions of what to do had no tie to deciding what to do, who treated such questions as mere theorizing on the properties of her alternatives. That's not conceivable; she wouldn't recognizably be asking what to do—beyond, perhaps, mouthing words she picked up from the rest of us. We should explain thinking what to do as moving toward action, and then explain the term 'ought' accordingly, as one I can use to couch my frame of mind when I decide. Don't look for some one property I can attribute which can serve as an all-purpose deciding factor, as if attributing a property could substitute for acting. When I speak of concluding "what to do", understand this to mean coming to a choice.

Far more needs to be said, of course, on the tie of *ought*s to action, and I develop my positions on all this in the following chapters. My point here is to worry how invoking a property, and saying that it is picked out by the term 'ought', could explain decision. How can all the questions I ask in deliberating be relevant only in bearing on the one question: which alternative has this special property?

Descriptivism downplays choice, we expressivists complain. Prop-

---

5. Jason Stanley and David Copp have pressed arguments in this vein on me.

erties are all, and acting an afterthought. This is equally the stance of naturalism and of non-naturalism. In thinking what to do, a theorist of either kind encounters the same question: how, on her view, do thoughts of what we ought to do bear on choice?

Sensible Knaves

Some naturalists renounce any search for some one, conclusive action-determining property. A "sensible knave", they say, might know all there is to know of what's right and wrong—but not care. An irrationalist might likewise know all there is to know of what's rational and irrational, wise and foolish, but likewise not care. Non-naturalists too might join in these contentions. I label such a position, naturalistic or non-naturalistic, *hyperexternalism*; it downplays choice with a vengeance. My choice may be left open, hyperexternalists agree, when all descriptive questions are settled and I know what I *must* do. At that point, I complain, such theorists leave us conceptually in the lurch, with no refined concepts for thinking my way to decision, and no refined language for thinking about it together. No subject matter addresses the residual question I ask myself in deliberating what to do: not ethics, not wisdom, and not anything else.

To be sure, we have a device for saying what to do that descriptivists recognize, namely, imperatives. I can tell myself to leave a burning building, or to choose real engagement with the world over a blissful life of simulation. But imperatives are syntactically rigid. They don't even fit into *if* clauses; we can't, for instance, say,

If prefer death to tyranny, then prefer skimping to tyranny. (1)

That isn't grammatical.[6] Would we could put the thought like this!

If tyranny is worse than death, then it's worse than skimping. (2)

But this, descriptivists tell us, isn't the same thing. Conceivably a person might be entirely sensible but indifferent to value. He, then, could

---

6. Hare, "Wanting: Some Pitfalls" (1971), renders hypothetical imperatives this way as a technical device.

accept (2) but ask, rhetorically, "How does that bear on any question of what to do?" He can't substitute (1), which is ungrammatical, and so he has no language for conditional reasoning on what to do.

Suppose Xanthippe is rational in every way. Then she will form correct fundamental beliefs as to what she ought to do, and go on to do what she is convinced she ought. She combines two kinds of rationality: she is rational in forming her *ought* convictions, and rational in acting on these convictions. But, say hyperexternalists, these forms of rationality are separable—if not with us humans as we are, then with people as we might coherently imagine them. Alcibiades, imagine, has perfect command of the concept of *ought*, and is fully rational in forming his convictions as to what he ought to do. In these matters of belief, he is altogether rational. Still, he does not regard what he ought to do as having much bearing on what to do. In this he is irrational, perhaps, but it is fully coherent to describe him this way: fully rational in belief as to what he ought to do, but irrational in acting.

This typology attributes distinctions where they can't be found. Tweedledum rationally forms all the right convictions of what he ought to do, and he reliably acts on them. His brother Tweedledee, though, is a convinced egoistic hedonist: he thinks that one ought always to do what most furthers one's own prospects for pleasure and lack of displeasure. This is not the rational view to have, let's imagine. (If you think it is, you can invent another, irrational view to attribute to Tweedledee.) Fortunately, though, Tweedledee has another deep irrationality: he doesn't see that what you ought to do has anything much to do with any question of what to do—with any question he must answer in moving to action. Indeed his actions and the considerations he cites in support of them coincide amazingly with those of Tweedledum. The two quarrel at great length about what a person ought to do. (They differ, to be sure, on what to *say* about actions, but let's confine our attention to choices apart from these.)[7] But in acting, in moving from the natural facts to choice, they are in full accord. Hyperexternalists take Tweedledee's disagreements with his brother at face value: the two, they say, disagree sharply and systematically on what a person ought to do. I myself think there's not much difference between them: they agree remarkably in thinking their way to decisions, and disagree only

7. Lenman, in "The Externalist" (1999), offers similar considerations.

on what to say about it and on the words with which to think about it. Their disagreement is verbal; they disagree on what words to mouth. They have no serious difference between them on what to do and why.

Descriptivists, in short, picture us as underequipped to ponder what to do, to think our ways to decision whether each by oneself or together in discussion. No naturalistic concept, after all, settles every question of what to do, beyond all need for further thought and discussion. A non-naturalistic concept, if there were such a thing, might succeed in closing discussion, but it is superfluous: why then think that deciding and thinking what one ought to do are separate activities? That leaves us with an extra burden, namely, to explain why the non-naturalistic answer settles the question we ask in deliberating. Hyperexternalists deny us the full use of reasoning and logic to settle what to do; we can use imperatives, but no action-concluding predicates.

Questions of living are inescapable and serious. Naturalistic findings won't settle these questions beyond all need for thinking and debate. Settle who will be happy and who not if, say, you apply yourself fully to the piano, losing sleep and shunning friends; settle what sounds will then come from the piano under your fingers and what critics will say; settle all such questions. There remains the question of whether to work so hard at the piano. We need language to discuss such questions, language with all the power and flexibility of language that is clearly descriptive—but with its tie to what to do built in. We need a predicate that conveys "to-be-doneness". With it we capture all the power of logic and reasoning that predicates give to language and thought. English may have such a predicate: 'ought' on certain readings, perhaps, or 'is the thing to do'. But whether English does or not, for crystal-clear thought about what to do we need such a predicate. If such language does not exist, we have to invent it. (And then we'll have a language that looks so much like our old one that it will be hard to say why we should judge that our language has changed. We've perhaps been speaking this expressive language all along.)

Driving What to Do Out of Ethics

What to do can be a serious question, the question I ask myself in thinking my way to a decision. Ethics concerns what to do. In morality figure injunctions "Thou shalt" and "Thou shalt not." These claims seem innocuous; how could anyone object? But moral realism of one kind or another can seem the sole alternative to moral chaos. The alternative, many philosophers think, can only be skepticism about all ethical claims.

This accusation of skepticism we can dismiss. Suppose, as I maintain, that ethical statements concern what to do. What, then, constitutes ethical skepticism? It must be the view that there's nothing to do—not just that the alternatives are always bleak or boring, but that nothing is ever the thing to do even given what choices we have. All answers to questions of what to do are mistaken, a skeptic must say to count as a skeptic. Or perhaps it's the view that even though some things are to be done and others aren't, we can never *know* what's to be done. Or it's the view that questions of what to do must always be nonsense, that an answer to such a question will never be right or wrong. 'Skepticism' is a loose term, and any such position might deserve it. Why, though, should anyone be committed to any of these views? Don't we often know full well what to choose? Opponents of expressivism, though, may themselves well be ethical skeptics by this test. They may think that all the real questions pertain to how things stand, in nature and perhaps outside of nature. There's never a real answer to what to do, never an answer we can know: answers and knowledge are out of place in the realm of deciding. And so, we conclude from this view, there's no such thing as ethical knowledge. Such a view is a form of ethical skepticism.

All this assumes, to be sure, that I'm right about what ethical claims amount to—and that is the very point at issue. Fair enough—but the point works in both directions. The critic of expressivism says that ethical statements mean such-and-such; and then if we are skeptical about this such-and-such, we count as ethical skeptics in his book. I myself am skeptical about non-natural properties; I think there are no such things. That only makes me skeptical of ethical claims if they consist in attributing non-natural properties to things—but whether they do is the point at issue. As for naturalists, I believe in natural properties by the millions, and think we can know about many of them. If you say that the phrase 'intrinsically good' means, say, happy on balance, I won't be skeptical of all ethical claims as you translate them. What I don't believe is that you gave a correct translation.

Some other forms of naturalism don't offer translations, but accounts of how ethical terms come to refer to natural properties.[8] What these views get right and what they get wrong is a tricky question, which I leave mostly untouched in this book; my main point is that whether or not parts of our language work as these theories describe, we still need—possibly in addition—the kind of language I describe in this book. And again, the point applies: when I disbelieve an *account* of ethical claims, that doesn't mean I disbelieve the ethical claims themselves.

No one, then, should reject expressivism because the alternative is moral skepticism. Not, that is, unless we should be skeptics on what to do—and on this score, a blanket skepticism seems absurd. As Korsgaard says, "If you think reasons and values are unreal, go and make a choice, and you will change your mind" (Korsgaard, *Sources*, 1996, p. 125). Expressivism, if right, wouldn't commit us to skepticism. Why else think that it's got to be wrong?

Some objections to expressivism really do assume the kind of skepticism on what to do that I've been dismissing. Agreed, there may be no real issue of whether to leave a burning building. But other questions are inescapably live: what, if anything, to sacrifice for the sake of other people? how stringently to treat one's promises when they'll cost yourself and cost others? how to choose between contentment and accomplishment? If there's a truth on these matters and we can find a firm basis for settling them, then our questions can be answered. Expressivism, though, leaves our questions hanging in midair, offering no firm basis for an answer.

Call this the "hard questions" worry. When questions of what to do are hard, we can't just claim to know perfectly well what to do and leave it at that. But to resolve these questions, can some naturalistic account or treatment help? Can some form of non-naturalism help? These positions just change the subject, we can see. We ask what to do, and they hand us analyses of a different question.

Take first naturalism. That I *ought* to help at grave cost to myself means that helping has such-and-such a natural property. Call this the property of being "natt", where the term 'natt', we suppose, has received some naturalistic treatment. 'Natt' may be analytically defined

---

8. See, for instance, Boyd, "How to Be a Moral Realist" (1988). I touch further on theories like this in Chapter 10.

in plainly naturalistic terms, or perhaps we have a story of how 'natt' gets its reference just as other terms of empirical science do. Suppose some such account is correct; does it answer our questions? Helping is natt despite its costs, or perhaps it isn't—but the question remains whether to help. Perhaps we can settle that helping is natt, and once we do, it will be obvious whether to help. But then what's the worry for expressivism? We've settled whether to help, and so we've settled whether we ought to help as the expressivist reads the word 'ought'. This is not a case where expressivism would leave us skeptics on what a person ought to do. Perhaps, however, although we can settle whether helping is natt, the answer doesn't settle whether to help. If so, then we've settled one question, but we haven't concluded our delibera-tions; we haven't settled what to do. To be sure, we've settled what we "ought" to do, if the naturalist was right, but this, we must bear in mind, isn't the question of what to do. It's all well and good to ask ques-tions we can answer, but doing so may still leave us without the answers we need. In short, if being natt settles what to do, then expressivists have their answers. If it doesn't, expressivists still have all the answers this naturalist has, and the naturalist lacks the answers expressivists lack. On either account, we know what's natt and don't know whether to do it.

What of intuitionism? I myself say there's no such thing as a non-natural property. But suppose there were, and to be "exnat" is to have that property. Perhaps settling what's exnat leaves open the question of what to do; then, as with naturalism, the hard question of what to do remains unanswered when all ethical questions are settled. Suppose, though, that intuiting that helping is exnat does settle whether to help. In deciding whether to help, I first learn all about what's involved in helping in this instance: what it will do for the other person and what I sacrifice. That's the natural part. From this I intuit that helping is exnat; that's the intuitive, non-natural part. And so I help. What part, in all this, is played by intuiting that helping is exnat? I settle on help-ing, and I do so because of the natural features of the situation—be-cause of what helping will do for the people I help, and despite the bur-dens. "I see what to do," as I might say. Do I need to "see" too, as a separate intuition, which act is exnat?

Life faces us with hard questions. I wish that questions of how to live had clear answers (though perhaps they do for the lilies of the field or for giraffes, and I'm not wishing I were one of them). In any case, neither naturalism nor non-naturalism resolves the uncertainties of living in a way that expressivism can't. When I deliberate, I ask myself what to do and I respond with a decision. Thinking what I ought to do amounts to deciding what to do.

If all this is right, though, can I ever be mistaken in an *ought* judgment? Mistakes can only be of fact, it may seem clear. I cannot be mistaken on what to do except by mistaking the natural facts on which I act. Normative claims, we think, can be mistaken, and so expressivism for normative concepts is faulty.

This kind of objection spurs much of what I do in this book. Note at the outset that the objection is no raw deliverance of common sense. People make mistakes; that's a truism. They make mistakes when they act; that's also a truism. It is no truism, however, that mistakes in action all boil down to mistakes of natural fact. That is a claim of philosophy—and a dubious one. Pluto, imagine, betrays his dear friend Minerva to get rich, leaving her impoverished and building a fancy house with the proceeds. Then in a fit of remorse and self-disgust, he burns down the house, even canceling the insurance so that his renunciation will be genuine. It's hard to claim that throughout this whole affair he acted without mistake. If it was fine to burn down the house, then it wasn't all right to betray Minerva in the first place. Were the errors of Pluto's ways all mistakes of natural fact? He thought he'd feel good about what he had accomplished, perhaps, and that was a mistake of natural fact. If he'd been clear how he'd feel, he would have made provision, carefully surrounding himself with other ruthless plutocrats, so that he could enjoy his riches unplagued by conscience. Would he then have acted unmistakenly? If not, what would have been his mistake of natural fact? If so, was he also unmistaken to burn down the house? Perhaps, indeed, you can resolve all mistakes in action into mistakes of natural fact—but common sense won't tell you how to do it.

Ethical questions, I argue at length in this book, are questions we ask in the course of thinking how to live. Their answers are not always settled by the natural facts; even when we make no mistakes on those natural facts, we can make wrong decisions. That's a view that each of us must take in her own deliberations, and it is a view we take together when we think together how to live a human life. All this is a picture to unfold in the chapters to come.

Minimal Facts

Are there facts concerning what's good, what's admirable, or what's sleazy? Are there facts concerning what I must do? Recent lines of philosophical argument suggest that there might not be much that can be made of a dispute over whether normative matters are matters of fact. Pleasure is worth having. Is that a fact? What would it mean to claim that it is? One question, of course, is whether pleasure *is* worth having—but suppose we agree that it is. Pleasure is worth having; what's further at stake in whether this is a fact?

Minimalists regarding facthood respond: nothing. If I assert "That pleasure is worth having is a fact," that is no more than a fancy way of saying that pleasure is worth having. The same goes for "Peas are yucky!" or "That's awesome!" If peas are yucky, then that's a fact. The same goes for truth: "That peas are yucky is the truth" just means that peas are yucky. So says the minimalist.

On the term 'fact', I won't be taking a stand in this book. Perhaps there is a distinction to be drawn between facts and non-facts, so that I could, for instance, think I ought to leave the building, but deny that it is a *fact* that I ought to leave. Or perhaps there is no distinction clearly conveyed by the word. It might be a deep feature of the human psyche that we mentally code matters as "facts" or not, so that the question of what is a fact and what is not seems clear and urgent—but these psychological findings wouldn't guarantee us that such a distinction withstands philosophical probing. In this book, in any case, I do not make use of such a general distinction. Neither do I deny that it could be drawn. As for the word 'true', I accept minimalism for the term as I use it, leaving it an open question whether there's a clear and more demanding sense of "truth".

Does all this leave anything distinctive in the position I'm calling expressivism? In many ways, I'll end up sounding like a non-naturalist, and in some ways, like certain kinds of naturalists. Am I, then, really a descriptivist in disguise, a moral realist?[9] Simon Blackburn calls his program *quasi-realism*, and with him I share a remarkable range of views. Much of this book is devoted to realizing the program he de-

9. Dworkin argues that a quasi-realist's expressivism, if it otherwise succeeds, fails to distinguish itself from realism. See Dworkin, "Objectivity and Truth" (1996), pp. 108–112.

scribes—though not always in ways he would accept.[10] Self-avowed realists, though, ask what's "quasi" about the program if it works. How does my position fall short of full ethical realism? Most of what I say on this score must wait for the theory itself, but here I'll say this much. Begin with the slogans I've been proclaiming: Questions of what we ought to do are questions of what to do. Finish your deliberation, conclude what to do, and you've concluded what you ought to do. These crude sayings will, of course, need qualification, but the distinctive claim of an expressivist is that dicta like these, suitably worked out, account for the subject matter of ethics.

If a self-avowed realist agrees, the two of us may have no quarrel. I don't, however, know of any "ethical realist" who accepts slogans like these explicitly. Indeed, many philosophers think that an explanation from the starting points I adopt can't be made to work; they think that what one could validly construct on these bases won't mimic intuitionism in anything like the fulsome ways I claim. These are intelligible denials—and I deny the denials. I later explain at length how expressivism does mimic a Moore-like intuitionism. If it is intelligible to deny this claim, then the claim, if correct, must also be intelligible. If sophisticated ethical theorists mostly reject this claim, then the claim itself isn't entirely truistic or undistinctive.

Our alternatives are three, as I have been talking: naturalism, nonnaturalism, and expressivism. The first two are forms of descriptivism, whereas we expressivists reject descriptivism. This taxonomy is old; apart from one newer label 'expressivism', it was commonplace half a century ago. Many current positions still fit these slots. This book presents a kind of synthesis of these positions; contrasts between these three families, I argue, are far less acute than is normally supposed. But of course there are more alternatives than these three, and far more alternatives than I can survey even in the whole book. Some current positions are sufficiently complex that no brief set of comments could begin to do justice to them.

10. For a compact statement of the program, see Blackburn, "Just Causes" (1990), p. 198. Blackburn champions such a view not only for moral thinking but for a variety of other kinds of thinking. He labels his program a combination of "projectivism" and "quasi-realism". See the introduction and many of the papers in Blackburn, *Essays* (1993). I develop some aspects of such a view in *Wise Choices* (1990), esp. chaps. 5 and 8–13.

In any case, much of this book is narrow in its ambitions. It is not, for
the most part, directly about ethics, or even about normative concepts
in general. Mostly I ask not whether an expressivistic treatment of normative concepts is true, but whether it *could* be true. I offer the possibility proof of which I spoke earlier. I say that normative concepts are
correctly explained expressivistically, and critics deny this. They don't
deny just that certain concepts—concepts we happen to employ—work
as I say they do. They deny that an explanation of the kind I attempt is
so much as possible. They deny that *any* concepts could work as I say
our normative concepts work. For the most part, it is this denial of possibility that I answer. I don't much ask whether this or that concept we
actually have works expressively: right, good, rational. Rather, I survey
a realm where expressivism has to be right: questions of what to do,
questions we answer by deciding what to do. Then I ask about the concepts that emerge, how they work. After that, we can go on to inquire
into our actual normative concepts, asking whether they too work this
way, and whether an expressivistic approach offers the best account of
what they mean—but this last is not my chief interest.

Almost all of what descriptivists insist on can be embraced and explained by an expressivist. That is a principal lesson of this book. Questions of what we ought to do are questions of what to do, questions
we pose in deliberation—and this explains the phenomena to which
descriptivists appeal. Indeed, I argue that a form of non-naturalism is
correct in a way, as far as it goes—but that it is incomplete. A non-naturalistic "moral realist" can present certain features of ethical concepts
as brute truths: that, for example, whether an act is right or wrong depends on its natural properties. No metaphysics of non-natural properties *explains* these truths; with this some non-naturalistic moral realists
agree.[11] Such a theorist, though, offers no explanation at all of the features of moral and other normative concepts. My aim in this book is to
render normative concepts unmysterious, to explain those features of
ethical concepts that such a non-naturalist can only treat as brute.

11. See, for instance, Dworkin, "Objectivity and Truth" (1996).

~ 2

Intuitionism as Template: Emending Moore

$\mathcal{N}$ORMATIVE CONCEPTS are concepts "fraught with ought", as Sellars put it. How do these concepts work? In this book I develop a hypothesis: normative concepts get their special characteristics, I propose, from their place in a broad kind of planning we carry out. For most of this book, I formulate this hypothesis and elaborate it, and then explore some puzzles of moral philosophy in terms of this hypothesis. Any hypothesis, though, requires testing: the one I propose will have to meet certain standards of adequacy—and so will any rival.

What these standards are is sharply contested. On one view, the young G. E. Moore set the problem of what 'good' means in his book *Principia Ethica* (1903). Moore's own solution to his problem was fantastical, but an adequate theory of normative concepts, this view maintains, must pass pretty much the tests that Moore devised. On an opposing view, Moore's tests misled generations of moral philosophers. Now, though, we can see through his tests and dismiss them as figments of semantics of a century ago. Still other philosophers continue to accept Moore's entire program; his tests work, they think, and he drew the right, non-naturalist morals from his tests.

My own view is that Moore's tests survive scrutiny to a remarkable degree. Not that we can accept what he says word for word—far from it. With judicious reading, extension, and revision, though, we can find in Moore the materials to construct a template that an adequate theory of normative concepts must match. In Moore's arguments, moreover, we can find clues as to what underlies the phenomena he discovered.

Good, Moore famously insisted, is "not to be considered a natural object" (1.12, p. 14). Good and bad are *simple* objects of thought—indeed, the only simple objects of thought peculiar to ethics (1.5, p. 5). Moore acquired a philosophical following with these views, but in the decades that ensued, non-natural objects came to look spooky. Moore's arguments against naturalism, though, had a longer run; they convinced many philosophers that ethical concepts are not purely naturalistic, that we can't develop a natural science of good and bad. The great emotivists of the 1930s fully accepted Moore's claims against ethical naturalism, though they repudiated non-natural qualities. The young Moore's arguments were loose, as he later acknowledged: his "naturalistic fallacy" had proved elusive, and his "open question" test was clearly defective. The question for us now, then, is not whether Moore was right in detail, but whether he was somehow "on" to something. Do any of his arguments point to considerations we must now take seriously?

I begin, then, with a motivated reading of Moore. I adopt some parts of what Moore says and drop others, and I interpret passing remarks in light of more recent philosophical developments. My aim in part is to construct a target theory, a target that an account of ethical concepts might hit or miss. Moore, on my reading, discovered the special behavior of a class of concepts, the concepts we now call "normative". The rest of this book develops a hypothesis to account for the behaviors that Moore discovered. Moore, then, on my reading, constructs a picture with many correct features, and we can test the hypothesis of this book by seeing if it matches these features.

Eventually, I depart from Moore in important ways. Moore spoke of *good* and *bad* as the simple, non-natural objects of thought that specially figure in ethics (1.5). I myself, in most of this book, will have little to say about good and bad. I don't think these concepts are simple; rather, I follow a later non-naturalist, A. C. Ewing: the term 'good', I take it, means desirable, and desirable means something like *to be desired* or *fittingly* desired (Ewing, "A Suggested Non-Naturalist Analysis," 1939). That places the burden of explanation on the construction 'to be' in 'to be desired', or on the term 'fittingly'. The special behavior of *good* that Moore more or less uncovers I'll attribute to Ewing's concept of what's fitting. Moore's own question, though, concerns *good*, and so for now I'll talk of good and bad.

What's at Issue?

How does Moore argue that *good* is distinct from all "natural" objects of thought? The arguments he offers are intricate, but persuasive enough that whether in detail they are correct or garbled, their force cannot have sprung from their niceties. As with many pieces of philosophical rhetoric, it is Moore's examples and the rough use he makes of them that carry the reader. Two interrelated lines of argument are the ones I find most convincing in Moore. One asks "What's at issue?" in a debate; the other appeals to coherent states of mind.

Two philosophers debate, Moore imagines; one claims that good is pleasure, the other that good is that which is desired. These are claims of identity in meaning: one philosopher claims that 'good' means the same as 'pleasant'; the other that 'good' means the same as 'desired' (or as Moore puts it, "that good just means the object of desire," p. 11).

The dispute is not verbal, Moore argues; it is not a dispute just about the English language. Whatever reasons we have, say, to go for pleasure don't rest on the meaning of a word in English—even the word 'good'. On this point Moore must be right: these two philosophers are *users* of English, who think in English or have thoughts that they express in English. The claim that good means pleasant, whatever it may amount to, would be expressed by a monolingual speaker of French as the last of the three statements below and not the first or second:

En anglais, 'good' veut dire 'pleasant',

En anglais, 'good' veut dire agréable,

Bon veut dire agréable.

If the issue, then, is not a verbal one about English, what is it? We have, I take it, a dispute about conceptual identity, conducted by us who alike use English to express our concepts.

First, then, the "What's at issue?" test. One philosopher—call him Désiré—claims that 'good' just *means* desired, and we want to test his claim. Another philosopher, Hedda, thinks that pleasure and pleasure alone is good, whereas Désiré rejects the claim that pleasure alone is good. What's at issue? We have two assertions:

Only pleasure is good. —Hedda $(\mathcal{H})$

Not only pleasure is good. —Désiré $(*\mathcal{H})$

Désiré and Hedda, Moore thinks we can see, disagree when they say these things. But Désiré can't express his disagreement with Hedda by saying:

Not only pleasure is desired. —Désiré $(*\mathcal{D})$

For Hedda can agree with this, though she still asserts $\mathcal{H}$, that only pleasure is good. The first two statements contradict each other, Moore thinks we can see: $*\mathcal{H}$ contradicts $\mathcal{H}$. The first and the last do not: $*\mathcal{D}$ does not contradict $\mathcal{H}$. It follows that Désiré's two claims $*\mathcal{H}$ and $*\mathcal{D}$ don't mean the same thing: one of them contradicts what Hedda says and the other doesn't. Whether or not what's desired is always good, 'good' doesn't *mean* 'desired'. This is the argument from "What's at issue?" It asks what's at issue between Désiré and Hedda.

This argument ties in closely with a test of *conceptual coherence*. Hedda cannot both think that $\mathcal{H}$, only pleasure is good and that $*\mathcal{H}$, not only pleasure is good—she can't think both these things and be coherent. She can, though, coherently think $\mathcal{H}$ and $*\mathcal{D}$: she can think that only pleasure is good, but that not only pleasure is desired. The two-person question of whether Hedda and Désiré are at odds in a set of claims boils down, then, to the one-person question: whether she could, without giving up her own claims, accept his claims and stay coherent.

Moore also made much of his "open question test", and often philosophers take this test to be crucial: whether Moore was right, they think, hinges on whether his open question test works. To test whether 'good' means desired, Moore proposed, construct the question "Is all that's desired good?" and see if the question is an open one. It's open, you'll see, whether all that's desired is good—and so 'good' and 'desired' can't mean the same. But this, critics respond, can't be a reliable test. Synonymy can be covert; if a philosopher labors to analyze a concept and discover the right analysis, the discovery won't be obvious on its face. The question whether the analysis is right will be open, because the analysis, correct though it be, is subtle.[1]

The tests I'm endorsing in Moore are more demanding. To apply the "What's at issue?" argument, we need not just uncertainty, but definite findings of which claims are in disagreement and which are not—as with Hedda and Désiré. To apply the coherence test, we need the definite finding that a state of mind is coherent; it won't be enough just to find the question of its coherence open.

These tests do, though, place a great explanatory burden on two notions: (i) one person's accepting or rejecting a claim of another, and (ii) a state of mind's being conceptually coherent. Notion (i), we should note, comes also in a one-person variant over time; we have the notion (i*) a person's sticking to a claim he previously held, as opposed to rejecting it. Moore's arguments require *claims* that can be accepted or rejected at different times and by different people, and *coherence* or incoherence in accepting a set of claims. With Hedda and Désiré, after all, Moore's argument starts from a datum: that it is *coherent* to accept both $\mathcal{H}$ and $^*\mathcal{D}$, that only pleasure is good, but not only pleasure is desired—whereas it is incoherent to accept $\mathcal{H}$ and $^*\mathcal{H}$, that only pleasure is good, but not only pleasure is good. Claim $^*\mathcal{D}$ is just $^*\mathcal{H}$ with 'desired' substituted for 'good'. Therefore, Moore's argument concludes, the concepts *desired* and *good* are distinct. Two concepts are distinct if they offer nonequivalent possibilities of coherent acceptance or rejection. If we can't ever recognize coherence or incoherence, disagreement or compatibility, we can't apply the tests.

My claim will be that we can't live and converse without these raw

---

1. Notoriously, Moore claimed too that a particular fallacy, the "naturalistic fallacy", underlay many forms of naturalism. He offered many characterizations of this purported fallacy, which now strike a reader as wildly non-equivalent (see esp. secs. 1.10 and 1.12); see also Frankena, "Naturalistic Fallacy" (1939). In his talk of a "fallacy", though, Moore seemed especially concerned with this pattern of argument: Proclaim that such-and-such is "the very meaning" of the term 'good', and offer this claim negligible scrutiny. Then use this claim about the meaning of 'good' to conclude, trivially, that all and only such-and-such things are good. See Moore's discussion of Bentham (1.4). Thinking that 'good' must mean something we can state in other terms, thought Moore, closes one's mind, and makes one dismiss questions that call for careful investigation, thinking them to be quickly settled by definition.

materials of Moore's tests. A thoroughgoing, lived skepticism about meaning would paralyze thought and discourse. Without judgments of disagreement and coherence, no one could navigate a conversation. We couldn't even navigate the inner conversation of our own thoughts. Quine famously challenges whether judgments of meaning can have a clear scientific basis, and this has led to a search for ways to do philosophy without relying on notions of analyticity and conceptual identity and distinctness. What's right about Quine's conclusions and what might be wrong are complex questions, which I won't attempt to sort out. Concede to Quine, though, that what Hedda means by 'good' is empirically indeterminate. Then if you confine yourself rigorously to empirically founded judgments, you can't consider what she says; you can't agree or disagree. You can't come to reject a thought that you yourself had entertained, for you don't know which thought it was.

We respond to possible states of mind as coherent or incoherent, and this, in part, is what enables us to "track" our conversations and our own thoughts. If these intuitions exist and work systematically, then we can meaningfully ask such questions as whether *good* and *desired* figure equivalently in our conceptual intuitions. How, after all, do we navigate a discussion? How can participants and observers track it? Sometimes we don't, and listeners are reduced to bafflement. Return to Hedda and Désiré, and their initial claims:

Not only pleasure is good. —Désiré $(*\mathcal{H})$

Tracking their conversation requires appreciating, implicitly at least, that these two claims are in direct contradiction. Faced with Hedda's claim $\mathcal{H}$, Désiré could not have responded, "Yes, but not only pleasure is good." To do so would draw bafflement; this we all recognize. On the other hand, he could intelligibly have said, "Yes, but not only pleasure is desired." Hedda might agree or disagree, but part of her conversational competence is to recognize that Désiré's 'Yes, but' here is linguistically appropriate, that she hasn't, in claiming $\mathcal{H}$, already rejected what he is saying.

Tracking a conversation, then, requires competence with logical terms like 'not'. But this may be uncontroversial: logic is one thing, and analyticity, insofar as it outstrips logic, is quite another. The word 'not' in English is a logical term, and tracking a conversation requires hearing simple logical contradictions as contradictions—with that pretty much everyone agrees. Quineans gladly accept logic as distinctive, but they deny that there are distinctively analytic truths and contradictions that are not logical truths and contradictions.

Imagine, though, this conversation.

Hedda: Only pleasure is good.

Waldo: Yes, but not only pleasure is desirable.

Hedda has every right to be baffled; Waldo's response doesn't "track". She can, of course, try to elicit what distinction he has in mind when he claims something to be "desirable" but not "good"; she can cast about for a charitable interpretation. What she cannot do is just take his words at face value, accepting or rejecting his position. Waldo isn't, in the narrowest sense, violating the logical rules of English; it isn't strictly logical terms like 'not' that cause all the problem. But he does seem to be trying to invoke a distinction that his words don't convey.

Is this phenomenon specially "conceptual"? There are many ways to draw a blank in conversation, and if Moore's diagnosis is supported by phenomena of bafflement, with signs that the conversation doesn't "track", this will require that the bafflement be distinctive in some way. It must be bafflement of a kind that is specially conceptual. Not that we need recognize it as such; Moore's taxonomies might be tenable even if we couldn't tell drawing a conceptual blank from drawing any other kind of blank. A theory of conversation and its pitfalls, after all, might classify kinds of bafflement in ways we couldn't recognize without the theory. Still, a claim that some kinds of bafflement are distinctively conceptual will need some kind of support or other.

When we draw a blank with Waldo's response, is our bafflement conceptual? What alternative hypothesis is there to invoke, what alternative that would dispense with an analytic/synthetic distinction? One is that the work is being done not by analyticity, but by manifest obviousness. A person should not be heard as accepting something that is obviously false; that is a prime maxim of interpretation. Now obviously, everything desirable is good, and so when Waldo appears to commit himself to denying this absurdity, we draw a blank. It is as if he had said, "That dog holds its breath when it chases rabbits."

Obviousness alone, though, isn't doing all the work. Clearly an important distinction can be drawn between the claim that something is desirable but not good and the claim that a dog chases rabbits without breathing. The first is false necessarily; the second is not. We can picture a dog chasing rabbits holding its breath; we know what it would *be* for a dog to do so, even if we expect it never to happen. In contrast, we don't know what it would be for a dog to sit on its own shoulders; there's no configuration, no way of coping with gravity and support, that would count as so doing. Likewise, we don't know what it would be for pleasure, or anything else, to be desirable but not good. We don't even know what it would be to *think* that something's good but not desirable.

Still, will Moorean tests work with harder cases? Philippa Foot imagines a man who insists that clasping one's hands is good, and for no reason but that it's the clasping of one's hands. Some naturalistic constraints, she concludes, are built into the very meaning of good. Does Moore have tests that let us assess Foot's claim? The hand-clasper does baffle us. (We're perhaps like the Masai boy in Kenya who flagged down a car with William Frankena in it with fellow bird-watchers: "What are they doing?" he asked the driver. "Looking for birds."—"Oh, to eat them?"—"No." Then after a pause, "Oh, they want the feathers?"—"No.") Like the Masai boy, we're baffled with the hand-clasper, because he's in a state of mind it's hard to imagine "from the inside", even in mental play-acting. Is he mixed up in his concepts, then? Not at all, I want to say—or he *may* very well not be.

But here I get ahead of my argument. Foot doesn't share my sense of the case, and so to speak with her I'd need more than my linguistic intuitions. I'd need some account of what our bafflement is, if it isn't bafflement with navigating his concepts—and the aim of this book is to develop such an account. Suppose, now, our man shows every sign of favoring hand-clasping, and no sign of having a rationale or of feeling in want of one. Then he's not mixed up in his concepts; he's got crazy views on what to do and why. Convince him that he's misusing words like 'reason', that an act's being a hand-clasping linguistically just doesn't count as a basic "reason", and he'll change his way of speaking, to be sure. But if he doesn't change his thinking on what to do, he'll still be crazy and unintelligible. And if he then does give up hand-clasping or if he then searches for a rationale for his practice, isn't he responding to the wrong kind of consideration? Won't Foot too recognize that? (I mean here, of course, Mrs. Foot of decades ago.) If we ourselves think whether to sacrifice anything else to clasp hands, what counts in English as "good" or as a "reason" won't remotely enter in. What's wrong isn't the hand-clasper's concepts, but his grounds for acting.

The Moore-like tests I support, then, do discriminate. I argue later, for instance, that strictly naturalistic ideal observer theories don't pass them. What, though, of the kinds of analytic equivalences I do accept? *To think something good is to favor it.* This no doubt needs refinement, but let's try it even in this crude form and see if it is a valid conceptual claim. Eve tells us "I favor this action, but I don't think it's good." Or she says, "I think that this is truly the very best thing we can do, but I don't favor it." We may on further questioning manage to give some sense to her words, but her bare words don't convey what contrast she's making. If she voiced this line in speaking, we might pick up a special sense of her words from her inflection—the "good" or "best" as goody-goody, or as all too decent when indecency is called for, or some such thing. We can't, though, simply tell from her words what she means. We know the language, but she isn't quite speaking it. It's as if she said "I think it's good, but then again I don't think it's good." With luck we'll discern what she means, but we can't just read off what possibility her words allow.

Property and Concept

By some accounts of what "naturalism" is, Moore might be read almost as a modern naturalist. "*The* good", he tells us, or "that which is good", is not indefinable. By "*the* good" he means "the whole of that to which the adjective will apply, and the adjective must *always* truly apply to it" (p. 9). "I do most fully believe," he avows, "that some true proposition of the form 'Intelligence is good and intelligence alone is good' can be found" (p. 9). A true proposition of this form, he explains, would be not a definition of good, but a definition of *the* good.

What, then, does Moore mean by '*the* good'? On one apparent reading, it is the extension of the adjective 'good', the set of all and only those things that are good. For all Moore's purely conceptual argu-

ments tell us, Hedda the hedonist might be right about what this extension is. She thinks that all and only pleasant things are good, and nothing in Moore's study of concepts alone refutes her.

Moore, though, demands something stronger than this of *the* good.
Suppose that Hedda is right, and suppose too that, in fact, only terrestrial beings experience pleasure. Then 'pleasure' and 'terrestrial pleasure' have the same extension: all and only terrestrial pleasant things
are pleasant, and so all and only they, on Hedda's view, are good. But
the good is pleasure, according to Hedda, not terrestrial pleasure. Being pleasant makes something good; being terrestrial doesn't. It might,
after all, have been the case, though in fact it isn't, that extraterrestrial
beings—beings, say, on a planet of Alpha Centauri—experienced pleasure too. This *might* have been the case, even if in fact, in the universe,
there happen to be no non-terrestrial beings that are capable of pleasure, even if there never have been and never will be. *The* good, Moore
tells us, is the whole of what the adjective 'good' "must *always* truly apply" to (p. 9); he thus uses the modal construction 'must *always*'. For
pleasure to be *the* good, we require that all and only pleasant things are
good not only as things in fact stand, but in every possible situation. In
this sense, 'pleasant' and 'good' must, for pleasure to be *the* good, be
coextensional necessarily.[2]

Is Moore, then, a believer in simple, non-natural properties? I mean
not the historical Moore, the Moore of the whole of *Principia Ethica*,
but a Moore we might read into the arguments and doctrines I have re-
counted. Moore draws from his tests a lesson about meanings: that
the term 'good' means something different from any naturalistic term,
from any psychological term or sociological term, for instance, from
any term that can figure in purely empirical inquiries. Still, he thinks,
some naturalistic formulation is coextensional with 'good' necessarily. Much work on properties in recent decades treats properties and
meanings as distinct. Writers differ on how the point is best regi-
mented, but one way is to speak of *concepts:* meanings are concepts, and
concepts aren't properties. Now if Moore had spoken this way, how
might he best have fit his tests and their lesson into this framework?
Suppose he distinguished properties and concepts. He would then

2. Of course, this isn't a necessary truth about the terms 'good' and 'pleasant' in
our community; we might have spoken differently. The point, rather, is that if
Hedda is right, then necessarily, all and only pleasant things are good.

need to ask whether it is the *property* of good or the *concept* of good that his arguments and core doctrines address.

Purported examples of a property/concept distinction abound in the philosophical literature of the past few decades.[3] The property of being me, I can say, is just the property of being Allan Gibbard. The two concepts I can entertain, though, are distinct: suffering amnesia but coming to know certain arcane philosophical writings, I might indignantly deny being Gibbard. Still, if I kept my logical cogency, I wouldn't deny my self-identity: "Of course I am me, but I am not Gibbard." The same might go for the concepts of being water and being H_2O, having a certain chemical structure: opponents of Lavoisier didn't deny that water is water, but they denied that water is H_2O. The concepts are distinct, at least for the naïve beginner in chemistry. As it turns out, though, the property of being water just *is* the property of being H_2O. Or so it is frequently claimed.

Properties go with necessity: in any possible situation in which I existed, I would be Allan Gibbard. I might not be called 'Allan Gibbard', for it is happenstance that, in our mouths, that name designates me; but I, as things stand, can say of any non-actual situation in which I would exist, "Allan Gibbard is who I would be." Likewise, in any possible situation water would be H_2O; if something other than H_2O behaved exactly as water behaves in everyday experience, that stuff still wouldn't be water. Identity of properties, however, though it yields necessary equivalence, does not yield *a priori* equivalence. Chemists, after all, required evidence that water is H_2O—just as I, were I amnesiac, might require evidence that I am Gibbard.

These glosses on the phenomena still no doubt require debate, but here I'll assume that they are correct and ask how to read Moore's views into such a picture. What position might his arguments and tests support? Hedda thinks that the terms 'good' and 'pleasant' are necessarily coextensive. Need she think, if she accepts Moore's arguments about meaning, that the two terms signify different properties? Nothing in the tests forces that conclusion, so long as the two terms express different concepts. Désiré, Hedda must recognize, is conceptually coherent if he denies that only pleasant things are good—just as opponents of

3. Putnam in "Meaning of Meaning" (1975) and Kripke in "Naming and Necessity" (1972) provide material for making such a distinction. Peacocke, in *A Study of Concepts* (1992), sharply distinguishes concepts from properties (p. 2).

Lavoisier were conceptually coherent in denying that all and only water is H_2O. That shows that the *concepts* of being good and of being pleasant are distinct. It doesn't show that two distinct *properties* are in play. Moore's tests show distinctness of concepts, not of properties.

If two terms stand for the same property, then they are necessarily coextensive. Does the converse hold? If two terms are necessarily coextensive, does it follow that they signify the same property? Different accounts of properties say different things on this score. Nothing I have ventured so far commits us on this issue, and so nothing so far commits my emended Moore to thinking that—on a conceptually coherent rendition of Hedda's views—'good' and 'pleasant' signify the same property. Still, I am arguing, nothing in Moore's arguments supports a conclusion that more than one property is in play. The most ontologically economical rendition of Moore's view, then, the view left after applying Occam's razor, might be that a conceptually coherent hedonist like Hedda will think that the property of being good and the property of being pleasant are one and the same.

Try reading Moore freely, then, as a non-naturalist for concepts but not for properties. This may not, of course, be what the historical Moore would have embraced if he had considered and accepted these purported distinctions. Still it fits his tests: what his tests support is claims of distinct concepts, not properties. Non-natural properties have ever since Moore seemed mysterious, and his arguments do nothing to establish them. The Moore to match in a theory of normative thought can drop non-natural properties and focus instead on normative concepts.

Concepts, we might say, can be naturalistic; these are the concepts that arise in strict empirical science and in everyday causal explanations of our experience and observations—explanations of a kind that might be elaborated into empirical science. Ethical theory, holds Moore, is not a purely empirical science; psychological and sociological claims, confined strictly to science, are not in themselves ethical claims. Claims are ethical, Moore thinks, when they involve, in an essential way, the specially ethical notions of good and bad. These notions are concepts, we can say, and they are non-naturalistic. Moore we can emend as proclaiming not non-natural properties, but non-naturalistic concepts. All *properties* are *natural*, but some *concepts* are *non-naturalistic*.

I now stipulate some terminology. If concepts, properties, and extensions are distinct, then a term like 'pleasant' will indicate each in a different sense. The term 'pleasant', then, I'll say

> *designates* its *extension*, the set of pleasant things (that is, the set of
> actual things that are actually pleasant),
> *signifies* the *property* of being pleasant, and
> *expresses* the *concept* of being pleasant.

According to Hedda, the terms 'good' and 'pleasant' signify the same property—a natural property—but express distinct concepts. This emended Moore thinks Hedda wrong on what property the term 'good' signifies, but thinks, like her, that it signifies some natural property. This property, on his own doctrines, is refined and complex, involving trade-offs of values and the ways more elementary natural properties combine in organic wholes. It's not, though, his arguments about meanings that are meant to establish this, and this difference in complexity isn't one of natural versus non-natural. The terms 'good' and 'pleasant' both signify natural properties, but the property that 'good' signifies is vastly the more complex of the two. So thinks my emended Moore.

Synthetic, *A Priori* Necessity

Hedda thinks that necessarily—in any possible situation—all and only pleasure is good. How does she claim to know this? Her friend Reg might offer an answer. Reg, too, is a hedonist: he agrees with Hedda that, necessarily, all and only pleasure is good. He also offers an account of knowledge of good and bad; technically, it might be called an "ideal observer account with rigidification". Good, Reg tells us, is whatever kind passes this test: every actual person would desire it to exist if that person were impartial, were normal as the actual run of people go, and had been aware, repeatedly and vividly, of all relevant facts. I'll call such a person *ideal-normal*. This definition rigidifies, in that even as it applies to wildly different ways human desires might have run, it signifies a single kind—picked out in terms of what actual people are prone to desire. A puzzle for ideal observer theories is how they apply to possible situations where the distribution of human characteristics are far different. What of a world of sadists, who, when impartial, thrilled to the thought of anyone's suffering and desired it? In thinking of such a world, says Reg, the standard is how the normal run of *actual* people, in our actual world, would, if rendered ideal, react to the world of sadists. (Here the term 'ideal' is given a technical meaning; an *ideal* observer is impartial and, vividly and repeatedly, aware of all relevant facts. It isn't built into the definition that an "ideal" observer isn't a sadist; that's a contingent, empirical matter.) If we normal people, rendered ideal in this sense, would want these sadists not to suffer, then their suffering is bad, not good. The dispositions of actual, normal people, says Reg, fix the property that amounts to being good. And that property, he agrees with Hedda, is the property of being pleasant. Necessarily, all and only pleasant things are good, and all and only unpleasant things are bad. Even in a world of sadists, suffering would be bad—though the pleasure others derive from contemplating it would be good. So says Reg.

Reg can't coherently make these claims *a priori*. His hedonistic claims rest on a purported empirical finding, a finding about the dispositions of actual people. The bulk of actual people, he claims, are disposed, when rendered ideal and thinking of non-actual situations, to prefer greater net pleasure in the world to less and to have no other intrinsic preferences. This kind of thing we could only learn from experience, by investigating what actual people are like—so Reg must agree. What, then, of his claim that the better is whatever most actual people would prefer if rendered "ideal"? If he claims to establish this on the basis of experience, that will push the question of how he knows one step further. Experience of type E, he will be claiming, establishes that his ideal observer test works. We can ask in turn how he knows that.

Intuitionists are *foundationalists*: they claim that such a regress cannot go on forever. At some point, they say, the claim to knowledge cannot rest on experience, but must be made *a priori*. A definitional naturalist will agree, but claim further that the *a priori* claim at the end of the regress is analytic, a matter of definition. Moore the non-naturalist must reject this, for if the regress ends in an analytic truth, then the concept of good turns out to be naturalistic. Imagine Reg as a naturalist of the ilk Moore rejects: he might end the regress of empirical support at the point we have reached, and proclaim it to be secured by definition. Reg then is a definitional naturalist. The concept of being better, he says, is the concept of being preferred by any possible ideal-normal observer— where by definition, an *ideal-normal* observer is one who is normal as the run of actual people goes, except that he has been repeatedly and vividly aware of all relevant facts. This is a naturalistic concept, and Moore thinks he can refute the view that it is the concept of good.

I haven't established that Moore is right in this. Moore may have thought he had shown that *any* version whatsoever of definitional naturalism falls before his catapults. In my own view, naturalistic analyses must be tackled case by case; I know of no argument that proves in advance that every such definition fails. I take up ideal observer definitions later.

Consider, though, an alternative kind of view that Reg might hold. He might end the regress at this point, claiming *a priori* knowledge, but not claim to have a correct analytic definition of good. What we know *a priori*, what we know but don't establish by experience, is that the better of two things is whichever would be preferred by any possible ideal-normal observer—with 'ideal-normal' defined as before. Suppose Reg takes this view of the matter. Hedda might claim to know *a priori* that the good is pleasure: that in any possible situation, all and only pleasant things would be good. If so, the grounds she cites will not include the upshot of observations; indeed she might see this as axiomatic, as clearly so on no further grounds at all. Hedda and Reg, then, are similar in important ways. Both are non-naturalists. They both think that the property of being good is the property of being pleasant. On how this is known, though, the two differ: Hedda claims to know this *a priori*, whereas Reg does not. Reg claims something else as axiomatic, *a priori* knowledge: that good things are those that would be desired by any ideal-normal observer.

Both, then, claim that the property of being good is a natural property, the property of being pleasant. Each is an intuitionist in that each rests this claim on a claim to *a priori* knowledge. The two differ, though, in the status they accord the claim that necessarily, all and only pleasant things are good. Hedda claims that we know this *a priori* and axiomatically; Reg that we know it *a posteriori*. Both claim that ethical knowledge rests on an *a priori* basis—but not on an analytic basis. If a faculty of basic, non-analytic *a priori* knowledge is called intuition, they both think that ethical knowledge depends, ultimately, on intuition.

A Template to Match

Here, then, is our Moore-like template. It is a naturalism for properties, but a non-naturalism for concepts. It denies analytic naturalism, the doctrine that 'good' can be defined, analytically, in naturalistic terms. It affirms, though, that some natural property is signified by the term 'good'.

I don't claim to have established this as the correct template to match. Moore did, more or less: he thought he had identified a "naturalistic fallacy" that all analytic naturalists commit, and he thought that once we surveyed a few possible versions of analytic naturalism, we could see how all such theories must fail. I myself claim that from Moore we can draw a powerful set of tools for refuting various forms of analytic naturalism. Do these tools, though, work against any form of analytic naturalism whatsoever? That I don't claim to have established. We must scrutinize each comer and see how it fares. In later chapters, I consider a few prominent forms of analytic naturalism, analytic versions of ideal observer theories in particular. I don't, however, discover a sweeping refutation, all in advance, of every possible form of analytic naturalism. Moreover, even refuting analytic naturalism in general, refuting it in all its possible forms, would not establish conceptual nonnaturalism; it wouldn't show that the concept of good is not a naturalistic concept. Another explanation of the phenomena, after all, might be that the concept of good is naturalistic but *sui generis:* that ethical concepts act just like other naturalistic concepts, in common sense or in the sciences, but still are not definable in terms of non-ethical concepts.[4]

I don't, then, take it that the Moorean phenomena I have been surveying refute all forms of conceptual naturalism. Rather, in much of the rest of this book, I develop a hypothesis to explain these Moorean phenomena. My aim is to prove that a *possible* kind of thought works much as Moore maintained. To show this, I won't consider specifically ethical concepts, and I won't study Moore's primitive concept of good. Instead, I take as my example the concept of being "the thing to do". For this concept, I stipulate a built-in *to-be-done*ness, and then I study how the concept must work. It turns out to work very much as Moore, on my reading, concluded that the concept *good* works.

Indeed, I attempt something stronger: I argue that as thinkers and planners in life, we are committed to concepts that behave as Moore expects—whether or not these are concepts we have words to express.

4. Nicholas Sturgeon has pointed out this possibility to me.

For many chapters to follow, I explore how these concepts behave, these concepts to which any agent is committed. Only later do I discuss whether these concepts include the familiar normative concepts that figure in our thoughts from day to day. Elsewhere I have studied a wide range of thoughts we do have and voice: thoughts about what it *makes sense* to do, about what things are *worth* seeking and worth having in life, about what acts are *right* and what acts *wrong*, and about what acts are morally *praiseworthy* and what acts *reprehensible*.[5] These thoughts, I have claimed, can all be explained on the pattern I explore in this book. These, however, are claims for elsewhere: My purpose in this book is to establish the possibility of such content and its intelligibility, and to show that we are all committed to such content—whether English gives us means to voice it or not.

Assume initially, then, that there are natural facts, and that we can think descriptive thoughts about them. Don't suppose, at this point, that there are any facts of what to do. Set aside for now all worries about what exactly "natural" facts are and whether we can make a sharp cleavage between them and facts that are laden with *to-be-done*ness. Seeming facts that hover near the gap will be for later. My claim now is this: that if clearly natural facts *were* all the facts there are, we would reason much as if there were facts of what to do. The concepts we use in this reasoning would behave, in many ways, like the non-naturalistic concepts proclaimed by my emended Moore. And reasoning with such concepts, as if there are such facts of what to do, is not to commit an error.

5. See my *Wise Choices* (1990), chap. 3, on what it "makes sense" to do, on right and wrong, and on the praiseworthy and reprehensible; see also my "Moral Concepts: Substance and Sentiment" (1992) and "Moral Concepts and Justified Feelings" (1993). On good and better, see my "Preference and Preferability" (1998).

~ II
The Thing to Do

$\sim$ 3

Planning and Ruling Out: The Frege-Geach Problem

$\mathcal{R}$ETURN NOW TO HOLMES, who as Moriarty draws nigh, decides to start packing now. His decision we can think of as expressed imperatively: to decide to start packing is in effect to tell himself "Start parking now!" There is not much difference, though, between "Pack now!" and the indicative "It's time to pack," or "Now I've got to pack." The import of the imperative may be much like the import of one of these descriptive-seeming claims. Could we, then, think that a decision can be expressed in either of two ways: as an imperative like 'Pack now!' or synonymously as a statement? As our canonical form for a statement expressing a decision, choose "Packing is now the thing to do."[1] Can we explain this predicate 'is the thing to do' as a device for expressing decisions?

Doing so raises the "Frege-Geach" problem for theories of content like mine.[2] Once we have such a predicate, it figures in a broad variety of contexts. Holmes can say to himself,

Either packing is now the thing to do, or by now it's too late to catch the train anyway. (1)

1. This phrase 'is the thing to do' was suggested by Railton, "Non-Cognitivism about Rationality" (1993), p. 42.
2. For expositions of the "Frege-Geach" problem for theories of meaning like the one I am developing, see Geach, "Assertion" (1965) and Searle, "Meaning" (1962).

He can then include this disjunction in an argument: join (1) with the premise

It's not even now too late to catch the train.   (2)

The conclusion seems to follow, therefore:

Packing now is the thing to do.   (3)

His conclusion (3), though, we have explained not by its truth conditions, but as an expression of a decision. How, then, do we explain the disjunction (1)? Not just any explanation will do: a satisfactory explanation must explain the apparent validity of Holmes's argument. It must explain why this validity seems of a piece with the validity of plain arguments of fact. These we standardly explain in terms of truth and truth conditions. Decisions don't seem true or false; how can they figure in ordinary-seeming arguments?[3]

The Frege-Geach problem can be solved, I claim: a good solution has emerged in publications over the past dozen years.[4] As it has been presented, though, this solution can look contrived and gruesome, motivated only by a determination to make things come out right. I claim, rather, that the moves an expressivist can use to solve the embedding problem are natural—and that they apply, in much the same way, to straight descriptive statements. Take the disjunctive syllogism Holmes uses: Why does reasoning on this pattern work even for prosaically descriptive statements? Answer this the right way, I suggest, and a like answer will apply to statements that interweave description with decision.

3. Whether explanations of logic in terms of truth conditions do any work is controversial. Horwich, in *Truth* (1990), adopts a "minimalist" position, according to which all there is to know specially about truth is contained in instances of a disquotational schema. Truth in this minimal sense, he argues, can't be used to characterize logical connectives. See also Dreier, "Expressivist Embeddings" (1996). I accept their arguments on this score. Horwich thinks, moreover, that there is nothing special for the expressivist who accepts minimal truth to explain. Dreier argues that there is. I accept Dreier's argument, which raises questions that are important for me to discuss. To discuss these questions, though, I need to place some apparatus on the table, and so I postpone discussion of these issues.

4. Gibbard, "Expressivistic Theory" (1986); Blackburn, "Attitudes" (1988); Gibbard, *Wise Choices* (1990, chap. 5); Blackburn, "Gibbard" (1993); Gibbard, "Reply to Blackburn" (1993).

In this chapter, I offer an initial formulation of this solution, and then refine it. In the chapter that follows, I explore some of the problems that critics might find with the solution, and ask what it is about choice and planning that makes the solution work. All this forms the first stage of a long two-stage argument: the argument starts from a view that reads decision imperatively and ends up mimicking a practical realism, a realism for being the thing to do. It mimics Moore's and Ewing's non-naturalistic moral realism, and in some respects it mimics a naturalistic moral realism. The second stage of the argument begins in Chapter 5: from the solution to the Frege-Geach problem, I there begin to argue, conclusions follow that sound like the tenets of a normative realism. Being the thing to do, I argue, *supervenes* on natural properties. And there is, moreover, a property that *constitutes* being the thing to do.

Indeed, far more follows—and these consequences will be subjects for further chapters. Something's being the thing to do can *explain* happenings in the world: it might explain why I did what I did, or why you were surprised when I didn't. In consequence, judgments of what to do act like perception or apprehension in some ways—though in other ways they act differently. In the third part of this book, "Normative Concepts," I turn to the concepts we actually have; in other writings too I touch on hypotheses concerning normative *value* of different kinds, *thick concepts*, and *morals*.[5] In part my treatments will be possibility proofs: armed with a solution to the Frege-Geach problem, we can see the possibility of explaining concepts expressivistically, and find that certain concepts, so explained, bear a tantalizing resemblance to familiar normative concepts. The work in these next few chapters, then, is the basis for much to come.

Suppose the concepts I'll be elucidating *are* our actual normative concepts, our concepts of being the thing to do, of value, and the like. Suppose in particular that I succeed in explaining our moral concepts expressivistically, to the extent that these concepts are clear. Then, it will follow, the bulk of things that "moral realists" of different varieties say to characterize their positions are things that I can accept and explain. The bulk of debate on "moral realism" in recent philosophy

5. I treat narrowly moral concepts in *Wise Choices* (1990) and "Moral Concepts" (1992); thick concepts in "Thick Concepts" (1992); value in "Preference and Preferability" (1998).

turns out to be irrelevant to any difference between that position and my expressivism. Those who see themselves as moral realists should perhaps welcome that outcome: many of the claims that they stress, I'll be showing, turn out to have more basis than just "what we think". Moral realists can welcome me into their fold, if they wish, as an adherent of their chief contentions. Still, though we agree on many of the phenomena that a theory of normative concepts must explain, the ways I explain these phenomena will be distinctive. I claim to explain aspects of warrant and value that otherwise we can only attribute to brute features of the normative realm.

Disjunction as Ruling Out: Decided States

How shall we understand the disjunctive claim Holmes makes?

> Either packing is now the thing to do, or by now it's too late to catch the train anyway.   (1)

To accept (1) all by itself isn't to accept any straight imperative. (1) involves *to-be-done*ness, true enough, but it doesn't proclaim it; it doesn't tell Holmes straight out what to do. As we have seen, though, it can make a difference in his reasoning on what to do. Put disjunction (1) together with the descriptive premise

> It's not even now too late to catch the train,   (2)

and he gets the practical conclusion,

> Packing now is the thing to do.   (3)

This last we explain as saying what to do. A piece of practical reasoning, then, has the familiar form *P* or *L*, not *L*, therefore *P*. In this case, though, the conclusion *P* expresses a decision.

What does Holmes do in accepting a disjunction like (1)? What, indeed, do I do in accepting *any* disjunction? I rule out a possibility. A disjunction *A* or *B*, as we all know, precludes the case where *A* and *B* are both false. The force of the precluding is this: if I accept *A* or *B*, I can't then come both to reject *A* and to reject *B*—unless, that is, I change my mind, either knowingly or by losing track of my thinking.

What, then, of an argument, *A* or *B*, not *A*, therefore *B*? With the first I rule out this: coming both to reject *A* and to reject *B*. With the second I reject *A*. The combined effect, then, is to rule out rejecting *B*. It would therefore be inconsistent for me to accept the premises and reject the conclusion: I would be doing what I had ruled out doing.

This explanation applies whether or not the disjunctive reasoning is couched in straight descriptive terms. It applies to reasoning from a descriptive disjunction *A* or *B*, and it applies equally to Holmes's reasoning from the disjunction (1). If Holmes accepts (1), he rules out the following: coming both (i) to reject its being too late to catch the train, and (ii) to reject deciding to pack. With (2), he rejects its being too late to catch the train. He has thus ruled out rejecting deciding to pack.

What do these states of "ruling out" or "rejecting" amount to? Consider plain belief: to *reject* belief in gods, as I mean the term, is to disagree with the belief that gods exist. The convinced agnostic does no such thing. She shuns belief in the gods and shuns disbelief in them too, but she doesn't, in my sense, "reject" belief in the gods. She suspends both agreement and disagreement with theistic belief. Likewise with packing: to reject deciding to pack is to disagree with any decision to pack. When Holmes rejects packing now, he not only shuns deciding to pack, he comes out in disagreement with packing. And "ruling out"? To rule out belief in gods, we might say, is to *commit* oneself to rejecting belief in them. To rule out packing is to commit oneself to rejecting packing. The inferential import of a state of mind, we can try saying, is a matter of the commitments one takes on in reaching that state of mind. Much more needs to be said about all this, of course, and I face some of the issues in the next chapter. (For one thing, the notion of a commitment is itself a normative notion—one that seems needed for any normative treatment of reasoning. Also, packing from preference is different from plumping for packing out of indifference, and for now I am fudging this distinction.) Here, though, let's postpone larger issues and pursue these rough thoughts: (i) one can disagree with an action, disagree with such disagreement, and the like, and (ii) certain states of mind have inferential import in that they rule out certain other states of mind.

It would be good to have a way to keep track of such inferential import. How might we code the inferential import of disjunctions and the like? Holmes's disjunction (1) rules something out: it rules out a combined state of describing and deciding, of judging how things are and settling what to do. Two issues are in play, one an issue of how things are, and one an issue of what to do: (a) whether it's too late to catch the train, and (b) whether to start packing. This makes for four possible combinations of pertinent settled belief and decision—four combinations that Holmes might come to if he settles his mind on both of these matters:

C_{LP}: Believing it's too late and deciding to pack.
C_{Lp}: Believing it's too late and rejecting deciding to pack.
C_{lP}: Believing it's not too late and deciding to pack.
C_{lp}: Believing it's not too late and rejecting deciding to pack.

Since these are the states of mind Holmes can be in if he has decided both what to believe and what to do, I'll call them *decided states*. We can now represent the content of the disjunction (1) by which of these decided states it rules out and which it doesn't. What it rules out is C_{lp}, believing it's not too late and still deciding not to pack. The disjunction rules out none of the other three decided states: C_{LP}, C_{Lp}, and C_{lP}. Say, then, that a judgment *allows* a decided state just in case it doesn't rule it out. (For a judgment to "allow" a decided state is not for it to *preclude* ruling that state out. One may go on to rule the state out with other judgments one makes. It is just for that judgment not *by itself* to rule out that decided state.) The content of the disjunction (1), then, we can represent by the set $\{C_{LP}, C_{Lp}, C_{lP}\}$ of decided states it allows. It rules out all decided states but these—namely, the single decided state C_{lp}.

We can also put all this in terms of changing one's mind or not. Decided states C_{LP}, C_{Lp}, and C_{lP} are just the ones Holmes could come to be in without changing his mind about disjunction (1), without coming to disagree with it.

Decided states thus work in a way isomorphic to the workings of truth conditions. That is to say, the structure of *allowing* decided states or not is the same as the structure of *being true* or not *under* determinate conditions. Just as disjunction can be treated as a truth-functional connective, we can treat it, in a like manner, as an "allowing-functional" connective. Instead of a table with 't' for *true* and 'f' for *false*, we can construct a like-appearing table where 't' means *allows* and 'f' means *rules out.* The standard things said of truth conditions then carry over to this new way of speaking: a disjunction, for instance, *allows* a decided state just in case at least one of its components allows that state. An inference is *valid* just in case no decided state is allowed by all of its premises but not by its conclusion.

We can switch back and forth, indeed, between talk of states of mind and talk of their "content", as we might say. This holds both for decisions and for beliefs. Instead of speaking in terms of decisions, we might speak in terms of a kind of content they have. Decisions, after all, do have content in a way: the content of Holmes's decision, we might say, is *to pack.* Can he, then, conjoin the content of the decision, in this sense, with the content of a belief *that it's not too late?* These, it seems, are two things that Holmes might settle on: to pack, and that it is not too late. This is intelligible as the content of a state of mind that is decided on whether to pack, and decided on whether it is too late. This maximally specific combination of decisional and factual content we might call a *fact-prac world.* It combines a factual condition with the content of a decision. The disjunction (1), we can say, *holds* for this fact-prac world, among others. And one is *in* what I've been calling a "decided state" of mind if and only if some fact-prac world is the content of one's combined beliefs and decisions.

In a different and more traditional sense, to be sure, one could treat a belief that I am about to pack and a decision to pack as having the same "content", *that I will forthwith pack,* toward which I take different propositional attitudes: belief, and deciding to actualize. The two attitudes have different "directions of fit", we can say, toward the same item of "content". Here, though, I am opting to transmute force into content: I speak of a single attitude "accepting" that one can take toward distinct items of content, *that I will forthwith pack* and the plan *to pack.*

Such talk of "content" in this non-standard sense, though, is optional. We can instead speak, as I did at first, not in terms of such content and such worlds, but in terms of decided states of mind a judgment allows and ones it rules out. This, I have been stressing, we can do even in purely descriptive, factual cases. Take thinking that snow is white or coal is black: this rules out rejecting jointly the thoughts that snow is white and that coal is black. It allows all other decided states of mind on whether or not snow is white and whether or not snow is black. Both with plain descriptive belief and with decision, in short, we can apply the structure of truth functions in either of two different ways: in terms of a kind of content, which may be either factual or decisional, or in terms of states of mind. The same structure emerges either way. On one interpretation, it is a structure of allowing or ruling out various decided states of mind; on the other, it is a structure of obtaining or not for various "worlds".

It is often thought that standard logic requires facts, that for logic to apply to one's thinking, the thinking must be descriptive of facts. Decisions too, though, allow for reasoning, and decisions in a sense have content. These things we can accept without thinking that to come to a decision is to come to a special kind of conclusion of fact.

Contingency Plans

At seven in the morning, Holmes concludes that it's too soon to start packing. At noon he decides that packing now is the thing to do. He hasn't changed his mind. After all, as his old school chum Edwin tells us,

> One cannot eat breakfast all day
> Nor is it the act of a sinner,
> When breakfast is taken away,
> To turn his attention to dinner.

Holmes may have planned all along to begin packing at eight, or he may have planned to start packing when he got word that Moriarty was drawing nigh. Disingenuous Edwin, in contrast, who has jilted his bride to be, has indeed changed his mind. As a love-sick boy he planned soon to marry her, whereas when the time came he changed his mind and broke his promise. (Moriarty, as an outright con artist, might have broken his promise without changing his mind.)

What a person sticks to or not in thinking what to do, then, is not a fixed policy of what to do next, but a plan. Likewise with beliefs: Holmes at seven thinks that Moriarty is still far away, and by noon thinks that Moriarty is close. In this case too, Holmes hasn't changed his mind; Moriarty has done just what Holmes expected. In a sense, Holmes correctly believes one thing earlier and another thing later—but in another sense, he believes the same things all along.

People can agree or disagree in belief, and they can, in a sense, agree or disagree in plan. This will require care in formulation. Holmes thinks that Moriarty is nearby, and Mrs. Hudson thinks that Moriarty is far away. The two aren't thereby in disagreement, if they are far apart from each other and they know it. Likewise, if Holmes decides to start packing and Mrs. Hudson decides to retire for the night, they don't thereby disagree on what to do. Mrs. Hudson may agree with Holmes on what to do in Holmes's situation; they may agree that in his plight, the thing to do is to start packing. Holmes, likewise, may agree with Mrs. Hudson that in her situation the thing to do is to go to bed. On the other hand, they might genuinely disagree as to what to do: it could be that Mrs. Hudson thinks that the thing for her to do is to go straight to the police, whereas Holmes, on the contrary, thinks that the thing for her to do is to stay in and project his cardboard silhouette on the window shade.

What are these thoughts that make up plans? Holmes plans, in advance, to start packing when Moriarty draws nigh. He plans too for contingencies: he can plan what to do, say, if he finds that his cab is being followed. He plans, in that case, to jump out of the cab into the bushes and have the driver speed on without him to the station. Such contingency planning has two aspects, just one of which chiefly concerns me. First, he asks himself what to do if faced with that contingency, and comes to an answer. As we might put it, he comes to a view on what to do in that contingency. Second, he expects that that thing is what he really will do if the contingency arises. He expects his thinking now to determine matters later: if he does find he's being followed, he'll already have settled what to do, and so he'll act on his earlier plan.[6] He comes to a view on what to do in contingency *C,* and expects that if contingency *C* arises, he will act on the view he now forms.

Holmes, I have been claiming, can also think what to do if faced with Mrs. Hudson's plight. In some ways, to be sure, this isn't full-fledged contingency planning. In the first place, he's certain he'll never be in her exact situation, down to every detail. In the second place—if the

6. See Bratman, *Intention* (1987) for refined and fascinating discussions of contingency planning, acting on plans, and changing one's mind. To understand planning, of course, far more would need to be said than I have just said. Holmes may expect not to rethink the matter, if the contingency arises, and instead just rely on the thinking he's now doing. If so, he is clearly planning what to do. Or he may expect to rethink that matter quickly, when the time comes, and come again to the same view of what to do. These differences don't matter for my purposes here; I instead focus on coming to a view on what to do in the contingency.

two aren't in communication tonight—he knows that his own thinking can in no way settle the question of what to do in Mrs. Hudson's own mind. She can't possibly act on his thinking, the way Holmes later on can act on the planning he's now engaged in. Still, this is in a way a kind of hypothetical planning: he thinks what to do if in a hypothetical circumstance. He's thinking as if he could plan what to do if in Mrs. Hudson's plight, and indeed, one aspect of contingency planning is fully in place: he is thinking what to do if in her situation, and coming to an answer.

My focus, then, is on coming to a view on what to do in a situation—even a situation one may fully know one will never be in. What is Holmes doing when he thinks that in Mrs. Hudson's situation, the thing to do is to project the silhouette and stay in? I don't want—at the outset, at least—to explain these thoughts as beliefs about a special property, a property of *to-be-done*ness or of being the thing to do. And we don't need to: Holmes's thought is intelligible as a kind that figures in planning, both planning for real and hypothetical planning. Holmes is planning hypothetically, we might say, what to do if in Mrs. Hudson's shoes. This is intelligible as a part of planning: in the fullest sense, one plans for a contingency when one expects, if the contingency arises, to then rely on one's present finding of what then to do.[7]

How much of her plight is Holmes planning for, hypothetically, when he comes to a view as to what is the thing for her to do? All of it, I answer. But this might introduce a worry: it is of course impossible for Holmes to be Mrs. Hudson. There is no possible situation, after all, in which Holmes—who in fact is not Mrs. Hudson and knows it—would be identical to Mrs. Hudson.[8] One response would be to say this: that

---

7. Hypothetical planning, in this sense, is not full-fledged, literal planning for a hypothetical contingency. It is akin, we might say, to make-believe planning: proceeding as if one could now decide what to do in that contingency. The preferences in play, though, are real. If I think that for Caesar on that day, crossing the Rubicon was the thing to do, then I prefer being Caesar in those exact circumstances and crossing the Rubicon to being he in those circumstances and taking any alternative. These are my actual preferences for a circumstance that's not actually mine. Cf. Hare, *Moral Thinking* (1981), chaps. 5–6; my "Hare's Analysis" (1988), p. 59.

8. We could worry too that since Holmes is fictional, there is in fact no possible situation in which Holmes figures at all: no possible situation would constitute Holmes's really existing. Consider my discussion, though, as a kind of make-believe. See Walton, *Mimesis as Make-Believe* (1990).

Holmes is planning for the case of being in a situation that is exactly like Mrs. Hudson's in its qualitative (or *universal*) properties, but not in the identities of the people concerned. Such a maneuver, though, cannot be needed: Anastasia, after all, if she had survived and suffered amnesia, would necessarily have been Anastasia. Still, she could wonder whether she wasn't—or even be quite sure that she wasn't.

The neat way to put these matters is devised by Lewis ("Attitudes," 1979). Beliefs, he proposes, are attitudes *de se:* in general, belief is self-ascription of a property. The same goes for the state of wondering whether such and such: if, strangely, I wonder whether I am Anastasia, the object of my doubt is a property. I wonder whether I have the property of *being Anastasia*. The same even goes for making fantastic suppositions. Holmes—under no doubt that he is not Mrs. Hudson and couldn't possibly be—can nonetheless plan, hypothetically, for the case of being her, in her exact circumstances. Being Mrs. Hudson in Mrs. Hudson's exact circumstances is a property; it is a property exemplified by her and only by her at a certain time.

Mrs. Hudson thinks that the thing to do is to go to the police, and that's what she will in fact do. Holmes disagrees with her plan: going to the police, he thinks, is not the thing to do in her situation. Now her situation—the situation that Holmes is pondering—includes her planning to go to the police. Can Holmes, then, decide, hypothetically, to stay away from the police in this very situation? Is this coherent? Can he ask what to do—and in particular, whether to go to the police—if in a situation that includes, as one of its features, that one will in fact go to the police?

Such hypothetical decisions are fully intelligible. Think of a binge alcoholic who every Saturday night comes to want to get drunk, but who spends the week hoping desperately that he'll get through Saturday night on the wagon. He can ask himself what to do if it's Saturday night and he comes to crave a drink; he can ask this knowing what he in fact will do. This is what I'm calling "deciding hypothetically": he can decide hypothetically for the situation he'll be in on the coming Saturday night. It is part of that situation, he knows, that in it, he will want to drink. He will intend to get drunk, and in the upshot he will get drunk. Still, asked Wednesday for a hypothetical decision whether to get drunk in his situation to come, he'll decide not to. Sadly, he can't make this hypothetical decision effective; he can't now make a real, full-fledged plan for what to do, for by Saturday night, he knows, he'll have changed his mind on what to do. But still, this is the answer he'll *now* give to the question of what to do next Saturday night: the answer is, he tells himself, to stay away from liquor. He can decide hypothetically, then, for the circumstance he foresees himself being in next Saturday night—a situation that includes the circumstance that he makes a different decision. (Think too of regret: it involves, we might say, hypothetically deciding, for a circumstance one was in, differently from the way one actually decided. If, after all, your policy is to drink and be merry with no regard for tomorrow, and you are suffering a grievous hangover from having done so yesterday, you may wish you had been prudent yesterday. But if you ask yourself what to do next time and your answer is to get soused, will your present preference really amount to regret? It seems not.)

Holmes, then, can not only decide for the circumstance he is in right at the time of deciding. He can decide for circumstances he expects to arise: to do this is to *plan*. He can decide for circumstances he might come to be in for all he knows: that is *contingency planning*. And he can carry contingency planning into more fantastic realms: he can plan hypothetically for circumstances that he knows won't arise—such as the circumstance of being Mrs. Hudson. He can plan ineffectually and know it, as with the binge alcoholic. Hypothetical planning differs from full-fledged planning in that one knows one's present planning won't affect what one does in the contingency. But it has in common with full planning that one answers a question of what to do in a situation.

Why carry thinking what to do to such fantastic lengths? That is a deep and important question about human life, one that I mostly postpone. For now, I am examining the logic of such questions without yet asking why they matter. Later we must also ask why it matters whether you and I agree or disagree over what to do in my circumstances.

As a start, though, we can say this: think of fantastic contingency planning as a kind of rehearsal for life. Chess players plan, hypothetically, for games that were played out long ago, and become better players thereby. I can wonder what to do if in Mrs. Hudson's plight and do this as a kind of practice, as a kind of play that prepares me for situations I might some day face. As with other kinds of play, we find thinking what to do fascinating in itself, entirely apart from the ways the practice might later come in handy: few readers of mystery stories seriously contemplate becoming detectives. Still, as with other kinds of play, we wouldn't be built to find the exercise rewarding if propensities to this kind of play hadn't tended to pay off—to pay off reproductively in ancestral populations. And as with other kinds of play, that we play at planning may still carry extrinsic rewards, rewards as reckoned in terms of what is worth caring about in life: this play can make us better deciders than we would otherwise be. And often, we will play best at this when we play together, agreeing and disagreeing about what to do in a situation.

Big Worlds

We need, I am claiming, to think not just of what to do now, but of contingencies: we ask what to do in a variety of situations a person might come to be in. How great must this variety be? Here we might go for either of two extremes. At the modest end, a "small world" plan will be the minimal sufficient for purposes at hand. I pictured Holmes, at the start of this chapter, planning just for the present moment and considering only whether he has time to catch the train. He can plan more extensively, though, thinking through, for instance, the implications of what his "small world" plan treats as outcomes. Or less modestly, as I have suggested, he can engage in imaginative exercises that serve, in a way, as rehearsals for plans he might have to make in the future. Were Holmes less single-minded in his musings, he might ponder what to wear if on the moon, or whether to cross the Rubicon if Julius Caesar on that day.[9]

At an extreme, then, we can construct the ideal of a "big world" hypothetical plan, of the plan that maximally "looks before it leaps". In what follows, I'll drop the qualifier 'hypothetical' and take it as understood: a "plan" will be a determination of what to do in various contingencies, expected or hypothetical; a "big world" plan provides for all

---

9. Savage, a pioneer of Bayesian decision theory, discusses the choice between a "big world" and "small world" in analyzing a problem; see *Foundations of Statistics* (1954), pp. 9, 15–17, 82–84. His use of the term 'world', though, is different from the philosophers' use that I am adopting; the world is "the object with which the person is concerned", and a possible world in my sense, big or small, is in Savage's terminology a state-act pair.

conceivable contingencies. Such a plan will provide for being Caesar at the Rubicon, for being Holmes on the train to Dover pursued by Moriarty—and indeed for every situation one might conceivably be in. We could call this a *maximal contingency plan*, or as I'll say more briefly, a *hyperplan*. Of course no one can plan maximally, and trying to approach this ideal would be a waste. Still, for logical purposes we can contemplate this ideal, and see what it has to teach us. If a person, fantastically, adopted such a maximal contingency plan, we can say, he would be in a maximally decided state, or a *hyperstate*.

Normal plannings and musings, of course, fall somewhere in between deciding just what to do right away and reaching a hyperstate. Holmes can decide to stop at the river if he walks to the station, and so rule out walking to the station without stopping, without yet having decided whether to walk.

How should we understand the content of these steps toward decision? The devices that worked before with small worlds apply to big world contingency planning as well. One way to think of fact-plan content is to mimic truth functions and quantification. I as a planner can combine partial contingency plans: "One if by land; two if by sea" as a plan to hang lanterns. I can reject a plan or partial plan: I can reject a plan to walk without stopping at the river. I can make general plans: to stop whenever I'd otherwise be run down by a carriage. These operations—*combining, ruling out, generalizing*—mimic standard logical operations on statements: conjunction, negation, and universal generalization.

At this point, though, we must introduce a crucial refinement, distinguishing two ways of choosing. One may choose out of indifference, simply because one must take one course or another. Buridan's ass might have been wiser, and a wiser ass would choose one bale of hay or choose the other. She wouldn't thereby *rule out* choosing either—or at least there's an important sense in which she wouldn't. She wouldn't be in disagreement with plumping for the other from indifference. It is in the nature of planning, after all, to distinguish rejecting an alternative by preference from simply not choosing it in that, from indifference, one chooses another. Rejecting an alternative is something more than just taking a different alternative when there is more than one alternative that one doesn't reject by preference.

Is this a distinction an expressivist can make? I regard some alternatives as *admissible* and others not, some as *okay to take* and others as *not to be taken*. This, we might worry, is not to decide but to describe. It is to regard alternatives as having or lacking a certain property: the property of being admissible, of being okay to take. This property may be "queer"—but is the lesson to draw perhaps this: that to plan, one needs to believe in such properties? Planning is one thing, an objector can say, and judgments of what's okay to do are another. A contingency plan need not settle whether the road not to take is worse; it just needs to settle whether or not to take it. To be sure, I plan on the basis of my judgments of which acts are admissible and which are not, but, the objector claims, to judge an act admissible or not is not in itself to decide for or against it. The judgment of okayness is cognitive; decision or planning is another matter.

This objection, though, seems a little fantastic. Must a planner settle questions of metaphysics, choosing sides in debates between naturalists and non-naturalists, in order sometimes to have preferences and sometimes to be indifferent? Must he believe in "queer" properties in order sometimes to reject an alternative, and sometimes just to plump for one out of indifference because one or the other must be chosen? Must a wiser ass than Buridan's be a metaphysician to choose one bale though finding nothing to choose between them?

The distinctions I'm relying on to speak of planning as I do traditionally belong within the realm of practical thinking: preference and indifference don't seem clearly to be apprehensions or misapprehensions of facts of a special kind. The distinction we need here is between permitting oneself an act and forbidding oneself, choosing something because I don't permit myself to omit it, and choosing among alternatives that I equally permit myself. Is there a difference, then, between rejecting an alternative—not permitting it to myself—and just not choosing it? Surely there is. The two differ in "valence" or oomph. To think this distinction intelligible, must I already think that permitting myself an alternative consists in attributing some special kind of property to it? No, distinguishing in this way is clearly a part of planning, but there is no need to think, at the start of inquiry, that distinguishing this way is a matter just of factual belief. My claims here concern what one commits oneself to in planning, and the facts I'm allowing at the outset are straightforward and prosaic. We can distinguish preference and indifference without first admitting facts of a kind more ethereal.

Once we distinguish permitting oneself an act from ruling it out, we accord contingency plans the following structure. A contingency plan deals with *situations* one might be in. In a situation there is a set of *alternatives* that are open to one. A plan is *complete*, for a situation, if for each alternative in this set it either rules out that alternative or permits it.

Permission here is stronger than just not ruling out: to permit an alternative for a situation, rather, is to *reject rejecting* it (where "rejecting" an action means rejecting it from preference). To permit an action is to disagree with disagreeing with the action. It is inconsistent to permit an alternative with one judgment and reject it with another: if one has permitted an alternative and now rejects it, one now does what one earlier rejected. One does this either unwittingly or by knowingly changing one's mind. One is in disagreement with one's earlier state of mind. To *permit* an alternative, then, as I am using the term, is not just to "allow" it in the sense I used that term. For a judgment to *allow* a decided state, in my technical sense, is just for it not *by itself* to rule that state out, not for it to *preclude* ruling it out. One may "allow" a decided state with one judgment and then go on to rule it out with another, all without changing one's mind or violating one's commitments. If, though, without changing one's mind, one *permits* an alternative in a situation and then proceeds to reject it, one has violated one's commitments.

An important requirement of consistency for a plan is that it must not rule out every alternative open on an occasion. A plan that did that—even a partial plan—would preclude offering any guidance on what to do on that occasion. A *hyperplan*, we can stipulate, covers any occasion for choice one might conceivably be in, and for each alternative open on such an occasion, to adopt the plan involves either rejecting that alternative or rejecting rejecting it. In other words, the plan either forbids an alternative or permits it. It follows that it permits at least one alternative in each conceivable occasion for choice and action. For there must be at least one alternative it does not forbid, we have said, and as a hyperplan, it permits that alternative.[10]

---

10. One might plan to hold still and "do nothing" on such an occasion, or to faint dead away, but if this course of action is open to one by choice, it is an alternative. One might faint from the terror of the choice without choosing to do so, but in that case, one's situation isn't an occasion for choice, and so a hyperplan need not provide for it. One might refuse to decide hypothetically for a conceivable occasion because the alternatives are each so horrendous, but in that case one simply doesn't have a hyperplan; one doesn't have a plan covering that occasion.

A couple of more comments about contingency plans: An occasion for action, a conceivable situation in which choices are open, is "centered" on an agent who must decide. A single possible world, a single determinate way things might have been, may contain many occasions for action, since it may contain many agents, and each agent must decide many times. We might think of an occasion for action as given by a triple $\langle w,i,t \rangle$ consisting of a possible world w, an agent i, and a time t at which agent i in world w has something to decide.

A plan must be one the agent can carry out with the information at her disposal. "Buy low, sell high," for example, is not a plan, if one has no way of telling whether prices have reached their peaks or their troughs. An *occasion*, as I have characterized it, contains much that the agent has no way of knowing, but one's plans must respond to features of the occasion available to the agent. Alternatives must be subjectively characterized, so that the same alternatives are available on subjectively equivalent occasions. And a plan must permit the same alternatives on subjectively equivalent occasions.

Back, then, to the ideal of a hyperplan. These are much like the possible worlds of the possible worlds semanticist. Just as possible worlds leave nothing indeterminate as to how things are, hyperplans leave nothing indeterminate as to what to do, on any occasion actual or hypothetical. All that is not permitted is forbidden, and all that is not forbidden is permitted.

The start of the chapter, then, presented "small worlds" that consisted of just one aspect of how things are and one aspect of what to do. Disjunctions and other "truth-functional" constructions that intertwine fact and plan—that intertwine *how things are* with *what to do*—I analyzed as allowing some small "fact-prac" worlds and precluding others. Now we can apply the same pattern to "big" fact-prac worlds, or *fact-plan worlds*. The content of a state of mind that mixes fact with plan, we can now say, *is given by the hyperstates that it allows* and the ones it rules out. Alternatively, we can speak not of states of mind, but of facts and plans themselves: a "big" fact-plan world $\langle w,p \rangle$ consists of a factual possible world w and a hyperplan p. Fact-plan disjunctions and the like *obtain* in some fact-plan worlds and not in others. These two ways of speaking—in terms (i) of planning, believing, and ways of thinking that intertwine the two, and (ii) of facts, plans, and content that intertwines the two—are isomorphic to each other. (Thus if you don't like "fact-plan worlds", you can instead put everything I'm saying

in terms of hyperstates, of possible maximally decided states of mind.)
Both these ways of representing plan-laden content, moreover, are isomorphic with truth-functional ways of speaking.

We pass easily, after all, between talk of the *mental activity* of planning, on the one hand, and the *content* of planning on the other. I reject
walking without stopping by the river, and thereby engage in mental
activity. But my planning, as a result, has some content: not, in any
case, to walk without stopping by the river. In this regard, planning is
like believing in matters of fact: I can reject a combination of believing
that it is snowing and disbelieving that the roads are slippery. My believing then has content: that it won't snow without the roads' being
slippery. Combining, rejecting, and generalizing apply to mental operations, which then have a content. The content is expressible with the
logical operators of conjunction, negation, and quantification. These
logical devices mirror the mental operations of combining, rejecting,
and generalizing.

Fact-plan worlds, then, give us a way of displaying entailment relations among judgments that intertwine fact with plan. The structure of
this apparatus is just the familiar structure of possible world semantics.
Logic, whether with factual worlds or with fact-plan worlds, is a matter
of the ways statements allow determinate possibilities and rule them
out. The logical import of a statement, we can say, is a matter of the
fact-plan worlds that it allows and the ones it rules out. This gives us a
way of thinking of the content of such judgments.

I started out with another way to think of plan-laden judgments, of
judgments that intertwine fact and plan. These judgments, we can say,
are built up recursively out of factual judgments and pieces of planning,
by combining, rejecting, and generalizing. If we start out this way, then
fact-plan worlds give us a way of keeping track of the import of a recursive sequence of such operations. With them we can keep track, say, of
rejections of combinations of rejections. A piece of planning P, which
permits or rejects an alternative on a subjectively characterized occa-
sion, *allows* a fact-plan world $\langle w,p \rangle$ only if P is included in hyperplan p.
A factual statement Q *allows* fact-plan world $\langle w,p \rangle$ iff Q holds in w. A negation $\neg P$ *allows* all and only those fact-plan worlds that P does not allow. A conjunction $P\&Q$ *allows* all and only those fact-plan worlds that
both P and Q allow. A statement *rules out* all and only those fact-plan
worlds it does not allow.

This apparatus lets us see what is wrong with inconsistency in combined belief and planning. A set of judgments is *consistent* if there is a hyperstate that every judgment in the set allows. It is *inconsistent* otherwise: it is inconsistent if every possible hyperstate is ruled out by one or another of the judgments in the set. If, then, my judgments are inconsistent, there is no way I could become opinionated factually and fully decided on a plan for living—no way that I haven't, with my judgments, already ruled out. Likewise, we can see what makes Holmes's practical argument valid. It took the form *F* or *P*, not *F*, therefore *P*. An argument of this form is valid, even if to accept *P* is to come to a decision. To accept the premises and reject the conclusion would be to rule out every way that Holmes could become opinionated factually and fully decided in his hyperplan.

～ 4

Judgment, Disagreement, Negation

$\mathscr{T}$HE ALTERNATIVE TREATMENTS I have been giving—invoking recursive mental operations of combining, rejecting, and generalizing, invoking maximally decided states of mind, or invoking the fact-plan worlds that are their content—address the "Frege–Geach" problem for expressivism. This problem has been widely discussed in the philosophical literature, and a wide variety of positions are now on the table. Indeed, it is controversial whether there even *is* any such problem. It is controversial too whether the problem, if a problem there be, is solved by a "minimal" conception of truth. And of course it is controversial whether published solutions work.

My own view of the matter is that (i) there is a problem, (ii) minimalism about truth won't take care of it, and (iii) the solution I have been offering does solve the problem. Claims (i) and (ii) have been beautifully argued by Dreier ("Expressivist Embeddings," 1996), and so I lay out my views on this quickly. As for (iii), that my solution does work, published discussions of the Frege-Geach problem may bear on this claim, but it is hard to pin down how they do. The solution, after all, hasn't previously been presented in exactly this form. In effect, though, it is my own previous solution with a somewhat different gloss. It is also equivalent to one aspect of a solution given by Blackburn.[1]

1. Gibbard, "An Expressivistic Theory" (1986) and *Wise Choices* (1990), chap. 5; Blackburn, "Attitudes and Contents" (1988).

I begin in this chapter with discussions by Horwich and Dreier. These have a crucial and far-reaching moral that I broach here and develop later, namely, that disagreement and ruling out are what underlies the possibility of logic. We can "disagree in plan", and it is this that makes for the fact-like comportment of questions of what to do. Later, I consider objections and grounds for doubt that arise in treatments of expressivism, logic, and the Frege-Geach problem. Can I distinguish negation proper from other forms of rejection or ruling out? How do I leap "Frege's abyss" and arrive at genuine judgment? Am I helping myself to materials to which I'm not entitled until the leap has been made? Is a state of mind intelligible that disjoins a plan with a factual proposition? Have I properly explained what this state of mind is, and can I be in that state of mind and yet neither plan nor believe? Published objections to programs like mine are mostly not directed precisely to what I have been saying, and so it is sometimes hard to calibrate the objections with my own program. Still, we need to see if reasons have been offered for doubting or turning away from the kind of program I have been advocating.

Dreier's Puzzle: Accostings and Headaches

Horwich develops a "minimal" conception of truth, and denies that there is any special Frege-Geach problem to be solved.[2] In the moral case, he proposes, a term like 'wrong' is fully explained with two theses. First, to call something "wrong" is to express an attitude of disapproval toward it. Starting with this thesis fits an expressivist's style of explanation. His second step, though, diverges from my own program. The term 'wrong', Horwich declares, works as a normal predicate—and this, he thinks, is all we must say to legitimize truth functions and quantification involving the predicate 'wrong', and to account for their logic. I myself accept, more or less, both of Horwich's theses: that (i) to call something "wrong" is to express an attitude of disapproval toward it, and (ii) the term 'wrong' works as a normal predicate. Thesis (ii), though, needs explaining: we need to establish how theses (i) and (ii)

---

2. See Horwich, *Truth* (1990) for his minimalist theory of truth, and "Gibbard's Theory of Norms" (1993) and "The Essence of Expressivism" (1994) for his take on expressivism.

can go together. Can cogent thought have a term to which both of these theses apply?

Truth, Horwich argues, does nothing to explain logic—even in the case of descriptive, baldly factual discourse. He advocates a "minimal" conception of truth, on which everything there is to know specially about truth is given by instances of a disquotational schema.[3] This precludes explaining truth-functional constructions recursively in terms of their truth conditions. For what Holmes can learn from the truth schema are things like this:

> That packing is now the thing to do is true iff packing is now the thing to do.   (1c)

> 'Packing is now the thing to do' is true iff packing is now the thing to do.   (1q)

But (1c) and (1q) both embed the clause 'packing is now the thing to do' in a biconditional—and so if the embedding poses a genuine problem for the expressivist, we'd need to have the problem solved before we could form the pertinent instance of the truth schema. (Indeed, if one takes Tarski's way of explaining such truth functions as conjunction and disjunction recursively, and plugs in instances of the minimalist schema that Horwich uses to characterize truth, the result, as Dreier shows, is empty. Dreier, "Expressivist Embeddings," 1996, pp. 32–38.)

Now I agree, in effect, with Horwich that logic is to be explained without appeal to truth. Disjunction and the like, to be sure, I explain in ways that mimic possible world characterizations, and possible worlds, we can say, give truth conditions: the possible worlds for which a statement obtains are the conditions under which what it says would be *true*. Truth, though, played no basic role in the explanations I gave of how disjunction works. I should, then, be able to welcome minimal truth—if minimalism turns out to be a plausible view of truth on other grounds. True, expressivism is often characterized as a view that, among other things, denies that normative statements are "true" or "false," and I myself have sometimes joined in such a characterization (Gibbard, *Wise Choices*, 1990, pp. 8, 10; also p. 92). My basic claim about normative thought and talk, though, I now realize, is not about

---

3. I discuss truth minimalism and its bearing on expressivism in Chapter 9.

aptness for truth. Rather, mine is a claim about how best to *explain* normative language.[4] An expressivist for a term like 'wrong' starts by explaining the state of mind that calling something "wrong" expresses. He does not, in the first instance, explain it just as the belief that such-and-such, but in some other, psychological way. If I can explain normative language in such a way that a minimal notion of truth applies to normative claims as I explain them, I can happily call many such claims true. Although expressivists about a discourse are often characterized as denying that the discourse is true or false—and I myself used to put my position this way—we expressivists about normative discourse can keep the term as labeling a distinctive position, and still welcome minimal truth for normative discourse.[5] Minimal truth may be welcome, and truth doesn't explain logic—though structures of being "true" or "false" can systematize what we say about the logic of connectives and quantifiers. On this, Horwich and I agree, and I appeal chiefly to Dreier's fine treatment to argue the case (Dreier, "Expressivist Embeddings," 1996). What, then, of Horwich's further claim: that there is no Frege-Geach problem to solve? Can we just declare 'is to be done' a normal predicate, and trust that normal logic will work from then on? Dreier gives an example of what we *can't* do along these lines. I'll first present his example, and then ponder what it should teach us.

I can say "Hey, Bob!" to *accost* him, to attract his attention. 'Hey!' of course isn't a predicate; the syntax of 'Hey!' is not that of a predicate. Couldn't we, though, remedy this? Let's invent a predicate, and imagine that it is a standard part of our language: saying "Bob *is hiyo*" in assertoric contexts, let's specify, accomplishes the speech act of accosting Bob—and likewise for saying that anyone else is hiyo. The predicate 'is hiyo', we further specify, functions logically as an ordinary predicate (Dreier, "Expressivist Embeddings," 1996, pp. 42–44).

4. Blackburn too thinks that a "projectivist quasi-realist" for morals can be happy with minimal truth, once he has "earned the right" to the notion, and that what is distinctive about the position is the kind of explanation it offers. See *Essays in Quasi-Realism* (1993), pp. 3–6; *Ruling Passions* (1998), pp. 317–319.

5. Some writers argue that expressivists can deny even minimal truth for the discourse they treat expressivistically. For debate on this, see Smith, "Why Expressivists" (1994); Jackson, Oppy, and Smith, "Minimalism and Truth Aptness" (1994); Miller and Divers, "Why Expressivists about Value" (1994); Field, "Disquotational Truth" (1994); Divers and Miller, "Platitudes and Attitudes" (1995); O'Leary-Hawthorne and Price, "How to Stand Up" (1996).

Dreier is clearly right that this won't do; the specification makes no sense. I can't now reason as follows:

The dingo is safe in its cage or Bob is hiyo,

The dingo is not safe in its cage,

Bob is hiyo.

As Dreier says, "It is obvious that the idea of inferring is out of place when the conclusion is a speech act of accosting" ("Expressivist Embeddings," 1996, p. 43).

What, though, accounts for the obvious truth that Dreier notes? Why can't I infer to a conclusion "Hey, Bob!"? Why can I still not infer to it once it is put in assertoric clothing? We sense that I can't, to be sure: to conclude that hey, Bob! is ungrammatical, and to conclude that Bob is hiyo is grammatical enough, but meaningless—at least for all we have so far explained. It does seem, in contrast, that a piece of reasoning can end in a decision: Holmes can infer that packing is now the thing to do. What explains the difference?

Part of the difference may lie in *expression*—as an expressivist like me might well suppose. The assertion "Packing is now the thing to do" *expresses* a decision; it expresses a state of mind. The assertion "The cat is on the mat" likewise expresses a state of mind, in this case a belief. One symptom of such expression is that, in either case, the assertion may be sincere or insincere. If the speaker is competent, we can say, his assertion is sincere just in case he is in the state of mind he expresses. Accosting, though, can't be straightforwardly sincere or insincere—for to accost someone is not in itself to express a state of mind. Agree with Dreier, then, that we can't explain what a predicate means just by declaring it a predicate, and then saying what speech act its ascription performs. Might we nevertheless explain a predicate by saying what state of mind its ascription expresses? Not all speech acts consist in expressing states of mind, but what of the ones that do?

We won't find that expressions of just any state of mind can embed in disjunctions and figure in inference. Groaning and holding my head can express a headache, perhaps. This isn't entirely a matter of convention, but could we set up an expressive convention for headaches? We do have 'Ouch!' and 'Yowee!' and we might try turning one of these into a predicate. "I am yowee", let's stipulate, expresses a headache. To say "I am yowee" is not to *say that* I have a headache; it is to *express* my having the headache: for me to accept that I am now yowee just *is* to have a headache. "I am yowee," a piece of language, replaces the groan that more naturally expresses a headache.[6]

Can I then accept this disjunction?

The cat is on the mat or I am yowee. (2)

Can I accept this without either accepting that the cat is on the mat or accepting that I am yowee? To accept that I am yowee is to have a headache, and so our question amounts to asking whether there is an intelligible state of mind that I can be in that consists in accepting (2), which I can be in without either accepting that the cat is on the mat or having a headache. Clearly not—and again we need to ask why. What divides headaches, on the one hand, from beliefs and decisions on the other? The answer might tell us much about logic—about what it is that allows an expression of a state of mind to partake in normal, propositional reasoning.

Disagreement as the Key

You can't disagree with a headache. You can't agree with it either, for that matter. It is this, I suggest, that debars headaches from figuring as premises or conclusions of reasoning. It is this too that debars them from being negated or disjoined. For beliefs, in contrast, there is such a thing as agreeing or disagreeing. Likewise with decisions, I have argued: there is such a thing as agreeing or disagreeing with a decision.

This means that a belief or a decision can have a special kind of stability over time and from person to person. Holmes can keep on agreeing with what he concluded earlier, whether it was the expectation that Moriarty would draw nigh at nine o'clock that night, or his decision to start packing then. He can step into the same belief or decision twice, either to hold to it or to come to reject it.

This is crucial to inference. Holmes can wonder whether to accept

6. Cf. Wittgenstein, *Philosophical Investigations* (1953), part I, sec. 244, p. 89: "the verbal expression of pain replaces crying and does not describe it."

or reject a conclusion, and then later come to accept or reject that same conclusion as the upshot of his reasoning. Holmes can wonder whether Moriarty will draw nigh at nine, and then later conclude that he will or that he won't. Holmes can wonder whether to pack at nine, and later conclude in favor or conclude against. Be it a belief or decision, it has a stable content, which Holmes can contemplate, come to accept—and perhaps later come to reject: he can "change his mind".

With a headache, it isn't like that: to stop having a headache isn't to change one's mind, to come to disagree with one's earlier headache. Likewise with accosting: if I accost Bob now and not an hour from now, I haven't thereby changed my mind about anything.

Hale entitles his critique of Blackburn "Can There Be a Logic of Attitudes?" For one understanding of the term 'attitude', we might say, the answer is that logic *pertains* to attitudes as such: there can be a logic of attitudes, and only of attitudes can there be a logic. Understand an "attitude", in the sense we need, as a state of mind that can be maintained over time by a person and shared between people, and also rejected—so that there is such a thing as agreeing or disagreeing with oneself at a different time, or with another person at the same time or a different time.

Beliefs clearly are attitudes in this sense. But we must be careful, as we saw at the start of this chapter: Suppose I believe that it is snowing and then later in the day I come to believe that it isn't snowing. I don't thereby disagree with my earlier belief: I may go on believing that it had been snowing earlier and now believe that it has stopped. Likewise the person in the tropical lowlands who thinks that it isn't snowing doesn't disagree with my judgment, in the northern winter, that it is snowing. Agreement and disagreement require a kind of stability of subject matter. So does reasoning, for the following would be fallacious: Just before noon, I accept two premises, namely, (i) my watch hasn't gone beep; (ii) my watch has gone beep or it's not yet noon. Just as my watch goes beep, I draw the logical conclusion from these premises: therefore, (iii) it's not yet noon. That's silly: I should come at noon to reject "It's not yet noon"—and this isn't to come to reject a conclusion that follows from premises I earlier accepted.

Parallel things hold for decision. At eleven in the morning, Holmes ponders whether to pack and decides not to; at noon he decides to pack. He hasn't thereby changed his mind; he hasn't come to disagree with his earlier decision. He can accept all along that eleven was too early and noon is just right. We need to think, then, not just of decisions for the very time of deciding. Holmes can change his mind about this plan and decide to act otherwise, but he doesn't change his mind by desisting until noon and then packing.

You and I too can agree with Holmes's strategy or we can disagree. We can decide, hypothetically, for the case of being Holmes in his exact situation at eleven, to start packing. In that case, we disagree with Holmes. We can disagree with him on what to do if one is he, in his situation.

What, then, of groans and accostings? To have a headache now and not in an hour isn't to change my mind. Could I change my mind, though, as to having a headache first thing in the morning? I can change my mind about whether I *will* suffer a headache first thing in the morning: I might expect one and then be pleasantly surprised. If I had enough control of my headaches, I might change my mind about whether *to suffer* a headache first thing in the morning, deciding the night before to have one and then changing my mind in the morning. But the groan that, in a sense, expresses my headache does not express a belief that I have a headache, nor does it express a decision to have it. (I'd decide otherwise if I could.)

With accosting, nothing is expressed in this sense at all: I can think that I'm accosting Bob and come to realize that I'm accosting a stranger. My decision can be to accost Bob when I see him, and I can then change my mind. "Hey, Bob!" though, expresses neither of these states of mind: it doesn't express the belief that I'm accosting him, and it doesn't express a decision to accost him. By saying "Hey, Bob!" I accost him; I don't assert that I'm accosting him, and I don't express a decision to accost him: "Hey, Bob!" doesn't mean "Let me now accost Bob." To be sure I *could* accost Bob by yelling "I now accost Bob" or by yelling "Accosting Bob is now the thing for me to do." With these calls, though, I don't *just* accost him. I can reason to a belief that I am accosting Bob, and I can reason to a decision to accost him—but "Hey, Bob!" expresses neither of these conclusions.

All this ties in closely with the treatment I gave of states of mind that mix believing with planning. For this treatment, the possibility of agreement and disagreement over time is crucial. It is this possibility that we exploit to characterize fresh states of mind. "Either it's now too late to catch the train," thinks Holmes, "or packing is now the thing to do." This, we explain, is the state of mind with which he would disagree were he to come to be in state C_{lp}—believing it's not too late and deciding not to pack—and agree otherwise: he would agree with it were he to come to be in any of the other decided states C_{LP}, C_{Lp}, or C_{lP}. The decided state, though he comes to it later if at all, must pertain to the time for which he is deciding. It is the intelligibility of agreeing and disagreeing with beliefs and decisions made at different times that enables all this to succeed.

I have reduced the possibilities of embedding and logic to the possibility of agreement and disagreement across time. This doesn't resolve all mysteries: we still have questions to ask about agreement and disagreement. What is it to agree or disagree? Why are some states of mind subject to agreement and disagreement and others not? Stevenson began his study of ethical language by studying agreement and disagreement: there can be disagreement, he argued, not only in belief but also in attitude. He was right, I am suggesting, to begin this way. What to say further about disagreement, though, is an issue I must postpone.

Disagreement in Plan

Believing and planning admit of agreement and disagreement, whereas accosting and suffering do not. This, I have suggested, is the key to why both act as kinds of judging: why plans and factual propositions—the respective contents of planning and believing—stand in logical relations to each other, and embed in more complex logical structures that can mix the two. In what, though, does disagreement in plan consist? Why can plans, like beliefs, be rejected or ruled out?

Disagreement in plan, as I am presenting it, might seem recherché. Suppose I disagree with Caesar on whether, if he in his shoes, to go to the Senate on that Ides of March. What sort of disagreement is this? To disagree with his decision to go, I don't need to be against it. Brutus too, after all, may well disagree with Caesar on this. For though Brutus plots desperately to ensure that Caesar come to the Senate that morning, he may nonetheless say to himself "If I am Caesar in Caesar's shoes this morning, let me stay home." (Brutus, in technical jargon, thinks Caesar to have agent-centered reason, all told, to stay home. At the same time, he thinks himself to have agent-centered reason, all told, to ensure that Caesar leave home and come to the Senate. He thus thinks that not all reasons stem from agent-neutral reasons.)[7]

Disagreement in plan, then, is not what Stevenson called "disagreement in attitude", as when two people "cannot easily agree on which restaurant to choose" for dinner together. People disagree in attitude, Stevenson explains, "when they have opposed attitudes to the same object"—one for it, the other against it—"and when at least one of them has a motive for altering or calling into question the attitude of the other" (Stevenson, *Ethics and Language*, 1944, p. 3). On one crucial question, Caesar and Brutus agree in attitude, in Stevenson's sense: they both favor Caesar's coming to the Senate that day. On this matter, Caesar has no attitude that Brutus need work to alter; they both favor the same thing. On another matter, to be sure, they disagree sharply in Stevensonian attitude: they favor vastly different upshots once Caesar arrives. Their disagreement in plan, though, in the sense I am taking as central, is not Stevenson's disagreement in attitude, but a kind of disagreement in *conditional* attitude: they disagree what to do *if* in Caesar's shoes.

The same kinds of contrast can be drawn between different times in the life of a single person. As a youth I prefer, of the packages on offer, to smoke now and suffer later. In middle age, dying, I prefer to be healthy now and so not to have smoked in my youth. This comes close to Stevensonian disagreement in attitude, disagreement between one person at two stages in life. Of course, my later disagreement with my earlier self is futile: I'm not exactly *content* with having had the attitudes I did as a youth, but there is now clearly nothing I can do about it; the youth I was is now beyond scolding. Still, I now prefer living the non-smoker's life history that was open to me, and earlier had the opposite preference. In something close to Stevenson's sense, I disagree in attitude with my earlier self.

Do I thereby come to disagree in plan with my earlier self? Probably—but possibly not. I might instead plan shortsightedly, and take good reasons to be "time-centered". That is to say, I might tell myself both the following things: first, "If a youth, let me smoke to impress

7. See Nagel, *View from Nowhere* (1986), pp. 152–158. In his *Possibility of Altruism* (1970), he speaks of "objective" and "subjective" reasons, and argues that "all reasons must ultimately be specifiable in objective form" (p. 98). He takes this back in the 1978 paperback printing; see "Postscript," pp. vii–viii.

the girls and other guys and to feel grown up. Let me smoke for the cool image, and chance the distant consequences." Second, "If middle-aged and endowed with powers of backward causation, let me prevent my earlier self from smoking." To this plan for how to decide in hypothetical situations, I might stick firmly, from youth to the end of my life. Nagel brands this a "practical solipsism" of the present moment—and it does indeed seem a weird state to avow. Some strong resistance to this pattern may well be part of what constitutes regarding oneself as a single person through the course of life.[8]

Whether cogent reasons can be, at base, time-centered and agent-centered is a central question of practical theory. My aim here, though, is not to settle these issues, but examine the concepts needed to pose them in the first place. Those who treat some reasons as basically agent-centered (and perhaps even time-centered) must read my "disagreement in plan" as different from Stevenson's "disagreement in attitude". Agents who work together must agree, to some extent, in Stevensonian attitude, but they need not agree in plan. For you and me to work to a common purpose, that is to say, I needn't agree with you on what to do if in your shoes, and you needn't agree with me on what to do if in mine. Bully and Martyr may agree that Martyr is to turn the other cheek and Bully is to strike it, though Bully disagrees with Martyr on whether, if Martyr in Martyr's shoes, to turn the other cheek—and Martyr disagrees with Bully on whether, if Bully in Bully's shoes, to strike Martyr's proffered cheek. In Stevensonian attitude they agree, but in plan they sharply disagree.

Isn't it, then, Stevensonian agreement and disagreement in attitude that matters, not agreement or disagreement in plan? To agree in attitude is to agree what is to be done—whereas to agree in plan is to agree on wild hypotheticals. Why should agreement in plan matter?

It matters because we share thoughts. Thinking is not something that each person can do entirely for himself alone. I don't mean that we don't each do much thinking for ourselves. Some of our thoughts will be downright secret, and inevitably, the bulk of our non-secret

8. Hare explores the possibility that part of what it is to regard the person who is about to suffer as oneself is to be averse to the prospect. See *Moral Thinking* (1981), pp. 96–99. Nagel, in *The Possibility of Altruism* (1970), along with Sidgwick in *Methods of Ethics* (1907) and others, argues from this case to the interpersonal case, and finds "agent-centered" reasons defective unless they are rooted in agent-neutral reasons.

thoughts we never get around to sharing. (It's an illusion, too, that the bulk of one's thoughts are easily shareable, as I have found when I've tried to use a micro-cassette recorder to keep track of my thoughts about student term papers.) But to some large degree, we learn to think by talking together, by sharing our thoughts in words.

Even the most private of thinking, I've been arguing, requires keeping track of one's thoughts enough to be able to combine them, reject them, and generalize on them. I work toward a plan for an occasion by considering possible options, rejecting some, and combining others. To plan competently, I must keep track of how one determination I might make in the course of my planning precludes another. I cannot plan at all if I can't keep track of these relations of precluding from second to second and from minute to minute, and I cannot work with yesterday's tentative planning if I can't keep track of these relations from day to day.

Why go interpersonal, though, in contingency planning? To manage the chess of life, I answer. Chess players develop refined and elaborate means of sharing and scrutinizing hypothetical plans for what to do in difficult chess situations. Life is far more complex than chess—and the object of the "game" is far less clear. Just as with the human urge to share plainly factual thoughts, so do we share planning thoughts in various forms. In conversation, I may let you do some of my thinking for me. I stand ready, of course, to disagree with you if I find disagreement called for—just as in my own thinking I stand ready to disagree with a thought of five seconds ago. In such conversation, a normal urge serves an ulterior purpose in two senses. First, a "purpose" of evolutionary design, long ago: crucial to our propensities to this urge must be the reproductive advantages, in ancestral human populations, of being disposed to share thoughts of many kinds, to think together on matters of life. Second, our own purposes now: we can find that our lives go better because we are not each entirely alone in our thinking. We think in devices we pick up from family, teachers, authors, and chums. This goes for planning as much as for thoughts of fact.

Evol. Fallacy

Rejection, Negation, and Practical Realism

In *Wise Choices, Apt Feelings*, I spoke of "ruling out" possibilities, and used this as the basis for normative logic. Here too I speak this way. I speak also of "rejecting" a state of mind, and I explain this as "disagreeing": to reject an action is to disagree with performing it, and to reject a plan is to disagree with the plan. You "rule out" an act, a plan, or something more complex, I said, if you commit yourself to rejecting it. That is, you commit yourself to rejecting it should you come to be decided on it—where to be decided on it is either to reject it or to reject rejecting it.

Is it intelligible, then, for one state of mind to "rule out" another? The philosophical questions of what it is to follow a rule—and how the rules one follows can have consequences such as ruling out—are daunting, and I don't here venture a solution.[9] Instead, I rely on an analogy: just as one belief can rule out another, so steps in planning can rule out other steps. We can take on commitments, in the course of planning, as to how plans may further be filled out. Then, just as a plainly factual belief can be seen as getting its import from the possibilities it allows and the ones it rules out, so other states of mind could be seen as getting their import in a like way, from more extensive possibilities they allow and rule out—possibilities that include not only how things are, but also what to do in possible cases. If we accept these things, then we understand why the logic of fact mixed with plan is the same as the logic of fact.

The simplest case is negation. Both with fact and with plan, accepting a negation is just what I am calling "rejecting" or "disagreeing". The expressivist's strategy is to explain negation by explaining the state of mind of accepting a negation. To accept the negation of *P,* I say, is to disagree with belief in it. This might seem truistic and empty—but Nicholas Unwin argues instead that it is wrong: negation cannot be explained in any such way. Consider theology: a settled agnostic rules out accepting that any gods exist. She does not, however, thereby accept the negation of the claim that gods exist: she doesn't accept that no gods exist, or even commit herself to so accepting. As a settled agnostic, after all, she equally rules out accepting that gods exist and accepting that no gods exist. To rule out accepting something, then, is distinct from accepting its negation (Unwin, "Norms and Negation," 2001).

Unwin finds this the Achilles' heel of expressivism. How am I to

9. See discussions, for instance, by Kripke, *Wittgenstein on Rules and Private Language* (1982); Boghossian, "The Rule-Following Considerations" (1989); Brandom, *Making It Explicit* (1994). My own preliminary attempt to grapple with these issues is "Meaning and Normativity" (1994).

explain negating a plan-laden judgment? If this is a problem, then permissibility is in trouble; the problem besets my treatment of being "okay" to do. To think an act not okay to do, say I, is to disagree with doing it. This is the most elementary plan-laden judgment I can make, and so let's find a single word to express it: if I reject an act, I regard it, let's say, as *Out;* I accept that it is Out. (I capitalize 'Out' to distinguish this use.) Holmes, imagine, standing above Reichenbach Falls, can now either jump, hide, or fight Moriarty. Hiding is Out, thinks Holmes, but fighting and jumping are each okay. Can an expressivist make sense of this?

Jumping is okay, we might try saying, if and only if it is not Out. Now, though, we must explain negation. The expressivist twist is to explain negation by explaining what it is to *accept* a negation. What, then, is this state of mind, accepting that jumping is not Out? It consists, I explained, in rejecting rejecting jumping. Such an account, however, loses the distinction between negation and settled agnosticism—so objects Unwin. Couldn't Holmes be a settled agnostic about whether jumping is Out? Or couldn't Mrs. Hudson, when she contemplates Holmes's plight? If so, we must distinguish two states:

(i) Rejecting the claim that jumping is Out.
(ii) Accepting that jumping is not Out.

My own account of the logic of expressivism explains only (i), whereas to explain negation, an expressivist must explain (ii). This is the crux of Unwin's critique.

When, in the last chapter, I derived a logic of plan-laden states of mind, I explained that "disagreeing" is what the atheist does, not the agnostic. Even the most settled agnostic doesn't disagree with the claim that gods exist; she doesn't in my sense *reject* theism. Unwin's challenge, I take it, amounts to whether I am entitled to disagreement in any such sense. The orthodox explain disagreeing with a claim as accepting its negation, whereas I go the other way around: I explain accepting the negation as disagreeing with the claim. Agreement and disagreement are what must ground an expressivistic account of logic. Is disagreement intelligible, though, without appeal to an apparatus of substantial truth, states of affairs, and the like—just the kind of basis expressivists hope to avoid?

In response, I note first that I have been talking of "disagreement" in

two different ways. On the one hand, you can disagree with an action
or a plan: your cousin marries a lowlife and you disagree with what she
does. Alternatively, you can disagree with her state of mind, with her
thinking and deciding as she does.

Consider first disagreeing with a plan. To speak this way is to treat
the plan as, in a sense, the *content* of a state of mind. (Orthodox,
Fregean philosophy of language, as I have noted, uses the term 'content' in a different way. In this orthodox sense, her plan to marry and
her prediction that she will marry have the same "content", namely, the
proposition that she will marry. She takes two different attitudes, believing and intending, toward the same proposition. But we can put
what's going on differently: she accepts, we can say, both the prediction
and the plan. We can speak of the plan, then, as something that she accepts—and this treats the plan, in an important sense, as the "content"
of her state of mind, as something she can accept or not.) Planning has
its logic, we can now say, and to accept the negation of a plan is just to
disagree with the plan. The syntax of imperatives doesn't work that
way, true enough; it doesn't let us negate plans. That's precisely the
reason to transform imperatives by embedding them into "thing to do"
language.

Proceeding this way might seem to be philosophical theft. The
scheme amounts just to helping ourselves to the notion of disagreeing
with a piece of content, be it a plan or a belief. A negation, we say,
is what one accepts when one disagrees—and this explains negation.
Now I wish, of course, that I could offer a deeper explanation of disagreement and negation. Expressivists like me, though, are not alone in
such a plight. Orthodoxy starts with substantial, unexplained truth, es-
chewing any minimalist explanation of truth. I start with agreeing and
disagreeing with pieces of content, some of which are plans. It's a thiev-
ing world, and I'm no worse than the others.

What, then, of disagreeing with a state of mind—responding to it
not just with "Don't think that" but with "No"? Realizing that your
cousin believes that the stars map our fates, you disagree, and realizing
whom she plans to wed, you likewise disagree. Again, if I take the notion of disagreeing with a state of mind as primitive, for the time being,
I may be no worse off than the orthodoxy that starts out with belief and
substantial truth.

Think of planning a chess game. My plan unfolds bit by bit as I accept a fragment here and reject a fragment there. I decide, say, not to move my queen unless I have already castled. If at first I accept a fragment and then come to reject it, I disagree with my earlier conclusion of what to do. Such disagreement is intelligible as part of emerging planning; conclusions of prosaic fact aren't the only conclusions that are subject to disagreement. We cannot informatively reduce disagreeing with a fragment of planning to other terms, such as commitment, or planning how to plan. On this point, Unwin is quite right. What we can do is recognize this mental operation as one we can perform. We can say what its marks are, we can recognize by these marks when a person is disagreeing with a fragment of planning, and we can find ourselves to be doing this. Disagreeing with disagreeing, for instance, is agreeing; that is one mark of the mental operation of disagreeing. Disagreeing excludes agreeing; that is another mark. In explaining negation of claims of prosaic facts, we would, after all, say like things about the marks of accepting a negation. If we can recognize this mental operation of disagreeing as one we perform as we develop plans, and if we can explain its marks, then what more can we ask? It is a mental operation that applies to plans and fragments of plans, as well as to prosaically factual beliefs.[10]

Expressing a State of Mind

The label 'expressivism' alludes to a way of explaining the meanings of statements in a public language. Holmes tells Mrs. Hudson, "Packing is now the thing to do," and we explain what he means by explaining the state of mind that he thereby *expresses*. Expressing we explain by analogy with prosaically factual statements: Suppose Holmes instead says, "Moriarty will shortly arrive." He thereby expresses a prosaically factual belief, his belief that Moriarty will shortly arrive. Expressing a state of mind works the same in these two cases, but the states of mind expressed are different. Holmes's conviction that Moriarty will shortly arrive is a prosaically factual belief (somewhat vague though it is). His conviction that packing is the thing to do is instead a fragment of a plan; it consists in planning now to pack. Whether this state of mind

10. I especially thank Robert Mabrito for discussion of these issues. Rosen raises some of them in "Blackburn's *Essays*" (1998), as does Hawthorne, "Practical Realism?" (2002), p. 176.

qualifies as "belief" in some queer, non-prosaic sort of fact we needn't say; what's important is that it can be explained as a piece of planning.

Expressivism is crucially, then, a way of explaining some class of judgments. Its account of public statements is an afterthought, an appeal to analogies with expressing beliefs. Still, many of the claims of expressivists may remain unclear until more is said about "expressing" a state of mind. Expressivists stress the contrast between expressing a state of mind and saying that one is in it. According to emotivists, for instance, to say "*X* is good" is to *express* one's approval of *X*, and decidedly not to *say that* one approves of it. How, though, is this contrast to be drawn?[11]

A Grice-like account of meaning may be helpful, but it leaves a residue of puzzles. When Holmes tells Mrs. Hudson, "Moriarty will shortly arrive", he intends to get her to believe that Moriarty will shortly arrive—and he intends to get her to believe this by means of her recognizing this very intention. Or perhaps he intends, rather, to get her to believe something slightly different: that he himself believes that Moriarty will shortly arrive—again, by means of that very intention. He then expects her, in consequence, to proceed to believe that Moriarty will shortly arrive, because she'll expect that Holmes wouldn't believe it unless it were true. How, then, shall we choose between these two variants of a Grice-like account? If we can't, then we'll have trouble distinguishing the literal meanings of the two claims "Moriarty will shortly arrive" and "I believe that Moriarty will shortly arrive." Hearing either statement leaves a trusting Mrs. Hudson in the same state of mind: believing both that Moriarty will shortly arrive and that Holmes so believes. What intention of Holmes's differs with the two assertions?

Indeed, a puzzle remains even if we ignore statements and keep to states of mind. Holmes believes that Moriarty will shortly arrive, and he believes that he so believes. These two states of mind go together, weird cases aside. What's the psychological difference, then, between these two states of mind? In a parallel vein, what's the psychological difference between planning to pack and believing that one so plans? The latter is a psychological belief, whereas the former is no prosaic belief at all, but a state of planning—that's the contrast that lies at the heart of expressivism. But again, these two states of mind go to-

11. See Jackson and Pettit, "A Problem" (1998).

gether, except in weird cases. What's the psychological difference between them?

Here again, I say, disagreement holds a key. We classify Holmes as
being in two states of mind because there are two things to agree or
disagree with him about. We can agree with him on whether he *believes*
that Moriarty will shortly arrive, but disagree with him on whether
Moriarty *will* shortly arrive. Likewise with disapproval: Holmes disapproves of Moriarty, and he believes that he so disapproves. We can, if
we are so minded, agree with his belief and yet disagree with his disapproval. Likewise with planning: Holmes plans to pack and believes that
he so plans. We can agree with his belief and disagree with his plan.

A statement invites agreement or disagreement. Expression and disagreement, we can now see, are linked as follows: to disagree with a
statement is to disagree with the state of mind it expresses. If Holmes
says, "I plan to pack now," I disagree with what he literally says if and
only if I disagree with the belief that he is expressing: the belief that he
plans to pack now. When he says, "Packing is now the thing to do," I
disagree, literally, with what he says if I disagree with his plan to pack
now—if, that is, for the case of being he in his exact shoes, I disagree
with now packing.

Holmes may, of course, intend to lie or to speak recklessly. When I
say he "expresses" a belief, I don't mean he has that belief. To express a
state of mind, as I use the term, is to purport to have it, whether or not
one does. Holmes is sincere in what he says if indeed he is in the state
of mind he expresses. When he says, "Moriarty will shortly arrive," he
is sincere if he believes that Moriarty will shortly arrive; when he says,
"Packing is now the thing to do," he is sincere if he plans now to pack.
(Or perhaps being sincere is a matter of *believing* one is in the state of
mind expressed—but cases in which *believing* that one is in a state of
mind comes apart from really *being* in that state are bizarre, and our
notion of sincerity may well not distinguish the two.)

Stevenson was a fairly late convert to full-fledged expressivism, but
when in the 1960s he did convert, he offered a further test for distinguishing an attitude from the belief that one has that attitude: the reasons that support these two states of mind are distinct (Stevenson, *Facts
and Values*, 1963, pp. 210–213). Holmes's plan to pack is supported by
Moriarty's imminent arrival. His belief that he plans to pack is, in contrast, supported by introspection (or in whatever other way we know

our own minds). The questions "Why plan to pack?" and "Why think that you plan to pack?" are distinct. A public statement is linked to the state of mind it expresses in this way: the reasons that support the statement are the reasons that support the state of mind. (In saying this, we must distinguish the reasons that support a state of mind—a belief or a plan—from reasons that support *wanting* to be in that state of mind. Reasons of current peace of mind may well support wanting to believe Moriarty far away and wanting to plan the impossible. Only evidence that Moriarty is far would support believing him far, and only reasons to pack support planning to pack. Nothing could support planning what one knows one cannot possibly carry out. The reasons that support the claim "Packing is now the thing to do" are the reasons that support a plan to pack, not the reasons that support wanting to plan to pack.)

What reasons support a belief or a plan is itself a planning question. Does the layout of fossils in layers support belief in an extremely ancient world of slowly changing fauna? That's a question of how to guide one's beliefs by empirical findings. Disagreement on this question consists in disagreement in plan for coming to beliefs. This disagreement in plan may well be rooted in disagreement in belief about what the empirical findings are: about which sorts of fossils are to be found where in the rock layers. Alternatively, it may be a planning disagreement fundamentally, an epistemic disagreement that would survive even full agreement on the empirical findings. Each side in the dispute, though, can use Stevenson's test to distinguish two states of mind: believing that the earth is old, and believing that one believes that the earth is old. Likewise, Stevenson's test distinguishes planning to pack from believing that one plans to pack. Why to pack is a different question from why to believe one so plans.

One further point about expressing: it might be thought that one could express a belief with an explicit performative, as with

I hereby express the belief that Moriarty has arrived.   (E)

But for the sense of the term 'express' that I intend, this isn't so. Holmes would normally express his belief that Moriarty has arrived by saying "Moriarty has arrived," and the logical force of this is quite different from the logical force of (E). For one thing, to pronounce (E) is to say something about what one is doing, whereas to say "Moriarty has arrived" is to do no such thing. But still, with (*E*) doesn't Holmes also express his belief that Moriarty has arrived? He may do something else as well, but doesn't he at least do this among other things? I think not. If Holmes expresses a belief, then you contradict what he says by expressing a contradictory belief. When he says "Moriarty has arrived," for instance, you contradict him if you say "Moriarty has not arrived." When Holmes utters (*E*), however, you don't contradict him if you say "Moriarty has not arrived." You contradict him by saying, "You don't thereby express that belief." In the sense of the term 'express' I intend, you express a belief by making a statement. You cannot, it now appears, do the same thing by uttering an explicit performative. All this applies as well to expressing your planning, or expressing a plan-laden judgment.[12]

Frege's Abyss: The Leap to Judgment

An abyss separates full judgments from sheer representations. This is another lesson to be drawn from Frege. The dog who chases a squirrel up a tree has an image of the squirrel, a representation, but perhaps doesn't fully judge that the squirrel has run up the tree. That is to say, it may be incapable of such things as disjoining one image with another. Full-fledged judgments, in contrast, can enter indiscriminately into logical relations. We, but perhaps not the dog, can judge that either the animal has run up the tree or it was not a squirrel and ran under the ground.

I am claiming to span this abyss, carrying planning across to the judgment side. Have I really done so—or have I cheated by covertly starting out on the judgment side, stealing materials from that side that were not mine to use? Isn't what's needed a more "slow track" quasi-

12. The same applies to stating. You can state that snow is white by saying "Snow is white," but you don't do the same thing with the explicit performative, "I hereby state that snow is white." I contradict your statement that snow is white by saying, "Snow is not white," but I don't thereby contradict the performative. Van Roojen in "Expressivism and Irrationality" (1996), pp. 325–329, constructs an elaborate critique of my position in *Wise Choices* (1990), but the critique depends crucially on thinking that, on my view, an explicit performative could have "the same content that 'Remaining silent is rational' has" (327). I owe aspects of my response to van Roojen here to Robert Mabrito.

realism, the honest toil of constructing an explanation of judgment with non-judgmental materials? These were worries that Simon Blackburn had about my earlier formulations of my treatment of the Frege-Geach problem.[13] Blackburn's point isn't that the abyss can't be crossed: he himself, he judges, has shown us how to bridge it, toiling with materials honestly acquired.[14] But in my own case, he feared, it was theft that allowed me to claim a quick victory on a field where honest victory must be Fabian: slow and achieved with dogged patience.

Now on closer examination, there seem to be not one but two abysses that expressivists must span. Whether and how they join together might be open to question. One we might call the gap between apprehending and real judgment; the other, the gap between representing something as fact and doing something else—deciding or planning, for instance.

Take first, then, the apprehension–judgment gap. This is a gap between two kinds of factual representation. A dog doesn't just have an image of a cat; it apprehends the presence of the cat, along with other things about the cat. That's what the dog needs if it is, for instance, to chase the cat. The dog, though, is not equipped, perhaps, to operate with disjunctions of such apprehensible contents.[15] Explaining how the dog represents facts doesn't by itself get us to an explanation of such possible thoughts as "The cat is on the mat or the squirrel is not in the tree." Perhaps only linguistic beings can think such things—or perhaps some of our non-linguistic ancestors had to be able to think such things before speakable syntax and semantic processes attached to syntax would be possible.[16] But in any case, with representation we get a gap between apprehending and full-fledged judgment. Items that combine truth-functionally, quantificationally, and the like are on the judgment side.

Turn next to the gap between representation and non-representation. We can be full-hearted realists about what the dog apprehends

---

13. Blackburn, "Gibbard on Normative Logic" (1993). My "fast track" formulations were in "An Expressivistic Theory" (1986) and *Wise Choices* (1990).

14. See especially Blackburn, "Attitudes and Contents" (1988).

15. Whether or not dogs are so equipped might be a difficult problem, in large part empirical. I don't mean to take a position on the issue; I'll just suppose for the sake of illustration that dogs differ from us in this way.

16. I owe this proposal to Robbins Burling.

and distinguish such apprehendings of fact from, say, the desire to catch the cat. The desire, we can maintain, isn't an apprehension of any queer fact that catching the cat is desirable. Representing facts, then, contrasts with doing other things, and this is a different contrast from that between apprehending and true judgment. The contrast has nothing directly to do with whether the state is linked by syntax to a rich space of possible states of mind that stand in logical relations to each other. The judgment–non-judgment gap, then, is not the factual–non-factual gap, and to cross one might not be to cross the other.

Once we distinguish these gaps, a strategy for the expressivist leaps to view. Take a class of states an expressivist might appeal to: particular decisions for actual and hypothetical situations, for instance, as in the treatment of the last chapter. These consist, recall, in one's rejecting some alternatives. Take such a class, and call its members *straight attitudes*. Straight attitudes aren't representations of fact, we may initially take it. In another way, though, they are analogous to apprehendings. Straight attitudes are sparse in that the class of them isn't closed under various kinds of syntax and semantics. We don't, for instance, promiscuously have a straight attitude that is the disjunction of any two straight attitudes. Now couldn't we try explaining judgments that encompass straight attitudes by analogy with plainly factual judgments? Here is a precept that might guide us: attitudinal judgments are to straight attitudes as factual judgments are to apprehendings of fact.

To say this alone, of course, would leave us with much work to do: we would have to say what this relation is. That is what I was trying to do in the last chapter. But to say this alone would leave work equally for the factualist and the non-factualist. The expressivist who is challenged that she cannot do something that she needs to do might well reply, "Show me how you do it in the strictly factual realm, and I'll mimic what you do in a broader realm that extends both factual apprehendings and straight attitudes."

I have explained how *I* do it, both with attitudes and with prosaically factual beliefs. Once a being is capable of agreeing and disagreeing with possible states of mind, both factual apprehendings and straight attitudes become members of larger classes: factual apprehendings become a special class of factual judgments, and straight attitudes become a special class of purely attitudinal judgments. Factual judgments and attitudinal judgments, moreover, are special cases of judgments in general: some of these judgments are attitude-laden (or plan-laden in the particular treatment in this book), and the remainder are purely factual.

If we adopt the kind of strategy I have sketched, we have ceased to be expressivists in a specially narrow sense. The *narrow* expressivist, let us specify, says that the statements he is analyzing all express straight attitudes. To proceed as I advocate is to be an expressivist in a broader sense. The *broad* expressivist says that attitude-laden statements express attitude-laden judgments—and just as factual judgments are to be explained partly in terms of factual apprehensions, so analogously, attitude-laden judgments are to be explained in terms, partly, of straight attitudes. Indeed, I cannot think of anyone recently who could even be suspected of narrow expressivism. Broad expressivism, moreover, is important: it makes a claim about the right order of explanation for a class of concepts. Start with straight attitudes, it says, and don't try to explain them as apprehensions of a peculiar class of facts.

Tied to a Tree

My treatment of plan-laden content involves a kind of automation. Some responses to the Frege-Geach problem consider particular constructions, one at a time, and show how to treat them. The hope is then that other constructions too can be satisfactorily treated as investigation proceeds (Hare, "Meaning," 1970; Blackburn, *Spreading*, 1984). Now where such piecemeal treatments are correct, they should have a pattern—a pattern that can be applied more widely. My apparatus of decided states is meant to help generalize this pattern. The apparatus does not do the explaining all by itself; rather, it offers a structure for generalizing the explanations that apply to simple cases, such as Holmes's inference P or F, not F, therefore P. Of course the apparatus doesn't handle every context by itself: asking plan-laden questions, for instance, remains to be explained. The great triumph of truth-conditional semantics, though, isn't with explaining such things as questions. Questions have to be explained separately—and what I'd do about questions is ask what to say about factual questions, and just say the analogous thing for the case of plan-laden questions.[17] The great triumph of truth-conditional semantics is that it handles iterated truth-

17. See Hare, "Meaning" (1970), pp. 13–15, for a discussion of questions.

functional and quantificational contexts. It is this generality I try to mimic with my apparatus of decided states.

Blackburn too develops a device of automation: the semantic tableau or "tree".[18] Accepting a normative statement, he says, is "being tied to a tree", and he explains what this consists in. Now Blackburn's talk of "trees" and my own devices, I think, are equivalent. Trees are a device for displaying "small worlds". A decided state—decided just enough for logical purposes at hand—corresponds to a path in the tree. The semantic tableau method keeps track automatically of which combinations of more decided states a set of states of mind allows.

Bob Hale, though, rejects Blackburn's tree explanation.[19] Hale himself seems confident that he has dispatched the kind of expressivism I advocate: the quasi-realist's "prospects ought by now to seem bleak," he writes just after he deals with Blackburn's talk of "trees".[20] The only hope that Hale still allows, at this point in his argument, takes him in a direction that I would emphatically reject (Hale, "Can There Be," 1993, sec. 6, pp. 353–358). Now in my own view, Blackburn's solution and my own are in essence the same.[21] With a few added glosses, I claim, these treatments solve the Frege-Geach problem. I need to ask, then, whether Hale has identified some grave problem with Blackburn's talk of tree-tying.

To calibrate Hale's critique with the view I advocate, I must ignore large parts of what he and Blackburn say. Blackburn speaks in terms not of decisions, but of attitudes of favor and disfavor. In the article that Hale attacks, he develops an elaborate logical treatment of attitudes ("Attitudes," 1988). Now I would hope that the kind of treatment I'm giving can work for favoring and being against; indeed, I take this up in

18. Blackburn, "Attitudes" (1988), pp. 192–193. See Jeffrey, *Formal Logic* (1991) for one presentation of the "tree" method. Blackburn's way of handling the Frege-Geach problem in *Spreading the Word* (1984) has been criticized by Scheuler in "Modus Ponens and Moral Realism" (1988), and in reply in "Attitudes" (1988), Blackburn develops a different treatment of the problem.

19. Hale, "Can There Be" (1993). See Blackburn's reply, "Realism: Quasi or Queasy" (1993) and Hale's "Postscript" (1993).

20. Hale, "Can There Be" (1993), p. 353. Some readers have taken Hale's critique of Blackburn as definitive; see Wright, *Realism, Meaning and Truth* (1993), p. 241.

21. Blackburn, "Attitudes" (1988), pp. 192–193; Gibbard, "Expressivistic Theory" (1986), *Wise Choices* (1990), and here.

Chapter 7. I am uncertain, though, on the kind of deontic logic that Blackburn develops, and don't want to assess Hale's treatment of this particular logic. It is Blackburn's diagnosis of "tying oneself to a tree" that I endorse. My question is whether Hale should regard his objection as carrying over from attitudes to decisions, and from aspects of Blackburn's treatment to mine. To what degree Hale's objections to Blackburn depend on the details of Blackburn's logic of attitudes and the glosses he gives it, I'm quite unclear. I'll read Hale's objection, then, as meant to apply to any expressivist quasi-realist who explains complex constructions as "tying one to a tree". And I'll leave open the question whether other aspects of Blackburn's system render him susceptible to Hale's attack. My claims are, first, that we can find a core of doctrine in Blackburn that resists Hale's attack, and, more crucially, that nothing Hale says tells against the system I've been laying out.

Hale's focus at the point I want to examine is on tree rules that "branch": rules for disjunction, the truth-functional conditional, and the like. I'll stick with the case of disjunction, though Hale and Blackburn often use conditionals as their examples. Since it is controversial whether "if . . . then . . ." is truth functional at all—and since I myself think that it isn't (Gibbard, "Two Recent Theories," 1981)—I'll rewrite what Blackburn and Hale say to near-quote them as if they too had spoken in terms of disjunction.

Blackburn uses 'H!' as a Hooray! operator, so that to accept H!q is to *endorse q*, to *insist on q*. To accept $p \lor$ H!q, according to Blackburn, is to be "tied to (either accepting that p, or endorsing q), where the parentheses show that this is not the same as (being tied to accepting p) or (being tied to endorsing q)." Blackburn's formulation here of what the person *is* tied to—"(either accepting that p, or endorsing q)"—may be misleading, since these words suggest that one must then go on either to do the one or to do the other. (Much of what Hale says, at crucial points, he links specifically to this formulation of Blackburn's.) As Blackburn indicates, though, commitment to a disjunction is *non-distributive:* one can be committed to a disjunction without ever becoming committed to either disjunct. Blackburn goes on to explain matters clearly: "The commitment is to accepting the one branch should the other prove untenable." (We might add also, it is to accepting at least one of the disjuncts should one become decided on both.)

Hale, though, states that this non-distributive reading of one's commitment to a disjunction "is fatal to the claim . . . that the usual tableau rule" can be applied. We should be puzzled why Hale thinks this. After all, the same thing goes for descriptive beliefs: one can be committed to *p* or *q* without being committed to *p* or committed to *q*—and a branching tableau rule validly applies. Why does Hale think the case is different for expressive embeddings?

I am quite mystified by what Hale has to say at this point, and so I can only near-quote extensively and intersperse a few comments. To pass from *p* ∨ H!*q* to a pair of alternatives *p* and H!*q*, writes Hale, "is precisely to treat the commitment as distributive. For it is tantamount to saying that if—in the actual world—you are committed to (either affirming *p* or endorsing *q*) then—in the actual world—either you are committed to affirming *p* or you are committed to endorsing *q*."[22] As I have noted, what Hale says here doesn't hold for descriptive disjunctions. We have to ask why it should hold, then, for disjunctions like *p* ∨ H!*q* that embed expressive language. Hale's attack here may depend on Blackburn's particular misleading formulation, that the person who accepts *p* ∨ H!*q* is "committed to (either affirming *p* or endorsing *q*)." Hale's words also may exploit the common confusion between expressivism and subjectivism: crucially, H!*q* does *not* mean "I am committed to endorsing *q*." To say H!*q* by itself, in assertoric contexts, is to *make* such a commitment, but it is not to say that one is so committed.

In any case, Hale goes on,

> To put the point slightly differently, if *p* ∨ H!*q* registers a *non*-distributive commitment to (either affirming *p* or endorsing *q*), then it has to be reckoned a possibility that this commitment goes unrealized in the actual (morally imperfect) world, just as any other evaluative commitment may go unrealized. The upshot is that, so far from facilitating the treatment of the evaluative inferences which concern us as straightforward instances of *modus ponens*, the proposed interpretation of disjunctions in terms of being tree-tied actually debars us from so treating them.[23]

Whether or not this passage applies to Blackburn's full formulation of his position, it proceeds in terms of a kind of commitment that figures nowhere in my own treatment of the problem. On my view, what ac-

22. Hale, "Can There Be" (1993), p. 353, with conditionals replaced by disjunctions, and appropriate changes in wording to accommodate this change.
23. Ibid., same passage, same kinds of alterations.

cepting $p \lor$ H!q commits one to is not both to disbelieve p and tolerate $\neg q$. It also, we might say, involves a *conditional* commitment: that *if* one moves into a decided state with regard to affirming p and endorsing q, *then* one is to do one or the other (or both). "The commitment", explains Blackburn, "is to accepting the one branch should the other prove untenable." If what Hale says applies fairly to part of what Blackburn says—and I am not clear whether it does, or just depends on a misleading formulation on Blackburn's part which Blackburn goes on to clarify—it doesn't apply to the interpretation I advocate. Blackburn's crucial tree-tying insight stands.

Further Note on Hale

I have near-quoted Hale in full at the crucial point in the text of Hale's article, but Hale also devotes a long note to the issue. Christopher Peacocke, Hale reports, defended Blackburn as offering inference rules for connectives like 'or'.[24] Writes Hale,

> But if it is granted, as it is, that for the expressive interpretation, the conditional cannot be truth-functional, then specifying the inference rules in this case ought to *distinguish* the special, expressive form of the conditional allegedly introduced from the ordinary truth-functional variety. Yet that the proposal manifestly fails to do, since the only inference rule proposed is just the usual tableau rule for the truth-functional conditional. . . . The trouble is that Blackburn wants '$p \rightarrow$ H!q,' etc., to have just the inferential liaisons of the ordinary truth-functional conditional. But then the proposal collapses. ("Can There Be," 1993, p. 361, n. 27)

This seems to me to equivocate on two senses in which a conditional might be truth functional. A conditional is truth functional in a weak sense if—in contrast, for instance, to the Adams conditional, the Stalnaker conditional, the Lewis counterfactual conditional, or the strict conditional[25]—it has the familiar logic of the truth-functional condi-

24. Hale interprets this as somehow combining with reading 'H!q' "descriptively", but since I—and I presume, Blackburn—want no such reading, I'll skip past this.

25. See Adams, *The Logic of Conditionals* (1975); Stalnaker, "A Theory of Conditionals" (1968); Lewis, *Counterfactuals* (1973).

tional. Among other things, if '→' is truth functional in this sense, then $p \to q$ follows from q, and from $\neg(p \to q)$ follow p and $\neg q$. We may use the terms 'true' and 'false' to keep account of this logical behavior, and say that the truth value of the conditional is a function of the truth values of its components. But this may be "truth" on quite a minimal conception, on which truth and falsity don't serve to *explain* logic, as opposed to systematizing it.[26] In a stronger sense, a construction is truth functional only if its behavior is explained in terms of some substantial conception of truth, in such a way that the truth value of the compound is a function of the truth values of its components. Blackburn is free to deal in conditionals and disjunctions that are truth conditional in the first, weaker sense, and these will have the familiar logic. He may then owe an explanation of the logic of such conditionals—and that is what both he and I have been trying to give. But the logical behavior explained may well then be the familiar (if quirky) behavior of the truth-functional conditional, and the familiar truth-functional behavior of inclusive disjunction.

26. See Horwich, *Truth* (1990, 1998).

~ 5

Supervenience and Constitution

$\mathcal{I}$s PLANNING A KIND of believing? Is it a matter of believing special kinds of facts, facts of what it is okay to do in a situation? I haven't committed myself to any view on this question. Rather, I stipulated that "facts" and "factual beliefs", as I am using these terms, will be of more prosaic kinds—facts that are more plainly and uncontroversially a matter of how things are. Planning I have treated as permitting or ruling out acts in situations, but I have not declared myself on the thesis that to permit an act is to attribute a property to it. In a fuller sense of the term 'factual', okayness may be a "factual" property or not, for all I have said, but "facts", as I'm using the term—by sheer stipulation—do not include facts of okayness.

Or at least, they don't unless the existence of such facts is a hidden consequence of things I am saying. Whether it is will be a chief topic of this chapter. In a sense, I conclude, there indeed is a property of *being okay to do* in a situation. On the other hand, thinking an act okay to do is not straightforwardly ascribing a property to it. It is permitting the act—and people who agree on what properties an act has in a situation can disagree on whether to permit it. They can disagree on whether the act is an okay thing to do in that situation. (I speak in this chapter mostly in terms of being "okay", not in terms of being "the thing to do". An act is the thing to do just in case it is, among the alternatives open on the occasion, uniquely okay, so that omitting it is not okay.)

88

Supervenience

Plans, I have said, I am treating initially as "non-factual" in their content: a situation *s* for which one can plan does not include facts of what is okay to do in it and what isn't. Think, though, of a universal plan *p*, a hyperplan. This, recall, is a fantastic plan that, for each act open in any situation anyone could be in, allows that act or rules it out. *Relative* to any such particular hyperplan *p*, there *are* facts of okayness. Given any hyperplan *p*, an act is *p*-okay in a situation or not—and whether it is is a matter of prosaic fact. An act is *p-okay* in a situation just in case plan *p* permits that act in that situation. Given a plan *p*, a situation *s*, and an act *a* open in *s*, whether *p* permits *a* in *s* is just a matter of what plan *p* is, of what it permits in what situations. A hyperplan *p* thus determines a prosaically factual property, okayness according to *p*.

Turn now from being *p*-okay to being okay, and to other, more complex plan-laden concepts. My way of treating mixed fact/plan judgments, we can now show, brings with it an important kind of supervenience. Whether an act is okay to do in a situation *supervenes* on the prosaically factual properties of that act in its situation. The argument for this takes up the next few paragraphs.

What is meant by 'supervenes'? One leading conception runs as follows: The aim is to define what it is for the properties of a class Y to *supervene* on another class X of properties. This means that any two possible items, in any two respective possible situations, differ in a Y-property only if they differ in some X-property. Kim (1993, pp. 149–156) labels this relation "strong covariance", and defines "strong supervenience" as this plus a kind of dependence.

My treatment will in the end involve dependence too; I shall show how being okay to do depends on prosaic fact—though I will not try in advance to characterize the kind of dependence that emerges. Supervenience as I treat it will not, however, be a relation between properties or between classes of properties: I will not show that okayness is a *property* that supervenes in this sense. My picture of supervenience, then, will turn out to diverge from this initial characterization. Still, we can take the more or less standard conception of supervenience as a starting point, and see how it would apply to okayness.

Being okay to do supervenes on the prosaic facts of the world, we can say, in this sense:

Supervenience. Two acts in two possible situations differ in being okay or not only if they differ, somehow, in their prosaically factual properties. That is to say, for any two possible situations s_1 and s_2, act a_1 open in s_1, and act a_2 open in s_2, we have the following: only if act a_1 in s_1 differs factually from act a_2 in s_2 will it be okay to do a_1 in s_1, though not okay to do a_2 in s_2.

"Factually" here, remember, means in matters prosaic. The prosaic facts it allows, though, can range widely: the ways in which two acts might differ factually include all the prosaically factual features of their contexts. Supervenience, then, does not rule out claims, say, that the ethos of one's group matters for what it is okay to do, or one's own inner commitments. Indeed, it does not, as a matter of sheer logic, rule out even such obviously irrelevant features as the positions of the planets or what intelligent beings do in the next galaxy. It merely says that *exactly* the same factual kind of act in exactly the same kind of factual circumstances will not differ in whether it is okay to do.

How can we show that being okay to do supervenes in this sense? Here I invoke a form of argument that proves immensely powerful; it is a form that I repeat time and again in what follows. Call it the technique of *proceeding from hyperstates*. Start first with a thinker-planner in a fully decided state: Hera, imagine, suspends no belief on matters of prosaic fact, and leaves no hypothetical bridge uncrossed in her planning. Every act open on every possible occasion for choice she either permits or rules out. In other words, the content of her beliefs and planning is a particular fact-plan world. This paragon of freedom from doubt, I argue, accepts the supervenience thesis. That is stage one of the argument.

Stage two concerns the rest of us: ordinary, doubt-ridden humanity, the everyday Joe. We still, though, impose one vast idealization on Joe: that he is consistent. (Only the possible states of thinkers who are consistent reveal the commitments our judgments carry.) Think, then, of the ways that Joe could become fully decided without changing his mind on anything. His doubts are all resolved, his doubts on how things are and his doubts on what to do in all kinds of situations. These ways are the hyperstates in terms of which we have been characterizing Joe's thoughts. Take, then, something *Q* that Joe would accept no matter what hyperstate he might come to be in without changing his mind about anything. This, then, is something to which Joe is committed: it is entailed by what he already accepts. In short, we have the following:

Principle of Commitment. A person is committed to a claim Q if in every hyperstate he could reach without changing his mind he would accept Q.

In other forms, this lesson should be familiar. It is the lesson displayed by Venn diagrams. The content of a hyperstate is a fact-plan world. A Venn diagram represents worlds by points in a rectangle. Items of content it represents by sets of points—*expanses,* let's call them. Consistency it represents by overlap, and entailment by inclusion: Q entails P if and only if the expanse representing Q lies entirely inside the expanse representing P. One is committed to everything the things one accepts entail, and the Venn representation of entailment reveals the Principle of Commitment: that a person is *committed* to content Q if Q *holds in every world that his judgments don't rule out.*

In particular, then, to show that Joe and the rest of us are committed to the thesis of supervenience, it suffices to show that Hera accepts the thesis. It suffices to show that anyone in a hyperdecided state accepts supervenience, that supervenience obtains in every fact-plan world. For if it obtains in every fact-plan world, then, *a fortiori,* it holds in every fact-plan world that Joe could reach without changing his mind.

Now a part of Hera's being hyperdecided is this: she has adopted a hyperplan, a plan for which acts to rule out and which to permit in every conceivable situation, actual or hypothetical. She has a hyperplan for life, which we can call p. Now in accepting plan p, she in effect does regard an act's being okay to do in a situation as supervening on matters of prosaic fact. If and only if act a is p-permitted in situation s does she think act a okay to do in s. If she thinks a_1 okay to do in s_1 but a_2 not okay to do in s_2, then a_1 is p-permitted in s_1, and yet a_2 is not p-permitted in s_2. This, we have said, is a prosaically factual difference: being p-permitted is a prosaically factual property.

Think of the matter another way: Hera accepts hyperplan p. She thus regards an act a as okay to do in a situation s if and only if her plan p permits a in s. But a plan can distinguish between situations only in terms of their prosaically factual properties, and it can distinguish between acts only in terms of the prosaically factual properties of those acts. If two acts in two possible situations differ in no prosaically factual way, a plan can't distinguish them, permitting one and ruling out the other. Either it will permit both or it will rule both out. Though plans, to be sure, are not determinations of prosaic fact, anyone who was fully decided on a plan for living—a hyperplan, which provides for every conceivable situation—would accept the dictum "No difference in being okay without a prosaically factual difference."

I have characterized "supervenience" as a modally strong kind of covariance, with no additional talk of dependence. We could add dependence as well, though, to our list of what is required for supervenience, and the same results still obtain. Like any of us, Hera the hyperdecided planner regards what to do in a situation as depending on the facts of the situation. So would Joe, were he to become hyperdecided without changing his mind about anything. By the Principle of Commitment, then, Joe is committed to thinking that an act's being okay to do in a situation depends on the facts of the situation. So are we all.

We end up, then, with a strong result: anyone who thinks and plans is thereby committed to the supervenience of being okay to do on prosaic fact. I myself am a thinker and planner, and so are you. I therefore invite you to join me in accepting and asserting something to which we are both committed: *being okay to do supervenes on prosaic fact.* This is an invitation, if I'm right, that you cannot consistently reject.

Supervenience so characterized is not, for anything I have claimed, a matter of classes of properties. I haven't claimed so far, after all, that being okay to do in a situation is a property of an act. I am thus not saying that one class of *properties* supervenes on another. Whether this is what I *should* say is a complex question, which gets a complex answer later on.

The thesis of supervenience is not prosaically factual; it is planladen. In it figures the concept of being *okay to do*, and this is not a concept that we have admitted as "factual". The claim of supervenience has an *a priori* status, in that everyone is committed to it, and not on the basis of any feature of experience that they share. It is, we can say, an *a priori practical* claim. To accept it is what we commit to by planning any aspect of our lives.

This claim of supervenience, that being okay supervenes on prosaically factual properties, must not be confused with the claim—for any

particular hyperplan *p*—that being *p*-okay supervenes on factual properties. The claim of supervenience is plan-laden, whereas the other
claim, that being *p*-okay supervenes on factual properties, is not. The
conclusion that an act is *p*-okay is factual, whereas the conclusion that it
is okay is part of a plan. True, if *p* is Hera's hyperplan, then she accepts
that act *a* is okay just in case she accepts that it is *p*-okay. Still, the two
claims are distinct: If hyperdecided Zeus and Hera agree on all matters
of prosaic fact but not on how to live, they will agree whether act *a* is *p*-
okay, but may disagree whether it is okay. To think the act okay is to
permit it, to disagree with disagreeing with doing it; to do this is to
reach a conclusion in one's planning. Being *p*-okay too supervenes on
factual properties, and indeed that it does figured at one stage in my
proof of the claim of supervenience. But this claim, with its prosaically
factual subject matter, is not itself the claim of supervenience.

Note that being "plan-laden", as I am using the term, is quite different from being "plan-relative". An act may be okay *relative* to plan *p* but
not plan *q*, and if so, these are claims on which everyone will agree who
is coherent and has the facts right. No planning figures in the claim
that the act is *p*-okay; a fanciful being could agree who was purely a believer in facts, for whom questions of what to do did not arise. That the
act is "_____-okay" is an incomplete claim; no one can agree or disagree until the blank is filled in. You could call such an incomplete
claim "plan-relative". Whether the act is okay or not, in contrast, is a
question on which only a planner can form an opinion. The conclusion
that the act is okay is *plan-laden*, in that to accept it is to engage in planning. As for the Claim of Supervenience, it is couched in the language
of planning, the language in which one plans—and not in language that
merely allows *describing* plans without concurring or dissenting.

If "supervenience" as I use the term is not a relation between distinct
classes of properties, can it really count as a relation of supervenience? I
proceeded in a way that was metaphysically lightweight: I characterized
supervenience not by speaking of "properties", but directly in terms of
being "okay to do". Being okay to do *supervenes* on prosaic fact, I said,
in that if two acts, in two possible situations, differ in whether they are
okay to do, they differ in some way that is prosaically factual. This
seems a standard and natural way to speak of supervenience, but it is
non-committal on the metaphysical status of supervenience. We have
seen that since the claim is not couched exclusively in "factual" terms, it

is not a prosaically factual claim. It is plan-laden in that it is a claim to which we are committed not as sheer observers but as planners, who can think in terms of plans and entertain a wide variety of plan-laden thoughts. If you think that "supervenience", strictly taken, must be a relation between classes of properties, you can call what I'm talking about "quasi-supervenience". Remember, though, that it was characterized just as we would have characterized the "supervenience" of being okay to do, if we had thought that being okay to do were a plain matter of fact.

If supervenience (or quasi-supervenience), so characterized, is not a relation among properties, what is it? A planner, we can say, has a *concept* of being okay to do, and so the supervenience of being okay to do on the facts, we might say, is a relation between this concept and the class of factual properties. The concept of being okay to do is one among a whole class of *plan-laden* concepts, and so the supervenience in question, we can say, relates the class of plan-laden concepts and the class of prosaically factual properties.

Factual Constitution

I'll now make a claim that might appear far stronger than the thesis of supervenience. Any planner is committed to a Claim of *Factual Constitution:* that there is a factual property that *constitutes* being okay to do. This too will be a plan-laden truth, not a truth of prosaic fact.

As for what this factual property is, we can be coherent and yet agnostic on the matter. Our friend Hedda, imagine, does have a view on what constitutes being okay to do. As a hedonistic egoist, she is hyper-decided; she has adopted a hyperplan. Her plan is, in every conceivable contingency, actual or hypothetical, to maximize her net prospects for pleasure. It is, in a term I will coin, to do whatever is *egohedonic*. According to her, then, an act is okay to do just in case doing it is egohedonic: maximizes the agent's net prospects for pleasure. Hedda, then, has a view as to what the property is that constitutes being okay to do: it is the natural property of being egohedonic. Our friend Thomas, in contrast, is more of a doubter, undecided on many practical questions. He is unsure, imagine, whether to be a hedonistic egoist, a universalistic hedonist, or some form of self-perfectionist. Still, I argue that Thomas as well, as a planner, is committed to thinking that there *is* some property that constitutes being okay to do. The property need not be "queer" or non-natural; it could, for all Thomas is convinced, be the property of being egohedonic. What I argue is this: if Thomas is ideally coherent, he accepts that there is *some* such property—even though he is avowedly unsure what that property is.

What do I mean here by "constitution"? Take a loose analogy: being water, we can say, is constituted by being H_2O; what would this mean? First, water is *necessarily* H_2O: in any possible situation, all and only water is H_2O. Being water and being H_2O are necessarily coextensional. Second, we might say somewhat vaguely, something's being water depends, explanatorily, on its being H_2O: water's chemical structure explains its characteristic properties. To speak of "constitution" in matters of plan, then, we can check for parallels. Since we are, in these chapters, *examining* plan-laden judgments rather than making them and propounding them, I won't make claims as to which property constitutes being okay to do and which properties don't; rather, I'll speak in terms of the coherent opinions of Hedda, Percy, and Thomas. Hedda, our hedonistic egoist, thinks that in any possible situation, all and only acts that maximize one's hedonic prospects are okay to do. In this sense, she thinks that maximizing one's hedonic prospects and being okay to do are coextensional. She also thinks that an act's being okay to do depends, explanatorily, on its maximizing one's hedonic prospects. (The explanations in this case are not purely causal explanations; they are explanations of why to do things or not.) In her view, then, maximizing one's hedonic prospects *constitutes* being okay to do in a way that roughly parallels the case of H_2O and water.

She may be right about this and she may be wrong, for anything I say here. She, of course, thinks she is right, but Percy, as a self-perfectionist, disagrees, and Thomas doubts. Each of them is conceptually coherent—and which of them is right is a question of how to live, a question we are not now engaged in settling. Whether or not, though, Hedda is right about what constitutes being okay to do, *some* factual property does constitute, in this sense, being okay to do. This, I will be arguing, is a plan-laden claim to which any planner whatsoever is committed.

In speaking of constitution, I'll focus on necessary coextensionality, and then just note informally that a kind of explanatory dependence seems to obtain. What I shall mean by this Claim of Factual Constitution, then, is this:

There is a prosaically factual property F such that for any act a open in any possible situation s, act a is okay to do in s just in case a in s has property F.   (C)

As an abbreviation of (C), I'll say,

There is a factual property that *constitutes* being okay to do.   (C*)

To this, I shall argue, planning commits each of us.

The argument for this claim (C), the Claim of Factual Constitution, proceeds much as before, starting with hyperstates. Consider first Hera, who is hyperdecided. In particular, she is a planner who is hyperdecided in her life plan; she has a hyperplan. She, we need to show, accepts the Claim of Factual Constitution. Since the Claim of Factual Constitution is accepted by any planner who is hyperdecided, it will follow, by the Principle of Commitment, that anyone who plans is already committed to the claim.

How, then, do we show that hyperdecided Hera accepts the Claim of Factual Constitution? She has a hyperplan, a life plan that is universal, providing for what to do in every actual and hypothetical contingency. The argument will be that this plan must amount to permitting all and only acts with some factual property P. That is, for any possible hyperplan p, there is a prosaically factual property P such that hyperplan p can be viewed as taking the following form: for any situation, actual or hypothetical, hyperplan p permits all acts with property P, and rules out all other acts.

A planner, after all, must identify acts in terms of their prosaically factual properties: a plan, say, always to do whatever is the thing to do is no plan at all. A hyperplan can take the infinite form, in situation S_1 do an act with property P_1, in situation S_2 do an act with property P_2, and so on. From this, we can construct the grand property, having property P_1 in S_1, P_2 in S_2, and so on. Call this property P^*; the plan is, then, in any possible situation, to do something with this grand property P^*. In a hyperdecided state, this shows, one accepts that there is a property that constitutes being okay to do—namely, P^*. And this property is constructed, finitely or infinitely, out of factual properties.

What, then, of the rest of us—ordinary, doubt-ridden humanity, who are far from hyperdecided? To elicit the logic of our concepts, I'll again work with the vast idealization that my doubting Thomas, uncertain though he is, is nevertheless consistent. We return now to the Principle of Commitment that I used in arguing for supervenience. Consider the many ways that Thomas could become hyperdecided without changing his mind on anything. Take a conclusion Q that he would accept no matter what decided state he might come to be in without changing his mind. This, then, is something to which Thomas is committed; it is entailed by what he already accepts. Now in any hyperdecided state whatsoever, we have been saying, Thomas would accept the Claim of Factual Constitution. *A fortiori*, he accepts the claim in any hyperdecided state he could reach without changing his mind about anything. The Principle of Commitment thus applies to him, and so he is committed to the Claim of Factual Constitution, whatever his other uncertainties. And so are you, so am I, and so is any planner.

Having established what we are all committed to, I can now assert it. *There is a factual property that constitutes being okay to do.* So say I, and so must you agree; this is the transcendental turn in the argument.

An argument like this one is *transcendental* in Kant's sense: I establish a claim by showing that anyone must be committed to it. Such arguments, though, prompt a worry: couldn't we all be wrong in this commitment? It's a commitment that we can't do without, if my argument is right; we can't be planners and not be committed to Factual Constitution. Perhaps, though, the worry goes, the claim is nonetheless false: in truth no factual property does constitute being okay to do. If this were so and my argument is right, the moral would have to be this: we can be planners only by committing ourselves to a falsehood. Such putative morals are not unknown in philosophical lore: we can be planners, some contend, only by committing ourselves to belief in free will, but we have no free will: to act at all, then, is to act under an illusion. I myself don't accept this, but have I shown that no such thing is so for Factual Constitution?

The Claim of Factual Constitution, remember, is plan-laden. Plan-laden dicta concern how to live, and there is no question of whether they are true or false apart from factual questions and questions of how to live. The Claim of Factual Constitution in effect says to live in a way that satisfies the following constraint: there is a prosaically factual property such that, if the plan to do what you do were completely filled out, it would amount to the plan always to do what has that property. This is no real constraint at all, I have been arguing; any way of living satisfies it, and so to reject it would be incoherent. There's no question whether the Claim of Factual Constitution is true apart from the question of whether to live in accord with it—and no possible way to live fails to satisfy it.

In metaethical discussions, people often talk as if certain properties were peculiarly moral. The question then seems to press theorists, whether these are some subclass of natural properties, or some special kind of non-natural property—or whether there are no such properties at all. Morality has not directly been my topic; I have rather been seeing what happens if we start in a realm in which expressivism has to be right, with expressions of decisions. My conclusions about practical thought have then turned out to mirror much of what Moore and Ewing say in a metaethical vein. The property that constitutes being okay to do might indeed be complex, the resultant of a balancing of diverse considerations. Even if it is, however, that leaves another contrast that is crucial to understanding practical thought. The pattern I have described, after all, applies even if the property that constitutes being okay to do is a natural property of a plain and straightforward kind. It applies if, say, an egoistic hedonist like Hedda is right, and this property is that of maximizing one's hedonic prospects. Moore's non-naturalism, I argued earlier, might best be freely read as a doctrine not about properties but about concepts. Let P^* be the property that constitutes being okay to do, and let D be a descriptive concept of this property. Moore's point, so emended, is this: people who disagree about what's okay to do don't necessarily disagree on which acts are D. Their disagreement may not be descriptive, but purely a matter of what to do and how to live. In philosophers' jargon, it may be practical.

Here, then, is a possible set of slogans: It is concepts, not properties, that can be descriptive or plan-laden. There is no such thing as a plan-laden property as opposed to a descriptive property. There are, however, plan-laden concepts. Properties are just properties, neither descriptive nor plan-laden. Some concepts of a property, though, are descriptive, and other concepts of the same property are plan-laden.

Broadly Natural?

Is the property that constitutes being okay to do natural? The argument for Factual Constitution went quickly, and we should investigate carefully the kind of property the argument establishes. Basically, the requirement is this: it must be a property that suits a hyperplan. Some possible contingency plan, ideally complete, must amount to the plan to perform, in any possible contingency, whatever act has that property.

Now for sure, this cannot be a natural property in the sense that we conceive the property, as we plan, in terms of fundamental physics. We cannot guide our lives by anything so esoteric: "Keep away from radio-activity" would surely be a good part of a plan for living, if only we knew how to tell what's radioactive—but it's not much help if we don't. Plans, it seems, must be couched in terms of features that we can recognize: features of contingencies and features of options. Both of these must be available to the person who follows the plan. "Buy low, sell high" is no plan we can implement. Plans must be couched in terms whose application we can recognize.

The property that constitutes being okay to do is constructed, I have said, from the properties of contingencies and options. A hyperplan could go, "In contingency C_1 do act A_1, in contingency C_2 do act A_2, and so on." It thus amounts to a plan to do all and only acts with this property: being act A_1 in contingency C_1, or act A_2 in contingency C_2, and so on. The building blocks A_1, C_1, and so on are, I argued, properties one can recognize. Suppose, then, we interpret broadly "natural properties" as including such "wild disjunctions" of recognitional properties, even if they are infinite. Then this is a broadly natural property.

Recognitional building blocks might be "natural" only in quite a liberal sense. If spooks and gods are recognizable, so that one can plan for the contingency of encountering one of them, then spooky and divine properties will count as "natural" in the sense we need. (This fits Moore's purposes, we might note; his arguments, he insisted, applied to supernatural, divine, and metaphysical properties as well as to "natural" ones. The distinctiveness that concerned him pertained to good, not to these other kinds of properties.) Natural properties, we might say, are ones that could figure in empirical science, and if spooks and gods were recognizable, they might be subjects of an empirical science.

Does our property, then, deserve to count as a "natural" property, even if it is wildly and infinitely disjunctive? Here I'll take the view of properties that model theorists often take. On the model-theoretic conception, a property is—or at least, corresponds to—any way of assigning to each possible world w a set of entities in w. Let a possible world be determined by the elementary natural properties that entities have in that world and the elementary natural relations in which things stand in that world. (Many of these will be natural magnitudes, and not simple yes–no properties.) A natural property, then, is given by any function N that assigns to each such possible world w a set $N(w)$ of entities in w.

On this broad construal of natural properties, the claim that a hyperplan determines one is fairly trivial. The property will just be that of being permitted by the hyperplan. As a function, it assigns to each possible world the set of all acts in situations, in that world, that the plan permits for the situation. Again, the point is that what's distinctive about planning concepts—being the thing to do, being okay to do—isn't a distinctive kind of property they pick out. It is how such properties are conceived.

Let me formulate the structure of such a property more carefully—but feel free to skip this paragraph. A *situation* s is a triple $<w,i,t>$ of a world w, an agent i in w, and a time t at which agent i in world w has a choice of what to do. For each such situation s, there is a set $a(s)$ of *alternatives*. These are maximally specific acts open to person i at time t in world w. A *hyperplan* p assigns to each situation s a non-empty subset $p(s)$ of the alternative set $a(s)$. The property N we are seeking pertains to acts open in situations, and so we can treat it as a property of pairs $\langle x,s \rangle$ such that $x \, \varepsilon \, a(s)$, an assignment of a set of such pairs to each possible world. But this property will just be that for situation s, plan p permits x. The property is just that $x \, \varepsilon \, p(s)$. In model-theoretic terms, we can say that property N is the function that assigns to each world w every pair $\langle x,s \rangle$ such that s is a situation in w and $x \, \varepsilon \, p(s)$.

On this conception, then, constitution is not a relation among properties. Only one property is in play: property N. I have not introduced an additional property of being okay to do. Philosophical lore would have it otherwise. According to this lore, supervenience is a way of avoiding property identity. It relates classes of properties, and a property can supervene on a class of properties and yet be distinct from every member of that class. I, on the contrary, am maintaining that there is no special class of plan-laden properties that includes okayness. In the only sense in which okayness is a property—that there is a property that constitutes being okay to do—the property is a plain old property, however complex.[1]

---

1. Kim, *Supervenience and Mind* (1993), pp. 149–155, argues along lines that may be similar. He argues that what he calls "strong covariance" implies reducibility,

Should we call it a "natural" property? It is constructed from natural materials, but the principle for constructing it may not be finitely statable, and may have no clearly naturalistic rationale. Moore himself should agree that the property of being good is natural in this sense, that there's a function from determinate ways the natural world might have been to the things that would have been good had those ways obtained. (It's fine with me to say that Moore accepts the Principle of Constitution; his non-naturalism, I argued in Chapter 2, really concerns not properties but concepts.) Two considerations, though, favor an extremely broad use of the term 'natural', a use that has all properties natural.

In the first place, there may be no interesting conception of "natural" property that is more restrictive. Take, for instance, properties finitely expressible in basic physical terms. We don't know what these terms are, but we know enough to be sure that even most of the things that physicists themselves study will not be so expressible: rigid bodies, fluid dynamics, coils and capacitors, and such more abstract phenomena as coupled harmonic oscillators. Multiple realizability abounds in physics: a piece of wood and a piece of metal can have the same moment of inertia around their centers of gravity. As for "wild" disjunctions, they often have a rationale, and often the best formulation would not be as an arbitrary disjunction but, say, as a formula, or as satisfying a certain set of constraints. Apart from the division, if there is one, between fundamental physical magnitudes and non-fundamental ones, there may well be no sharp, principled, and interesting division between "physical" properties and properties that aren't themselves "physical" but that supervene on "physical" properties.

Now "natural" properties, as I use the term, might well not be physical. They include psychological properties like pleasure and belief—indeed, as I have insisted, the properties available for planning must be subjectively available in the situation planned for. But still, I see no more interesting prospects for a clear "natural/non-natural" divide among properties of interest for planning than I do for a clear

---

and allows that the property that a supervening property is reduced to may consist in an infinite disjunction of properties in the domain supervened upon. Kim argues that it is reasonable to accept this for plausible cases of supervenience. For another argument that supervenience of the ethical on the descriptive entails that ethical properties are descriptive properties, see Jackson, *From Metaphysics* (1998), pp. 121–128.

physical/non-physical divide among the properties that interest physicists.

A second reason to go for the liberal conception of natural properties is this: nothing in what I have been saying depends on whether the property that constitutes being okay to do is a fairly straightforward property involving, say, pleasure, or a complex property that, say, trades off pleasure, integrity, treating people as ends, justice, decency, courage, triumph, achievement, and the like, and then in hard cases privileges inaction over action. In either case, there is a natural property in my sense that constitutes being okay. In either case, one can coherently though mistakenly ascribe being okay and deny the property, or *vice versa*. It is, of course, a matter of great importance how complex this property is. The logical features of planning and being okay that I am exploring, though, are independent of this question—and these logical features too are important.

Recognitionally Grounded Concepts

Is calling an act okay to do, then, the same as saying that it has property *N*—where *N* is the property that constitutes being okay to do? Not at all. Hera and Zeus, suppose, are both hyperdecided, but their hyperplans are different. Hera is an egoistic hedonist: for any occasion for action, actual or hypothetical, she admits all and only those acts that hold out maximal prospects for the agent's net pleasure. Zeus is a triumphalist: he has a conception of triumph, and for any occasion for action admits all and only those acts with maximal prospects for the agent's triumph. For the case *s** of being Zeus in the form of a bull, Zeus plans to pursue Europa. He realizes that when in the form of a bull, cows hold out greater prospects for pleasure: that's in the nature of bulls. Still, for case *s**, he plans on the act he finds more triumphant. Hera's hyperplan is to go for cows in case *s**, taking the greater prospects for pleasure that cows offer anyone who is in the form of a bull. Hera, then, thinks that for case *s**, it is okay to pursue cows, whereas Zeus doesn't. According to her, the property that constitutes being okay to do is this: holding out maximal prospects for the agent's net pleasure. Call this property *H*. Zeus agrees that for case *s**, chasing cows has property *H*, but he denies that it is an okay thing to do in *s**.

Hera, then, coherently maintains the following:

Property H is the one that constitutes being okay to do. Zeus agrees with me that for situation s^*, pursuing cows has property H, but he denies that pursuing cows is okay to do in s^*. Zeus is mistaken about what to want in life, but he isn't incoherent or confused conceptually. So, even though H is the property that constitutes being okay to do, the case of Zeus shows this: thinking something okay to do is one thing; thinking that it has property H is another. For Zeus—coherently though mistakenly—thinks the second but not the first.

I have put the argument in Hera's mouth, since she has a firm and simple opinion of what property constitutes being okay to do. My own views on the matter are less clear and firm, and in any case, in a discussion of the *logic* of being okay to do, I don't want to foist my own fragmentary plans on you the reader, plans that give far more regard to Europa's preferences, choices, and feelings than do Zeus's. Still, Hera's conclusion in its general form is one to which I am committed: Whatever the property N is that constitutes being okay to do, I maintain, to think an act okay to do is one thing; to think, in a descriptive vein, that it has property N is another. A person can, coherently though mistakenly, accept one and yet deny the other. To these theses, if I am right, we are all committed.

You and I, then, cannot coherently reject the following two theses:

  (i) There is a property that constitutes being okay to do.
  (ii) To think something okay to do is not to ascribe that property as such.

What is it, then, to ascribe a property "as such"—the property, say, of being egohedonic? By this I mean simply thinking with regard to an act, "That's egohedonic". Thinking "That's okay to do" is not ascribing a property as such—even if Hera is right and the property of being okay to do just *is* the property of being egohedonic. For suppose Hera is right. We then have two concepts of the same property, the concept of being egohedonic and the concept of being okay to do. In a loose sense, therefore, we can "ascribe" this property to an act in either of two ways, by calling it "egohedonic" or by calling it "okay to do". Only calling it "egohedonic", though, counts as ascribing this property *as such*. The concept of being egohedonic attaches to the property di-

rectly and conceptually, whereas we can wonder whether all egohedonic acts are okay to do and suffer no purely conceptual confusion.
That is why Hera understands Zeus's claims, though she disagrees.
They share the concept *egohedonic*, and they share the different concept *okay* to do. Zeus joins these concepts in a thought when he says,
"Sometimes what's egohedonic is not okay to do." Hera understands
him and dissents.

A plan, then, is couched in concepts, not in properties apart from
how they are conceived. I don't follow a plan just by glomming on to a
naked property, but by conceiving it in terms of certain concepts. It's
with concepts, not properties directly, that we recognize our circumstances and alternatives. "Don't get wet" is an adage a small child can
often follow; "Don't have H_2O adhering to you" is not. These properties are identical, but the concepts are not the same. I should be talking,
then, not in the first instance about the property that constitutes being
okay to do, but about a concept of it.

Speak, then, of a factual concept that *realizes* being okay to do, and a
chemical concept that *realizes* being water. I form thoughts of what to
do with concepts I can use in recognizing my circumstances and my alternatives. Earlier I spoke of "recognitional properties", but it is concepts that primarily can be recognitional or not. Plans, we can say, must
be couched in recognitional concepts. As for the concept that realizes
being okay to do, this, I have been arguing, must be composable—
though perhaps only infinitely—from concepts I can use in planning.
Call such a concept *recognitionally grounded*: a concept is recognitionally
grounded if it is composable, finitely or infinitely, from recognitional
concepts. In the jargon I have been devising, we can now say this: the
concept that realizes being okay to do is recognitionally grounded.

The relation I have been treating as constitution, then, begins with a
relation among concepts, the relation of a concept's realizing being
okay to do. We start with a planning concept, the concept of being
okay to do, and now see that some recognitionally grounded concept
realizes it. By that I mean, at least in part, that necessarily all and only
acts that fit this concept are things to do.

This concept is the concept of a property, but other concepts too will
be concepts of this same property—esoteric scientific concepts, for
instance. Only recognitional concepts figure in plans fully specified.
There is a property that constitutes being okay to do, and a recog-

nitionally grounded concept of this property realizes being okay to do. (Hedda thinks that it is the concept of being egohedonic.) This recognitionally grounded concept and the pure planning concept *being okay to do* are distinct concepts of the same property.

Many philosophers besides Moore, to be sure, contrast ethical and natural properties. Can any sense at all be made of this talk, apart from saying that they have misspoken, and the contrast should be put in terms of concepts? I have not, of course, established that my treatment has anything to do with ethics, or with any normative concepts in everyday thought—but suppose it does, and familiar normative concepts are plan-laden. Some properties, we can say, are more interesting than others. Some are interesting naturalistically: concepts of these properties figure importantly in naturalistic explanations. Others are interesting normatively: concepts of these properties figure importantly in normative explanations. The same property may be interesting both naturalistically and normatively; ethical hedonists think that the property of being pleasant is a case in point. Anti-hedonists, though, may claim that the most normatively interesting properties are naturalistically uninteresting. In my terms, they can say that the descriptive concept that realizes being okay to do is naturalistically uninteresting. For purposes of naturalistic explanation, of explaining why things happen as they do, this concept is unsuited. Indeed, no concept of the property that constitutes being okay to do figures, in a significant way, in any purely naturalistic explanation of human affairs.

Is that right? Whether it's right is a question of how to live; it is not settled by the logical analysis I am offering. Moore may have thought it right, since he holds that what's good is a matter of complex organic wholes. That part of Moore's doctrine, though, is independent of the points he makes in Chapter 1 of *Principia Ethica*, the metaethical part of the book. For those purposes—if what I have been doing applies to the questions Moore posed—there is no contrast to be drawn between ethical and natural properties. The contrast is between ethical and naturalistic concepts.

Names and Recognition

A concept that realizes being okay to do is, I have argued, constructable out of recognitional concepts. The construction, though, might be infinite, for all the logic of planning by itself establishes; only in this loose way has the concept been proved naturalistic. I myself would find it bizarre if what to do were infinitely arbitrary, without discernible rationale. To think that it is would be to settle on leading one's life without discernible rationale. That is not, I am sure, the way to live—but nothing in the proof I have given speaks to this further claim. The question is an aspect of how to live: whether being okay to do has an intelligible rationale. Answering this is beyond the powers of sheer logic, the logic of how to live.

Does logic tell us anything further? Will the concept that realizes being okay to do be in any sense universal? Non-universal concepts are built from proper names or demonstrative concepts—such as admiring Jill, or honoring my mother, or hailing that man over there. For purposes of planning, I would claim, these boil down to universal relations to the subject in a situation. Pointing invokes a perceived relation to the thing one points at. Memory too invokes a relation of a different kind, a relation of the present thinker to the remembered event.

As for proper names, we can say this: to think in terms of a proper name is likewise to invoke a relation to the thing named. Imagine a doppelgänger of mine on a twin earth, who calls himself "Gibbard" but whom, to avoid confusion, I'll call "D-gibbard". The woman he thinks of as "Beth" is not my wife but his. She is like my wife Beth in all her universal characteristics, but distinct and far away. Still, D-gibbard's situations are subjectively just like mine. Suppose, then, that for situations that arise in my own life, I plan to cleave to Beth alone. That commits me likewise to cleaving to D-gibbard's "Beth" for the case of being he in his situation. I track Beth's identity, after all, with mental identifiers. What, then, makes these identifiers refer to Beth my own wife and not to D-gibbard's wife? It must be some relation I bear to my own wife Beth. This will be a complex historical relation, and it may have aspects of which I'm not aware—if not with names for one's spouse in most cases, surely with many historical names. Still, this relation is a universal: just as I stand in it to Beth, so any true doppelgänger of mine stands in it to a counterpart he thinks of as "Beth".

A property that one of my concepts snares, then, like *belonging to Beth*, may be non-universal, and had by nothing in D-gibbard's vicinity. Still, the relation is one we both stand in, I to the property *belonging to Beth* and he to the property that he would signify as 'belonging to

Beth'. Like comments apply to the earlier cases of pointing and memory: D-gibbard's memories and mine may pick out different people and properties, but they do so through universal relations we each stand in—I to the objects of my memories and he to the objects of his.

This picture may seem unduly phenomenalistic. Surely I form my plans not in terms of purely recognitional concepts, but in everyday terms, terms that inevitably put me at risk of mistakes. I can plan to cleave to Odette but then mistake Odile for Odette; I can plan to stay away from ghosts, though I then risk errors. All true enough—but that just shows that our plans aren't hyperplans. A plan to stay away from ghosts is incomplete; it can be supplemented with directions for what to take as signs of ghosthood. My incomplete plan "Stay away from ghosts" commits me to this: if I am to conclude that something is a ghost, then I am to stay away from it. This amounts to a restriction on hyperplans; it fits some hyperplans and not others. Still, the hyperplans themselves will be couched fully in recognitional terms. My plan to stay away from ghosts is couched in terms of its objective import, but it can be cashed out as a restriction on hyperplans couched recognitionally. Once my plan is refined enough so that I can begin to apply it, in that it now includes tests for ghosthood, I now risk performing these tests and getting erroneous results, and so I now risk hobnobbing with a ghost unbeknownst to me. If I do, I have made a mistake—though I perfectly carried out all recognizable features of my plan. That it is a mistake can be explained in the following way: my plan told me to think the form not a ghost but in fact he was, and my plan told me to keep away from him if I was to think him a ghost, but I hobnobbed with him.

In the other direction we might worry that hyperplans, as I characterize them, are restricted too little. I have said something about which differences in fact can make a difference to what it is okay to do in a situation. The facts that bear on planning must be conceived in recognitionally grounded ways, and in ways that invoke universal relations to the protagonist of a situation. Surely, though, there is much that is utterly irrelevant to planning that these strictures do not rule out. For few situations is it relevant, say, how tall is the highest mountain on the other side of the moon—if the agent knows. Hedonists, indeed, go farther: they hold that the *only* features of a situation that bear on what to do are features that bear on prospects for pleasure. Even the most truis-

tic aspects of relevance, though, don't follow from the arguments I
have been laying out. Which recognitional features bear on what to do
is, rather, a question of how to live.

I have been studying what we are committed to simply in virtue of
being thinkers and planners. In this sense, I am studying the sheer *logic*
of planning. In thinking about how to live, we will commit to far more
than logic. We might, for instance, join the bulk of economists in concluding that irretrievably sunk costs don't weigh on what to do next.
We may conclude that personal ties matter more than sheer ambition.
Neither of these, though, is something we're committed to simply in
being planners. These are not conclusions that govern the sheer logic
of thinking.

Thick Apprehension

In planning what to do, must we really stick to the facts—the prosaic,
natural facts, free of all hint of plan-ladenness? Indeed, can we assume
that there *is* such a thing as one's known subjective situation, apart from
any judgment of what the situation "calls for" or "demands" by way of
action? A prominent current philosophical view is that we can't. Understandings of one's situation cannot always be factored into separate
components of how things are, on the one hand, and what to do on the
other. I may just "see", for instance, that Jack is sensitive, and seeing
this can't be separated from finding reason to spare his feelings. Jack's
being "sensitive" is already practically laden for me: in finding him sensitive, I am already motivated to tread carefully on his feelings.[2] (Or if
I'm a bully, I am already motivated to bait him.)

Now this, if it is right, might seem to impugn the picture I have been
sketching. If I recognize my situation by its demands, won't I, in my
planning, have to include these demands in my specification of the circumstances for which I plan a given response? If so, it may seem, then I
cannot have my sharp distinction between *what to do* and *how things are*,
the distinction I have helped myself to throughout my argument. What
to do is built into circumstances for which I must plan.

Let me accept that apprehensions of one's situation can be heavy

---

2. For this contention and the example, see McDowell, "Are Moral Judgments
Hypothetical Imperatives?" (1978).

with demands for action. I may just perceive maggots on a slab of meat as disgusting, and to do this is to shy away from the scene. Feelings may come before recognition of an object, so that, say, disgust comes before recognizing the maggots as such. You do not, then, apprehend the scene in terms free of all valence for what to do, and then proceed to make your decisions. The same will no doubt go for more complex apprehensions of social situations: often, apprehending how things are won't be separate from having a strong sense of what to do.[3]

All this I am eager to accommodate—in the right way. Distinguish two ways in which we might try to accept these points. Only one of them is tenable, I'll argue; the other would yield monstrous directives for how to live. On the one hand, I'll agree, among an agent's circumstances is the fact that she has the sense she has of what her situation demands. Realizing that Jack is sensitive might involve having a sense that the way Jack is tells against joshing him. That Jill *has this sense* may indeed be part of her situation. It is, though, a psychological aspect, not plan-laden in itself. Describing Jill as having this sense does not at all commit us, logically, to being protective if in her shoes. A bully might plan for the case of being like Jill and so having this sense that Jack is not to be teased, but dismiss her concerns as wimpish, planning to weigh Jack's hurt feelings entirely in favor of ribbing him. The bully is depraved but not thereby short on logic.

A stronger claim on this score must, though, be rejected. The untenable claim is that we must accommodate more than this, that when Jill finds her circumstances to carry protective demands, we must recognize, as among her circumstances, that the situation indeed *does* carry these demands. If we were to accept this, we would not be describing her situation in the kinds of terms I have in mind in speaking of plans for living. The terms we use will then not bracket all questions of what to do.

The principle we'd need to accept in order to do this, though, is appalling. More to the point, the principle constitutes no demand of practical reason; it is one that a planner can reject without confusion. Our contingency planning, after all—even that of the most virtuous person imaginable—can include hypothetical decisions for the case of being vicious. Indeed, part of genuine human virtue surely consists in

3. Zajonc, "Feeling and Thinking" (1980).

just this: potentials for responding viciously are in us all, and we need to be prepared. Now, the vicious as well as the virtuous can experience a situation as demanding action. Turned vicious, I might find that a man's sexual persona demands bashing him up. I might be incapable of untangling my factual basis for this judgment from the glory, as I see it, of bashing up such a pathetic excuse for a man. A hyperplan covers all possible circumstances a person might be in, and so it covers this situation among others.

How, then, should I plan for such a plight? By discriminating, we might try answering, between virtuous and vicious sensings of what one's situation demands. What is it, though, when I view a hypothetical situation, to regard the demand-sensings I'd have in it as virtuous? Isn't it just to fall in, in my contingency plans for the situation, with the demands that I'd be sensing? Isn't it to give some weight, hypothetically, to meeting those seeming demands in that situation? What kinds of being "wimpish", as some would describe it, are vicious and what kinds virtuous? The answer doesn't come in advance of thinking how to live and what matters in living with others. Join me in thinking, then, what to do in the bashing case. In the situation we're planning for, one senses a seeming demand to bash, and we—the real we who are deciding hypothetically for that circumstance—can resolve to resist. We can each say to ourselves, "If something about a man I can't put my finger on seems to demand bashing him, don't bash, and work to get rid of my proclivity to sense such a demand."

As theorists of contingency planning, then, we need a framework that allows raising the question of whether a seeming demand is veridical, whether it is a demand to fall in with. We must distinguish, in contingency planning, whether a sense I might have of what my plight demands is virtuous or vicious. And this brings us back to the first way of accommodating the psychological point that situations may be recognized by their seeming demands.

Indeed, we could lead ourselves back to that way just by thinking about contingency planning itself. It is no part of contingency planning to decide, hypothetically,

If something about a man, one can't say just what, *really* demands bashing, then bash him!   (1)

Or at least this is no part of contingency planning on the plainest interpretation of this dictum (1). On this interpretation, the imperative (1) is
analytic, but it applies to no possible circumstance. It is analytic in that
it specifies the circumstance as one in which the man *is*, for no clear
reason, to be bashed. It is inapplicable, though—and this is a substantive claim about how to live—in that there are no such circumstances.
To make the principle a genuine candidate for inclusion in a contingency plan, we would have to interpret the antecedent psychologically:

> If something about a man, one can't say just what, *seems* to call for
> bashing, then bash him!   (2)

But then the hypothetical decision is one a planner can reject—and
that I hope we all do reject.

~ 6

Character and Import

$\mathcal{F}$OR *BEING OKAY TO DO* as the notion crops up in decision, the position that has emerged is quasi-realist. The term is Simon Blackburn's, and the point is this: thinking what to do remarkably parallels thinking, prosaically, how things are. The concepts that figure in thinking prosaically how things are I am calling *descriptive*—leaving this notion loose, so long as claims on what to do don't themselves count as "descriptive". Examples of clearly descriptive language are easy enough to find, and much theory of language and thought is trained on the descriptive.

How such language and thought works, though, is controversial. I need to say more about a picture of descriptive thought that fits with my picture of plan-laden thought. The treatments in this chapter will be somewhat technical, and you may reasonably decide to skip this chapter or skim it. Still, if I claim that plan-laden language mimics descriptive language, I need to be explicit how I take description itself to work. No one account of descriptive thought and language is widely accepted and clearly satisfactory, and terminology in this realm flies easily out of control. In this chapter I quickly lay out a familiar but controversial picture, not much defending it. Then I go on to indicate how this framework expands to handle mixed fact-plan thinking, thinking that is both plan-laden and prosaically fact-laden. As a bonus, the expanded framework then applies as well to purely descriptive thought: it applies not only to thinking that mixes description and planning, but also to purely descriptive thinking. It applies too to pure planning. I'll use the term *fact-plan thoughts* to cover the contents of all these kinds of thinking.

Reference is far from accounting for all aspects of thought and meaning, we know. Frege adduced the Morning Star and Evening Star, and I have alluded to the discovery that water is H_2O. Concepts can differ, it seems, though they share reference. In the last chapter I argued that, for all our concepts tell us by themselves, being okay to do might be *constituted* by the property of being egohedonic. Is this the same phenomenon as with descriptive concepts, when different concepts somehow involve the same property? I shall answer no: Moore, I think, was pointing to a further dimension on which concepts can differ. When we account for such phenomena as indexicality and the contingent *a priori*, we're still missing a feature that is crucial when concepts are plan-laden.

Explaining all this requires starting with concepts that are descriptive and then later examining what planning adds.

Term, Property, Concept

Begin with *concepts* and *properties*, thinking again of water and H_2O. The concepts are distinct, in that it once came as news that water is H_2O, but the properties, we may think, are identical. Two people might both grasp the naïve concept of water, and both understand molecular construction in general. Still, they could dispute whether water is H_2O, with neither of them being confused linguistically. If disagreement is the key to when concepts are distinct, then these concepts are distinct.[1] The property of being water, though, we can try saying, just turns out to *be* the property of being H_2O. The properties are identical, though the concepts are distinct.

Whether concepts can be characterized so that distinct concepts can pertain to a single property is, of course, highly controversial among philosophers of language. Here I won't go into the many issues that arise in this regard, but sketch without much defense a framework that

---

1. See Kripke, "Naming and Necessity" (1972), pp. 126–129, on water as a natural kind in counterfactual circumstances.

seems to handle some prime cases, descriptive and plan-laden.[2] In particular, I have my eye on objects of belief that can serve as objects of credence or subjective probability, and so let us account for dispute and discovery.

Supervenience and constitution I'll portray as pertaining not to properties but to concepts. Manifest physical qualities supervene on microproperties, and in particular, being water is constituted by being H_2O. This constituting is not a relation between two distinct properties, as I treat matters, for the properties in play are identical: the property of being water just *is* the property of being H_2O. It is the *concepts* that are distinct, and so constituting—if it is something other than identity—pertains at least in part to concepts. We could treat it as a relation between a concept and a property, as I have been doing: the concept of being water and the chemical property of being H_2O. Or we could speak of it as a relation between two concepts: the naïve concept of being water and the chemical concept of being H_2O.

With being *okay* matters are not entirely parallel, but they do share these structural features. Picture two people who dispute whether being okay to do is being egohedonic—offering maximal prospects for the agent's net pleasure. Egoistic hedonist Hedda thinks that it is; self-perfectionist Percy thinks that it isn't. Again, neither of them need be confused linguistically. Hedda thinks Percy mistaken, but she agrees that he is making no sheer conceptual mistake. His mistake is in his planning; it is a mistake of how to live. It betrays no defect in his sheer mastery of concepts, for the planning concept of being okay is distinct from the naturalistic concept of being egohedonic. Being okay, Hedda says, is *constituted* by being egohedonic. This is a matter of two concepts but a single property, namely, that of being egohedonic.

Here is the picture that emerges from this line of thought: Some concepts are specially plan-laden; the concept of being okay to do is a prime example. But no *property* is plan-laden—or at least, no property is plan-laden as a sheer matter of how concepts and properties work. Percy and Hedda share a concept, but they differ on which property constitutes it. Neither is mistaken conceptually. Being right on this is thus no purely conceptual matter; it is a matter of being right about how to live. There are, to be sure, properties of special planning import. The property that constitutes being okay to do, whatever it is, is the best example. Hedda thinks that this is the property of being egohedonic. Claims like hers, though, are plan-laden; accepting her claim consists in planning to live in a certain way. Such claims are not descriptive, and they are not purely conceptual. Some concepts are plan-laden; they are non-descriptive concepts that figure specially in thought about how to live. In contrast, there's no such thing as a non-descriptive property.

What I am saying applies not only to thought, but to language that expresses the thought. We need words for the chief broadly semantic relations between term, concept and property. Consider first the descriptive term 'water'. We are distinguishing, as I'll put it, (i) the *term*, (ii) the *concept* it expresses, and (iii) the *property* the concept is of. We have, for example, (i) the term 'water', (ii) the concept of being water, and (iii) the property of being water. Let us adopt the following technical vocabulary:

(a) The term *expresses* the concept.
(b) The property *realizes* the concept.
(c) The term *signifies* the property.[3]

With plan-laden discourse, relations among term, concept, and property parallel these, but with differences. The term 'okay', we can say, *expresses* the concept of being okay. Hedda, if she joins in these ways of speaking, will claim further that this concept is *realized* by the property of being egohedonic. This is the property, she will claim, that the term 'okay' *signifies*. Here, though, Hedda is making claims that are not purely descriptive. They are not purely matters of linguistic fact, or of

3. Writers may sometimes use terms like 'refers' or 'designates' for what I am calling "signifies". Sturgeon in "Contents" (1991), pp. 20–27, frames issues of communication chiefly in terms of "referring"; he speaks of whether speakers might be "referring to the same properties with their moral terms". He may have in mind as moral terms not predicates like 'just' but nouns like 'justice'. For descriptive parallels, I would say this: the noun 'wetness' does refer to a property, but the predicate 'wet' *signifies* this property. On my view, a predicate might best be seen as "referring" to its extension. The term 'water', for instance, refers not to the property of being water, but, perhaps, to all the water in the universe, or the set of all portions of water in the universe. ('Water' is a mass noun, and whereas a noun of divided reference like 'man' standardly has as its "extension" in each world the set of men in that world, how the term 'extension' applies to mass nouns doesn't have a standard answer.)

linguistic and psychological fact combined—as she herself can recognize. If the property of being egohedonic "realizes" the concept of being okay, that is a matter of how to live; accepting this claim consists in accepting the hedonistic egoist's hyperplan. If the term 'okay' indeed signifies the property of being egohedonic, that is partly a matter of linguistic fact—that 'okay' expresses the concept of being okay. (That's not a fact of ordinary language, but a matter of how I have stipulated the use of the term 'okay' for purposes here.) Partly, though, which property the term 'okay' signifies is a question of how to conduct our lives—namely that, supposing Hedda right, the property of being egohedonic realizes the concept of being okay. Parallel claims with 'water' are matters of linguistic and chemical fact: the property of being H_2O realizes the concept of being water, and this is a fact of chemistry. The term 'water' signifies this property, and this is a matter of chemical plus linguistic fact: the chemical fact that water is H_2O, plus the linguistic fact that 'water' expresses the concept of being water.

In expressing my views and Hedda's, I might not have used the unadorned terms 'signify' and 'realize' to make claims that are plan-laden, claims that are in part matters of how to live. I might instead have said "quasi-signifies" and "quasi-realizes". A term quasi-signifies a property p if and only if either it signifies p descriptively—as 'water' signifies the property of being H_2O—or it does what a hedonistic egoist like Hedda thinks the term 'okay' does with the property of being egohedonic. The term 'okay', I might have said, has a "quasi-extension"; Hedda thinks that its quasi-extension is the set of all acts that maximize the agent's hedonic prospects. The quasi-extensions of the predicates 'is okay' and 'is egohedonic', she thinks, are the same. This, she reasons, is partly because of how English works and partly a matter of how to live. She thinks that in English, the two predicates are necessarily quasi-coextensional, so that maximizing one's hedonic prospects "quasi-constitutes" being okay.

These "quasi-" terms, though, will be characterized in the same ways as they are when stripped of the hedge 'quasi-'. Take extensions and quasi-extensions, for instance: the extension of the predicate 'is egohedonic' is the set of all acts that are egohedonic, and the quasi-extension of the predicate 'is okay to do' is the set of all acts that are okay to do. The qualification 'quasi-' may be useful in marking out relations that are plan-laden, and so are not just a matter of language and the prosaic facts—chemical, psychological, and the like—to which the language applies. Since plan-laden matters of quasi-extension so closely parallel prosaically factual matters of full-fledged extension, however, I shall mostly dispense with the prefix, and so save ink and effort.

Here, then, are some of the slogans of this take on language, expressed in the jargon I have laid down: Ralph, suppose, is a naturalistic practical realist. He claims that there are only natural properties. In this, I conclude, he is right, so long as the term 'natural' is understood sufficiently broadly. (He may be right on a narrower understanding of the term too, one that excludes theological, spooky, and metaphysical properties, but my argument here does nothing to show that he is.) Ralph claims that the term 'okay' signifies a natural property—though we may not know which natural property it is. (That is to say, there might be no descriptive expression couched in psychological terms and the like that signifies this property and that we accept as doing so with confidence or with truth.) Give or take a few prefixes 'quasi-' inserted as hedges, Ralph has this right too: there is a broadly natural property that constitutes being okay (or quasi-constitutes it, if you prefer), and the term 'okay' (quasi-)signifies this property. We may be undecided as to which property constitutes being okay, and people may be wrong in their views of this property. Having dropped the prefix 'quasi-', I can say what Ralph says. Whether we mean the same thing, and whether we have remaining disagreements, are questions for later discussion.

Character, Concept, and Signification

Concepts of a single property can differ, as with water and H_2O. The phenomena that underlie this claim are familiar enough, though theorists dispute the diagnosis. One prominent diagnosis looks to indexicality: the naïve concept of water is subtly indexical, it is proposed, just as terms like 'I' and 'here' are blatantly indexical. Our concept *water* hooks up to whatever property chiefly explains our experience of clear liquid in rivers, lakes, faucets, and drinking glasses. So just as the pronoun 'I' in different mouths picks out different people, and just as the word 'here' picks out different places on different occasions, so the term 'water' might signify different properties in different contexts and still express the same concept. We can tell a fantastic story of a twin Earth, in a far part of the universe, where the same concept is realized by a different property. As employed on Earth, this fantasy goes, the term 'water' signifies the property of being H_2O, whereas as employed on the twin earth, the term still expresses the same concept, but it signifies a different property. It signifies the property of being XYZ, a different substance from H_2O. What property it signifies depends on context.[4]

This diagnosis I accept. Indeed, I'll lay out a schema to accommodate it, a schema found in the literature but far from standard. My point, though, will not so much be to stress an analogy of plan-ladenness to indexicality.[5] Such an analogy can be drawn, but my main point is this: plan-ladenness is a further dimension of conceptual variation. Co-signifying concepts may differ because of matters indexical, true enough. But concepts with precisely the same indexical behavior may differ even so in another way. They may differ because one is plan-laden, whereas the other is purely naturalistic.

Important dimensions of descriptive claims apply to plan-laden claims as well. Two concern being necessary and being *a priori*. Hedda the hedonistic egoist thinks her doctrine necessary, and she thinks it *a priori*. This means that according to Hedda, all and only acts that are egohedonic are okay to do. This, she says in the first place, is a necessary truth. If counterfactually, for instance, push-pin's hedonic prospects beat those of poetry and all other pursuits, then push-pin would be the activity to pursue. In full generality, Hedda maintains necessity in this sense: no matter how things were, the egohedonic act would always be the thing to do. In every possible world, that is to say, all and only egohedonic acts would be okay to do. This claim, she maintains in the second place, is *a priori*. That is to say, she doesn't rest the claim on empirical evidence in light of some deeper principle of planning. Another hedonist might—as I explain in due course.

4. The example is from Putnam, "The Meaning of Meaning" (1975), though he does not himself diagnose the term 'water' as indexical. Many philosophers reject the claim that we and those on Twin Earth, if it existed, would share a concept, rather than just the sound 'water', as we English and German speakers more or less share the sound 'hell' without in any way attaching it to the same concept. The Twin Earth story, though, is of chief interest as a parable for an epistemic situation. Whether the parable works will be legitimately controversial. But we'd better have some schema that lets us credit Lavoisier with a discovery—and if according to the schema he didn't discover that water is H_2O or he did discover that water is water, the theorist has much to explain away. I'll adopt a schema that offers an account of these phenomena, without trying to establish that it is best.

5. See Dreier, "Transforming Expressivism" (1999) for the analogy, important aspects of which I accept.

I'll start, in the next section, with a schema to handle these two dimensions on which Hedda makes her claims. The schema concerns indexicality and belief in response to evidence. In the first instance, it applies to descriptive, naturalistic concepts. Later, we see that a plan-laden concept and a naturalistic concept can coincide in all the features I study in the next section, and still be distinct concepts.

Each concept, I'll say, has a *character*. The character of a concept gives its extension—its truth value, what it designates, or the like—as the concept is applied from various standpoints—mine now, yours at the millennium, Napoleon's if he had just shot Wellington—to various possible ways things might have been. Character is always natural, in the sense that some broadly naturalistic concept might share this character. With a plan-laden concept like being okay to do, what its character is will be a planning question, a question of how to live. The character of the concept *to be sought* is a matter of what to seek. Hedda thinks that the concepts *to be sought* and *is pleasant* have the same character. This contrasts with the case of a naturalistic concept, whose character is settled by the concept alone. But of course I'll have to explain "character" before I go far into these conclusions. The scheme I end up with will still turn out to mimic a view that is freely Moorean in its structure and expressivistic in the ways it explains its Moorean structure. It will still turn out that naturalists are right in many ways. So are non-naturalists: if a concept is plan-laden, then it will be distinct from any naturalistic concept.

Naturalistic Concepts

To claim that plan-laden concepts mimic naturalistic concepts, I need a view of how naturalistic concepts work. I'll begin, then, with a schema that is meant to cover some crucial aspects of naturalistic concepts and their hook-up to the world.[6] As stock examples to handle, I'll take kind terms like *water* and indexicals like *I*, *here*, *now*, and *actually*.

6. The schema is closely related, in ways I mostly won't try to delineate, to work of Stalnaker, Lewis, Davies and Humberstone, and Chalmers. See Stalnaker, "Assertion" (1978); Lewis, "Attitudes" (1979); Davies and Humberstone, "Two Notions" (1980). See also Segerberg, "Two-Dimensional" (1973); Aaquvist, "Modal Logic" (1973); Kamp, "Formal Properties" (1971); Van Fraassen, "The Only Necessity" (1977). A highly accessible exposition is in Chalmers, *The Conscious Mind* (1996), pp. 57–70. My own version is much like Chalmers's, though I do not endorse the conclusions about consciousness that he goes on to derive.

David Lewis depicts the plight of a man who, in a sense, knows everything there is to know about himself—but doesn't know who he is. (I'll vary the story in minor ways.) Philosopher Adam Lingens has read his own biography, *Lingens: A Life*, which is complete in every detail. But he is amnesiac: he doesn't know whether the book concerns himself or someone else. He has read another biography, *Lauben: A Life*, on the philosopher Bengt Lauben, and for all he knows, he is Lauben. He knows he is in the stacks of a library, and that Lingens is in the stacks at Stanford and Lauben in the stacks at Harvard. Smoke wells up and he hears cries of "Fire!" The exit at Stanford is up the stairs, he knows, whereas at Harvard it is down. He knows everything about each man's situation, but doesn't know which way to go.

Lingens knows, then, everything that could be in a book describing the world; he knows which possible world is actual. What he doesn't know is his own position in it; he doesn't know which of two people he himself is (Lewis, "Attitudes," 1979). There are two standpoints, then, for thinking in the space of possibilities he contemplates, the standpoint a of being Adam Lingens and the standpoint b of being Bengt Lauben—though in this story there is just one world to think about, the world w_0 that Adam knows himself to occupy. The thought "I am Adam Lingens" has the truth table shown as Table 1, which gives its truth value as thought from each standpoint a or b in world w_0 that Lingens, for all he knows, might occupy. (The table is two-dimensional in a sense, but since only one possible world w_0 is in question, the vertical dimension is squashed down to a single entry.) "I am Adam" as thought by Adam is true, whereas "I am Adam" as thought by Bengt is false (all this as thought in world w_0 about world w_0).

The terminology needed to develop such a framework isn't standard, and so I'll stipulate some usages, trying to maintain some tie with the suggestions of ordinary language and traditions among philosophers.

Table 1

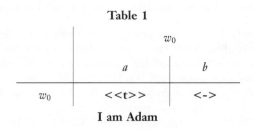

	w_0	
	a	b
w_0	<<t>>	<->

I am Adam

Words *express concepts*, I say. One crucial kind of concept is a *thought:* a concept expressed by a typical full declarative sentence in good order. I'll often glide between talk of a word and of the concept it expresses, though of course we should bear in mind various complications that I'll gloss by: that in different languages the same concept is expressed by different words, and the same word in the same language can express different concepts. Mostly I'll be speaking of concepts, pretty much helping myself to the notion. In any context of employment, a given concept has a number of characteristics that need to be distinguished. These are what I'll now be schematizing.

As an example, take first the naturalistic concept of *being water.* With us, it turns out, it is a concept of being H_2O, but for all anyone knew a few hundred years ago, it might have been the concept of a substance with quite a different structure. Return to Hilary Putnam's legend of Twin Earth far away (or "Twearth," as I'll call it). On Twearth, experience before 1750 was just as it was here, but the stuff they called "water" in Twin-England had quite a different structure from water, namely, XYZ. Of course in fact, Twearth doesn't exist, but we can contemplate how things might have been if it had. A speaker of English or Twenglish in 1750, if told the full layout of the universe, would still have to locate herself in it, as on Earth or Twearth. On that would hinge, as she might put it, "whether water is H_2O or XYZ".

To simplify representing her concept water, let's suppose there are just two possible worlds, ours the actual world w_1 with Earth but no Twearth, and another double world w_2 with both Earth and Twearth—call this the *tworld.* In the tworld w_2, I'll suppose, there are just two standpoints of thinking, theirs and ours, whereas in the actual world w_1 there is just one, namely ours. (Let e be our standpoint, and let t be theirs.) We can think about how things would be in the tworld w_2, and our twins on Twearth, if they existed, could think how things would be in a world like ours. The extension of the concept water in a thinker's mind, then, depends on the standpoint of the thinker: Earth in the world, Earth in the tworld, and Twearth in the tworld. We on Earth in the world w_1 can say, "If Twearth existed, water would still be H_2O."

That gives us a matrix: its dimensions are 3 by 2, where the "2" comes from two worlds w_1 and w_2 to be thought about, and the "3" is for the three standpoints for thinking, e in w_1, e in w_2, and t in w_2. A subject occupies one of these standpoints and thinks about a world, her own or another. As she does so, her concepts determine an *extension:* with the concept *being water,* for instance, the extension is all the H_2O in that world or all the XYZ in that world. Table 2 shows the matrix. The top entry in the center column, for instance, "all H_2O", is the extension of the predicate 'is water' as it could be applied on Earth, if Twearth existed, to the (then counterfactual) situation of there being no Twearth but just one Earth-like planet. I'll label what is shown in this matrix the *character* of the concept of being water. I double-bracket the entry for thinking from the actual standpoint in question about the way things actually are, and I single-bracket all other entries for thinking from a standpoint about the world of that standpoint (entries on the *diagonal* of the matrix). Perhaps more tractably, we could look also at the truth value of "Water is H_2O", and so display the character of this thought as shown in Table 3. (True is **t** and false is -.)

In these matrices, a given column has only one value. For the term 'water' is a rigid designator, picking out the same stuff in any world the term is applied to. These characters, we'll then say, are *rigid.* Different columns in these matrices have different values, because of the indexicality of the term 'water'. A matrix might also have identical columns, even if different rows have different values, as with "More than one planet superficially like this exists", which, wherever thought, is true as

Table 2

	w_1	w_2	
	e	e	t
w_1	<<all H_2O>>	all H_2O	all XYZ
w_2	all H_2O	<all H_2O>	<all XYZ>

is water

Table 3

	w_1	w_2	
	e	e	t
w_1	<<t>>	t	-
w_2	t	<t>	<->

Water is H_2O

Table 4

	w_1		w_2	
	g	n	g	n
w_1	<<t>>	<t>	-	t
w_2	-	t	<t>	<t>

H: I am here

applied to the tworld w_2 but not to the world w_1. In that case, the character is *standpoint-independent*.

Sometimes, though, indexicals combine to form contingent truths, and have characters that are neither rigid nor standpoint-independent. Consider the claim "I am here." I can apply this claim to a counterfactual situation; if Twearth existed and I were there, I wouldn't be here. Suppose that in the double world w_2, I'd be on Twearth and Napoleon would be on Earth—perhaps under the delusion that he was Gibbard. Thus, we get the matrix shown in Table 4 for the thought "I am here." (Again, the double bracket indicates my own actual standpoint.)

These vastly simplified matrices display what I'm calling the "character" of a concept or thought. The character gives an extension for every standpoint for thinking and every possible world to be thought about. In the case of full thoughts, the extension is a truth value. Thus in a finite universe of possibilities, the character can be represented by a matrix, like the matrices I have been using here. In a miniature, toy universe of possibilities like the ones I have been using, the matrix can be tractably displayed.

Each column of the matrix for a thought, we can say, gives a *state of affairs*. Take the first column: this represents the state of affairs *Gibbard's being on Earth*. From my actual standpoint, that of being Gibbard in our actual world, this amounts also to *my being here*. States of affairs, then, are individuated down to necessary equivalence, to having the same extension in each possible world.[7] For a one-place predicate, a column gives a *property*, again individuated down to necessary equivalence. We need a general term for what a column picks out, and I'll use the highly technical term *intension*. Properties and states of affairs will be prime examples of intensions.

7. States of affairs are sometimes called "propositions"; see, for instance, Lewis, "Attitudes" (1979).

Perhaps even more interesting, though, is the *diagonal*, the entries for which the standpoint of thinking is within the world thought about. In the character matrices I give, I have bracketed entries on the diagonal. Here is a slogan I'll be explaining: *Belief pertains to the diagonal.* Take the thought "I am here." This thought is *a priori*, in that it is true wherever thought; from every standpoint of thinking, it is true for the world of that standpoint. In its matrix, this is displayed on the diagonal: every value on the diagonal is **t**. As for "Water is H_2O," my credence for that—my subjective probability—is a matter of how I distribute my credence over standpoints I might be occupying: being on Earth in our own world, being on Earth in the tworld, and being on Twearth in the tworld. To read off my credence, we take my distribution of credence over standpoints for thinking, and see how much of it has **t** in the diagonal. In this sense, belief and credence (subjective probability, partial belief) pertain to the diagonal.

I've gone over this all very quickly to set the stage. It presents us with a complex structure to match with plan-laden concepts. Alas, we don't have standard names for most of the significant structures that can be read off the character matrix. I claim later that, with plan-laden concepts, at least, the character of the concept doesn't exhaust the concept; distinct concepts can share one and the same character. We'll need to distinguish, then, a concept from its character. A concept is expressed by some linguistic item, suppose, a word, a phrase, or a sentence. I'll speak of a *term* expressing a concept, and apply my technical vocabulary indifferently to the term and to the concept it expresses. The term (or the concept it expresses) *invokes* a character, I'll say. A special case is the thought expressed by a sentence; its character I'll call a *proposition* (though tradition uses this term for what below I'll be calling "states of affairs").

The character of a concept, along with one's standpoint of thinking and the world one is thinking about, determine everything else I'm talking about with regard to naturalistic concepts. Given all these, we can say, a term *designates* an *extension*. Given a standpoint of thinking, let us say, a term *signifies* an intension: a sentence signifies a state of affairs, and a one-place predicate signifies a property. (I'll also say of the concept the term expresses that it designates an extension and signifies an intention; thus a thought designates a truth value and signifies a state of affairs.)

Table 5

The term or concept	In general	For thoughts	For 1-place predicates	Matrix representation
designates an	extension	truth value	set of individuals	single entry
signifies an	intension	state of affairs	property	column
conveys an	import	doxon	guize	diagonal
invokes a	character	proposition	quality	full matrix
expresses a	concept	thought	attribute	

That leaves terminology for objects of belief. When they are newly believed we might call them "news-items", but it may be best just to coin the term *doxon* for the objects of belief that, for instance, subjective probability theorists study. These will be individuated down to *a priori* equivalence: when you learn something, you learn everything that is *a priori* equivalent to it. (This of course is an idealization, but the apparatus I'm developing—like the standard apparatus of decision theory and subjective probability theory—isn't suited to handle limitations in appreciating *a priori* relations.) As for a more general term covering predicates and individual terms, when you learn something, you revise your beliefs accordingly, and so we could call what the diagonal of a character matrix gives the *import* of its concept. (A doxon, then, is the import of a thought.) The whole, unfortunately complex scheme with the labels I have proposed is laid out in Table 5.[8] (The last row, of course, tells us only what's expressed by a term, not by a concept; concepts don't express anything. Rather, a concept may itself *be* a thought or an attribute.) As an example of what this table proposes, the sentence 'I drink H_2O' conveys an import that is a doxon, represented by the diagonal of the character matrix for the sentence (each entry of which is a truth value); this doxon is something one learns in learning chemistry. The one-place predicate 'drink H_2O' designates an extension that is a set of individuals (the set of all individuals who drink H_2O), represented by a single entry in the character matrix for the predicate.

Without much argument, I shall take this taxonomy as the one to

8. Chalmers calls the import of a concept its "primary intension", and its intension (as I call it) he calls its "secondary intension". Although he speaks of two dimensions, he doesn't much speak of matrices; still, he does in effect tell us that the diagonal gives the import.

match, insofar as plan-laden concepts mimic naturalistic concepts. A plan-laden thought, it will turn out, shares its character with a naturalistic thought. In this sense, just as there is no such thing as a non-natural property in the scheme I'm giving, there's no such thing as a non-natural character or non-natural import. There is, however, such a thing as a non-naturalistic concept: a plan-laden concept and a naturalistic concept are always distinct, even if they share a character. And all this, I'll be claiming, will fall out of the expressivistic treatment that is forced on us for plan-laden concepts.

Character and Constitution

What I'll be trying to show is this: *any plan-laden concept has a broadly natural character.* Take a plan-laden concept such as *to be sought* or *okay to do.* Anyone who plans, I'll argue, is committed to treating this concept as if it had a natural character. Hedda treats the concept of being okay to do as the same, in natural character, as the naturalistic concept of being egohedonic. She thus accepts the Principle of Natural Character, and we who are uncertain in our basic principle of planning likewise are committed to accepting it. As planners, then, we can make the transcendental move, voice the commitment, and proclaim, "It is as if this concept had a natural character."

If this can be shown, we will then have a broad choice of ways to talk. We can choose to sound like realists: when plan-laden concept C acts as if it had M as its character, we can say, let's go ahead and just call M its character. Then most of the things we say about naturalistic concepts we can say about plan-laden concepts too: the concept invokes a character, and so it signifies an intension and conveys an import. Alternatively, we may want to sound more "quasi" in our quasi-realism about plans, insisting on the "as-if"ness of it all. To do this, we can add the prefix 'quasi-' to everything we say: a plan-laden concept quasi-invokes a character, we'll say; it quasi-signifies a property and quasi-conveys an import. In what follows, I'll insert the prefix 'quasi-' in some of the things I say, just to distinguish what's plan-laden from what isn't, but I won't try to settle which is the better way of speaking.

The difference isn't in what we say about the abstract objects in themselves that are character, extension, intension, and import. It's how we speak of their relations, the relations of these abstract objects to concepts. Our choice is like choosing whether to speak of stepfathers as "fathers": the issue isn't the nature of the entities that are stepfathers; stepfathers are men, as are fathers, and the stepfather of one child may be the father of another. Likewise with characters and quasi-characters: on either way of speaking, quasi-character M is the same kind of abstract object, a "character" in the sense of a special kind of function—in my toy examples, a function that can be displayed by a matrix. On either way of speaking, M can perfectly well be the character of a naturalistic concept; as I insist, there's no natural–non-natural distinction for characters. The choice we face concerns how to speak of the *relation* between plan-laden concept C and function M: on one way of speaking, C "invokes" M; on the other way of speaking, C "quasi-invokes" M. Like remarks apply to property, guise, and the like: given property P, which is a natural property, we can say that concept C "signifies" P or that C "quasi-signifies" P. Again, the choice is one of how to speak of this relation, not how to speak non-relationally of the objects related.

Different character means different concepts. I'm claiming, though, that plan-laden concepts differ not just when they differ in character. A plan-laden concept can share its character with a naturalistic concept, but the two concepts will still be distinct. To illustrate how all this works, think again of Hedda the egohedonist and suppose she is right about how to live: that by *a priori* necessity, all and only acts that are egohedonic are okay to do.

Like any concept, the concept of *being egohedonic* has a character. That also, then, will be the character of *being okay to do*—or its quasi-character, if you wish. This just amounts to saying that by *a priori* necessity, the two concepts are coextensional. For what is the character of a word or a concept, as I'm using this technical term? The character is a function of standpoint-world pairs, a standpoint s of thinking paired with a world w thought about. For each such pair $\langle s,w \rangle$, the character gives an extension, the extension of the word or concept from standpoint s in world w. That is to say, take any standpoint s and any world w. Suppose that s is one's standpoint, and from standpoint s one is thinking what would be okay to do in world w. To the pair $\langle s,w \rangle$, the character of *egohedonic* assigns those acts that would then be egohedonic. To the same pair, the character of *okay to do* assigns those acts that would then be okay to do. Since, by hypothesis, egohedonism is correct, the acts that would be okay to do are just the acts that would be egohedonic.

The two characters therefore take the same value for this standpoint-world pair. The argument is general, and so they take the same value for every standpoint-world pair, and so they are the same function. The two concepts share a single character.

Hedda, then, accepts the Claim of Natural Character: that the concept of being okay to do invokes a natural character, a natural quality. So does Thomas who doubts; the argument extends as before from the hyperdecided to those who are merely consistent. Suppose no longer that Hedda's egohedonism is correct. Still, we could say, some view of how to live is correct. For some particular broadly natural quality Q and naturalistic concept N that invokes it, holding this correct view will amount to thinking the following: no matter what we learn of our standpoint, still for any possible situation, all and only acts with attribute N would be okay to do if that situation obtained. Thus there is a broadly natural quality Q that is, in this sense, the character (or quasi-character) of *thing to do*.

We can put this in terms of hyperdecided views that a thinker-planner could come to have without changing his mind on anything. Again, to take any such view would be to accept the Principle of Natural Character—and so any thinker-planner is already committed to the principle. A hyperdecided thinker-planner Hera has a hyperplan, a full plan p for what to do in any possible subjective contingency. She considers, then, that the character of *okay to do* is just that of *allowed by plan p*. Since plan p is couched in broadly naturalistic terms, the character of *allowed by plan p* must be an ordinary, natural quality, a function from standpoint-world pairs to sets of acts open at some standpoint in that world. She thus accepts the Principle of Natural Character: the concept *okay to do* has a broadly natural character.

We now proceed as before. Any consistent thinker-planner among us, if he became hyperdecided without changing his mind about anything, would be like Hera: he would accept the Principle of Natural Character. He is therefore already committed to the principle. We who are committed can now make the transcendental move and voice this commitment: the concept *okay to do* has a natural character.

Quasi-Character and Extended Character

A plan is characterized by its import, the import of the claim that one is conforming to it. The import of a concept, recall, is the part of its char-

Table 6

	w_1	w_2		w_0	
	t_1	t_1	t_2	t_1	t_2
w_1	\<t\>	t	-	t	-
w_2	-	\<-\>	\<t\>	-	t
w_0	-	-	-	\<\<-\>\>	\<\<-\>\>

I now turn

acter matrix that lies on the diagonal; the import of a thought we call a doxon. A doxon amounts to a property; in forming a belief, one self-ascribes a property.[9] In believing that water is H_2O, for instance, I self-ascribe the property of being such that water for one is H_2O. News comes by the acquisition of doxa, and credence pertains to doxa. Same doxon, same plan: with the plan to do what's egohedonic goes a doxon, the import of "I do what's egohedonic." This is the property of doing what's egohedonic. Two plans are distinct only if I could believe that I am following one and not the other, and so that I am following one and that I am following the other must differ in import.

Consider the absent-minded driver of game-theoretic lore. His route takes him past two opportunities to turn left, but he can never re-member which intersection he is at. He does best if he turns at the sec-ond but worst if he turns at the first; driving straight at both is interme-diate. The character of "I now turn" could be as shown in Table 6. There are two standpoints for action: the time t_1 of arriving at the first intersection and, if he has driven straight through, the time t_2 of arriv-ing at the second. There are three possible worlds: w_0 in which he goes straight both times, w_1 in which he turns at the first intersection, and w_2 in which he turns at the second and not at the first. Imagine he goes straight at both intersections so that w_0 is the actual world. The import of "I now turn" is the diagonal of the matrix, the property of its being a time when one turns. To each world it assigns the set of times when the driver turns in that world: $\{t_1\}$ to w_1, $\{t_2\}$ to w_2, and the empty set to w_0.

What is the quasi-character of "I now act okay," that I now do some-thing that's okay to do? That is a question of what to do as an absent-minded driver—a question decision theorists debate. I'll ignore mixed strategies, which settle what to do by use of a chance device. For some

9. See Lewis, "Attitudes" (1979).

parameters of the problem, a mixed strategy is perhaps the one to adopt, but let's keep matters simpler. If only going straight is okay to do, then the character of "I now act okay" is the same as that of "I now go straight." If only turning is okay to do, then the character of "I now act okay" is the same as that of "I now turn." Which is its true character is a planning question, a question of how to live, a question of what to do if in this driver's plight. Like things go for import. (They must, since import is given by a part of the character matrix.) Which is the import of "I now act okay" is a planning question; if going straight is the thing to do, then its import is that of "I now go straight."[10]

With plan-laden discourse, then, meanings alone don't settle character. To settle the character of 'okay', we must settle how to live. And so meanings alone don't determine signification and import, which are aspects of character. How to live is crucial to what their character and import are. Plan-laden concepts have character, and so they have import and signification—but not just in virtue of which concepts they are. That's why we may want to add the prefix 'quasi-': questions of the quasi-character of plan-laden terms aren't purely linguistic and conceptual, and they aren't purely factual. They are in part questions of how to live.

We can, however, extend our matrix representations to display what plan-laden concepts settle on their own. I'll speak now of the *extended character* of a thought, and so of its *extended import* and its *extended signification*. I do this roughly by following a general scheme proposed by James Dreier. It mimics the way signification is extended to character to account for the indexicality of concepts. Take a complete thought, that one now drives straight, or that driving straight is now the thing to do. Signification is an assignment of truth values to worlds; it occupies one dimension. Character extends this to two dimensions; it assigns truth values to world-standpoint pairs.[11] Extended character

---

10. With mixed strategies ruled out, the answer to the puzzle might seem clear. Always going straight gives a higher payoff than always turning, and so the thing to do, presumably, is to go straight. But if the thing to believe of yourself is that you reliably do what's the thing to do and so go straight, then turning is the better gamble: it loses you little if you are at the first intersection, and gains you much if you are at the second. Ruling out mixed strategies makes the situation paradoxical; cf. Gibbard and Harper, "Counterfactuals" (1978), pp. 157–159 for a similar case.

11. Or as Dreier represents this, isomorphically, it is (in my terminology) a function assigning significations to standpoints. See "Transforming Expressivism" (1999).

adds another dimension, the planning dimension. It assigns truth values to triples of standpoint, world, and hyperplan. They are (i) a standpoint from which one can think, (ii) a world about which one can think from that standpoint, and (iii) a hyperplan. Take again the absent-minded driver, who thinks to himself "I now act okay." He has two pure hyperplans available: turn and go straight. A triple $<w,s,p>$ gets value $\mathbf{t}$ just in case plan p says to do, at the time of standpoint s, what one does in world w at that time.

I don't know whether the extended character of a thought exhausts its content, so that plan-laden thoughts with the same extended character are the same thought. I do think that the framework I've given makes all the distinctions needed to handle indexicality and Moore-like phenomena. It handles the Frege-Geach challenge, since we can construct the extended characters of disjunctions, counterfactuals, and the like from the extended characters of their components, and treat analytic entailment among plan-laden thoughts in the usual way: that for any triple to which the extended characters of the premises all assign 'true', so does the conclusion.

Return, now, to the relation between extended character and character. Extended character is a purely conceptual matter: Hedda and Percy disagree on how to live, but if they understand each other and aren't conceptually confused, they will agree on matters of extended character. Take the claim "Dad has made mistakes", meaning "My father hasn't always done what was okay." The extended character of this thought includes both triples with Hedda's egohedonistic hyperplan and triples with Percy's perfectionistic hyperplan. It includes, for instance, triples with (i) the standpoint of you at the dawn of the third millennium, (ii) a world in which, in the second millennium or earlier, your father always has done the egohedonic thing but not always the self-perfecting thing, and (iii) perfectionism as a hyperplan. But still supposing that Hedda is right on how to live, the character of this thought doesn't include such standpoint-world pairs. To get its character, we restrict its extended character to those triples with the correct, egohedonistic hyperplan, dropping the hyperplan dimension.

Turn now to plan-laden conviction. I spoke earlier of the diagonal of the character matrix as pertaining to belief and giving the *a posteriori* "import" of a thought or other concept. We need to stress the "*a posteriori*" here, though, and remember that the root answer to how to live must be *a priori*. I don't mean that when I decide what train to take, my thinking has two components, a general *a priori* view on how to live and an *a posteriori* naturalistic belief about the standpoint I occupy. I mean that my view would have these two components if it were hyperdecided, and my decision will be consistent with some such hyperdecided fact-plan views and not with others. We can represent my decision, I'm saying, by the set of such hyperdecided views that it fits.

Plan-laden conviction, though, pertains not to the diagonal of the character matrix, but to the diagonal with a hyperplan dimension added. It is given by a diagonal plane in the extended character matrix. We can talk now of the *extended import* of a thought or other concept. When I accept what someone says on his authority, it is the extended import of what he says that gets communicated; I come to accept it. Suppose the guru I trust advises me to take the 11:20 train. He thinks what to do if in my exact circumstance and expresses to me his hypothetical decision; in that I treat him as a guru, I let him do my thinking for me, making his hypothetical decision my actual one. I accept his advice. This may consist in updating my views, restricting my previous credal-planning state to ones that fit the extended import of what my guru said. Earlier I was undecided whether to take the 11:20 or the 9:40; now I reject all hyperplans that have me taking the 9:40. (Of course there's more to be said: I'm also continually transforming my credal state to allow for the passage of time, and I have to center my guru's indexicals onto a conception of him—but let's pass over these matters here.) Or alternatively, my change may take the form of a conversion rather than updating: previously I thought to take the 9:40, but now I change my mind. In any case, my views change to be consistent with the extended import of what my guru says.

Note that if my fundamental views on how to live are misguided, I can accept the extended import of what someone says but reject its import as naturalistically framed. Hedda, Percy believes, has always done the egohedonic thing. A perfectionist friend tells him that Hedda has made mistakes in her life, and Percy accepts this. But the import of this—still supposing egohedonism is the way to live—is that she hasn't always done the egohedonic thing. And this Percy rejects. Extended import is what is conveyed when the hearer accepts what he hears, whether or not he has correct *a priori* views on how to live. Import, in contrast, is *a posteriori*, only available to those whose *a priori* views on how to live are complete and correct.

I have been quickly sketching some of the niceties of a rather complex view, but I don't know how to reduce the complexity. Character matrices do seem to tell us something important about concepts, and their diagonals do seem to give the *a posteriori* import of a thought. I have been considering states of mind that mix planning with naturalistic belief, and we must ask how plan-laden thoughts work with regard to character and import. A fundamental answer to the question of how to live would claim *a priori* status—and given that answer, a plan-laden thought has natural character and natural import. We don't, though, have a full, agreed answer to how to live, and so plan-laden claims also have an extended character and an extended import. We'll agree on what these are if we're communicating, for this is solely a conceptual matter, solely a matter of the meanings of our words.

I have been working to characterize, in these terms, what is right about practical naturalism and what is right about practical non-naturalism. Given all my terminology, the Moorean things I have said could be packed into these slogans: A plan-laden thought has a broadly natural character (or quasi-character). What this character is is not purely a conceptual question, but a question of how to live. What its extended character is, in contrast, is purely a conceptual question. This extended character, though, is not naturalistic: to deduce from a term's extended character what its extension is, we must settle how to live. In this sense, the doctrine that has emerged is non-naturalism for concepts but naturalism for character. And since import and signification are aspects of character, this yields naturalism for them as well (but not for extended import or extended signification).

∼ III
Normative Concepts

~ 7

Ordinary Oughts: Meaning and Motivation

$\mathcal{T}$HUS FAR, this book has been devoted to plans and plan-laden judgments. Plans, I argued, are judgments, in that they can act in many ways like beliefs in plain fact. They combine with beliefs in all the ways that beliefs can combine with each other. Standard logic applies, explained in a way that also explains the logic of belief. Plans and factual beliefs, then, belong to a larger class of fact-plan judgments. Those judgments that aren't purely factual beliefs are *plan-laden* judgments. And planning concepts—being okay to do and the like—are, in a sense I explained, concepts of broadly natural properties.

The assumptions needed to derive these conclusions were sparse. We can plan, I supposed, not only for situations we expect to arise, but for ones that are wildly hypothetical. Plans, as I pictured them, reject some courses of action as a matter of preference, but allow too for indifference. We can combine states of mind, rule out states of mind, and generalize over a class of states of mind. Finally, I supposed, we can share our planning thoughts, agreeing or disagreeing on what to do in a circumstance.

What does all this have to do, though, with judgments we make and voice, with judgments we already have words for? I have appropriated a couple of turns of phrase in English to express planning judgments: if *A* is "the thing to do," as I'm using the expression, that rules out doing anything else; if *A* is "okay to do," that rules out ruling *A* out. One of these expresses a requirement laid down in one's plans, the other a permission. I am not claiming, though, that in ordinary English these turns of phrase work these ways. The term 'okay' clearly doesn't; in English it has a wide range of uses that my stipulation doesn't cover: interpersonal permissions ("It's okay if you go now"), expressions of satisfaction or toleration ("Russia got the bomb, but that's okay"), and many more. 'The thing to do' may work better, but even this phrase I won't claim as meaning in English exactly what I'm using it to mean. I haven't so far, then, been making any claims about English—or, indeed, about thoughts we actually have.

Do we, then, make the kinds of planning judgments I have been exploring? Do sentences of a natural language like English express such judgments? In this book, I have not so far inquired whether we do; I have kept away from our ordinary concepts. My purpose has not so far been to make claims about English or any other ordinary language—or about ordinary thought.

Here, though, is an obvious hypothesis to explore: that a wide variety of the judgments we do make are plan-laden, and a wide variety of the terms we use are terms for expressing plan-laden judgments—the terms, that is, that we think of as "normative" terms or as "value" terms. This hypothesis would explain a number of features that normative and value terms seem to display. In particular, it would explain features of 'good' that G. E. Moore thought he established for the use of the term that interested him. Like the term 'good' according to Moore, a term expressing a plan-laden concept won't be synonymous with any purely factual, naturalistic term. Still, Moore spoke of a "natural object" which he termed "*the* good." This I've been reading as, in my own terminology, the natural property that constitutes being good.

The claim I'll press, though, is more qualified than this hypothesis. With normative language, we do mix plan with fact—on this point I insist. An everyday normative term, though, may not express a plan-laden concept at all straightforwardly. Talk can be loose, and so there may be no clear fact of the matter just what a term expresses in a given use. A term may carry presuppositions that blur the gap between plan and fact—and it may even be indeterminate just what presuppositions a term carries. Terms can draw their meanings too from an explanatory role they are meant to play, including their role in explaining what to do and why. My claim, then, is not that certain terms clearly express plan-laden concepts, always and definitely, with no ambiguity. But plan-laden concepts, I insist, have much to do with what these ordinary terms express. It follows that if we ignore plan-laden concepts, we won't understand how familiar normative terms work.

In this chapter, I start with how presuppositions about how to live might lie behind the use of a normative term. The ordinary terms 'good' and 'rational' might perhaps be understood as carrying such presuppositions; saying this might be the best way to accommodate contentions that substantive features of what is good or what is rational are built into the very meanings of these terms—such as that the good must have to do with typical human goals. For these two particular "thin" terms, I argue, the best accounts are more straightforward: a presuppositional analysis would be the best way to incorporate such constraints if they were needed, but with these two terms, I argue, they aren't needed. Other normative terms, though—"thick" terms that seem somehow to combine description with assessment—do carry pre-suppositions about how to live. These come in later chapters. In Chapter 8, I explore a complex pattern on which concepts can be plan-laden: they might pick out "normative kinds", invoking a conceptual role in explaining matters of what to do. Normative kind concepts will carry complex presuppositions about ways to explain aspects of how to live.

First, though, later in this chapter, I look at another principal reason many philosophers have for denying that familiar normative concepts are plan-laden: the implication that, as a sheer matter of meaning, no one can be indifferent to questions of what he ought to do. Chapter 9 returns to questions about the kind of theory I have developed: whether it is a form of "realism", or at any rate cheats by helping itself to the materials of realism. I ask too what is gained by the expressivist's Copernican revolution in explaining normative concepts.

Tracking Thoughts

When I ask about meanings, my guiding concern is how we can engage each other's thoughts. How can I engage your thoughts in conversation—and how, indeed, can any one of us manage a train of thought of his own. Dealing with anyone's thoughts, or an important part of it, consists in tracking agreement and disagreement: we respond to what agrees with what; we monitor what there is to be thought, and how some possible claims are allowed or excluded by a thought. We track, in effect, the logic of what a person is saying and thinking. All this has been a chief theme of this book. In asking how our actual normative concepts might be plan-laden, I'll focus on how we can engage each other, agreeing, disagreeing, or suspending judgment. I'll focus too on ways we can fail to engage each other's thoughts when we voice them to each other, finding ourselves unable to agree or disagree, and not from lack of convictions on the subject.

My devices for analysis are technical, but the questions are live. When do diverse people's normative judgments concern the same topic, and when do they only appear to do so? Are we separated from the ethical thoughts of those whose ways of life are not live options for us, because we cannot share the "thick" ethical concepts that guide distant and complex ways of life? We and a Bronze Age chieftain, say, will find ourselves baffled by the refinements of each other's ethical thinking; we can perhaps agree or disagree only on the thinnest of issues of what's all right to do and what isn't.[1] Now all this might well be right, but it would be good to understand better how inaccessible concepts could work. Can we regard the Bronze Age Achaeans as genuine users of concepts we cannot fathom? Or are our alternatives just two: to suppose they think much like us, or regard them as mouthing meaningless sounds?[2] Can we think that they really engage each other with claims and counterclaims, even though we ourselves cannot agree or disagree with them? These are not questions I'll try to answer, but I will construct patterns of meaning that could account for engagement and non-engagement with the concepts of others.

My chief device of analysis will be the one I have used throughout the book, namely, hyperstates: hyperdecided fact-plan states of mind. We can represent the meaning of a claim by asking in which such

---

1. Williams (1985) speaks of "thick concepts" (esp. pp. 143–145) and a "relativism of distance" when another's way of life is not a "live option" for us (esp. pp. 160–162). Williams's own views on these issues, though, are complex and tentative, and although I borrow some of his terms and examples—and although some things he says might suggest the kind of view I am sketching—I don't think that attributing quite this view to him would be accurate. What his position is in this fascinating chapter and what's right or wrong about it would require far more study that I should attempt in this book. See my "Reasons Thin and Thick" (2003).

2. On such questions, see Davidson, "On the Very Idea" (1974).

hyperstates a person would agree with it and in which she would disagree. Hyperstates, then, make for a canonical way to tally agreement and disagreement in the realm of judgments that bear on what to do. In this chapter and the next, I exploit this method to construct models of how everyday normative meanings might work.

Do I think, then, that when it comes to questions of what agrees with what and what contradicts what, there are definite facts of the matter? Do I, in other words, think that there are definite facts of meaning, with a clear analytic-synthetic distinction for human languages? A mixed planning language like mine gives us a stock of candidate meanings, a stock of possibilities for what terms in a natural language might mean. In this artificial language of planning, meanings are stipulated, and so for this language, which claims are analytic and which synthetic is clear enough: the answers follow from the stipulations. If, then, a natural language like ours translated into this mixed planning language, with a clear fact of the matter which translations are right, then analyticity would carry over to the natural language. I won't be claiming, though, that matters are so straightforward. The correspondences between English, say, and my artificial language may be complex and indefinite. Plan-laden concepts, in short, offer definite meanings, meanings that can be clearly the same or clearly distinct, but the meaning of a term or an utterance in our lives might be indefinite.

Still, we shouldn't think that the meanings of our terms are indefinite without bounds. If a term were utterly indeterminate in meaning, there would be no "tracking" the discourse using it—no agreeing or disagreeing, and so no engagement with the thoughts of others. The meaning of an utterance need not be sharp, but we must treat the things we say as having rough meaning, at least much of the time, if we are to think and converse.

The words to which the models and hypotheses of these chapters apply I term "normative". What might this mean? I can no longer just stipulate that the concepts I'm after are plan-laden; that, rather, is a hypothesis I want to explore. The exact scope of this hypothesis won't much matter here, but I can start out with a theory-light characterization of "normative" terms. There seems to be a common and problematic element in the bulk of 'ought's we use, and this element is shared by a large variety of other terms. The light bit of theory the term 'normative' presupposes is that such a special set of terms exists, terms problematic in a way that has some uniform explanation. These, if there is such a class, will then be *normative* terms.[3] If any terms are normative in this sense, then something special characterizes them; that follows from the characterization. My hypothesis will be that what's special, what explains the behavior that Hume and Moore noted, is that they express concepts that are in some way plan-laden.

With my theory of plan-laden concepts, then, I have been offering candidates for our everyday normative terms to mean, candidate claims we can agree with or disagree with. What this has to do with meanings our terms already have must be a long story—but I'll suggest some likely patterns.

Presuppositional Equivalence

One kind of slack in meaning will figure ubiquitously in our talk: the kind that doesn't matter. Dialogue proceeds with a stock of assumptions that are common knowledge or mutually manifest among all parties.[4] Utterances have their point against this background. Two meanings, then, will be equivalent in what they communicate if they expand this stock in the same way. Schematically let Δ be manifest background, and suppose Δ entails that P iff Q. Then against this conversational background Δ, claims P and Q are equivalent. Accepting the background with P added is exactly the same as accepting it with Q added.

Consider the term 'good', as applied to a state of affairs, a development or eventuality. Roughly, I'd say, it means "to be sought". A refined treatment of the term would add some qualifications: what to seek depends on what can be had, though how good it is doesn't—grapes out of reach are not thereby sour. Good ties in with a scale of what's better than what, and so the prime term to explain is 'better': the *better* of two ways things may go is the one to prefer. The good, then, we explain in terms of the better. The terms 'good' and 'better' suggest a common standpoint: that in the context of discussion, what's to be preferred doesn't change from person to person. Roughly, though, to

3. I suggest this characterization in "Meaning and Normativity" (1994), p. 97.

4. Lewis speaks of "common knowledge" in *Convention* (1969), and Sperber and Wilson speak of being "mutually manifest" in *Relevance* (1986, 1995). There is a large literature on these and related notions, which figure crucially in the theory of communication and in game theory.

settle what's good is to settle what to seek. Good developments are ones for us all to favor.[5]

Naturalists, though, object to any such analysis. It carries the concept of good too far, they say, from what makes things good and what doesn't. As Philippa Foot long ago noted, for instance, an act can't be good solely in that it consists of clasping one's hands, with no further explanation of its goodness.[6] And George Nakhnikian asks this non-open question:

> Is a thing good which is so constituted that it would reinforce the desires, sustain the interest, and occasion the satisfactions and enjoyments of everyone who had a mature and comprehensive grasp of that thing's scientifically discoverable and imaginatively explorable properties and relations? ("On the Naturalistic Fallacy," 1963, p. 149)

Whether or not, then, the meaning of a word like 'good' can be put purely and entirely in naturalistic terms, there are, it seems, naturalistic constraints on its meaning.

The analysis of 'good' I have sketched, then, might well not be the whole story. 'Good' might not mean "to be sought", even with the afterthoughts I added. For a term like 'good' might acquire its meaning against a background of presupposition—and the presuppositions might themselves be plan-laden. Let's explore how such a thing might work.

First we need to invent a descriptive term to abbreviate the qualities Nakhnikian cites: anything that fits Nakhnikian's rich description is *nakhy*. This term is for our own use, and gets its meaning by our stipulation; we aren't imagining that it is a term that anyone uses but us.

Now consider a population that speaks a language much like English; call it "Zinglish". These people all accept that anything that is nakhy is to be sought because it is nakhy. This, indeed, would strike them all as a truism; it is part of what is mutually manifest in all their conversations. They wouldn't put things this way, since 'nakhy' isn't one of their terms. Neither, imagine, is 'to be sought', which we our-

5. See my "Preference and Preferability" (1998).
6. This example is from Foot, "Moral Beliefs" (1959), p. 85.

selves reserve to express features of our plans; they have no concept so "thin". The point is rather that all their contingency plans give weight to attaining those things that fit Nakhnikian's description.

Zinglish speakers, imagine, do have a term that they apply to all and only the things they find nakhy: the term is 'zowy'. Our question is what they mean by this term. Two candidates are obvious:

(i) Nakhy.
(ii) To be sought because it is nakhy.

Which of these, if either, do they mean by 'zowy'? Since it is truistic for them that anything nakhy is therefore to be sought, the following would also be truistic for them: a thing is nakhy if and only if it is to be sought because it is nakhy. Thus (i) and (ii) are equivalent in the sense that it is mutually manifest, truistically, that the one applies if and only if the other does.

Perhaps, then, there's no fact of the matter whether (i) or (ii) is the right interpretation of the Zinglish term 'zowy'. Not that what we've said settles the matter: there might be further tests that would allow us to choose between the two interpretations. Speakers of Zinglish can be invited to try thought experiments. Engage fancifully in planning for life and for hypothetical contingencies in a way that gives no weight to bringing about that which is nakhy. In this make-believe state of mind, do you call nakhy things "zowy"?[7]

We might find that when it is clear that people have entered into this make-believe, they find it clear what to call "zowy"—and that people agree with each other on this. The answer they give, then, can be used to choose between candidates (i) and (ii). Or alternatively, many speakers of Zinglish may find the answer clear, but some choose one answer and some the other. This would support the view that idiolects of Zinglish differ, in that some individuals treat 'zowy' as meaning nakhy, whereas others have candidate (ii) as their meaning of the term. Finally, speakers of Zinglish might each find they don't know what to say: it is so obvious that what's nakhy is to be sought that in a feigned state of mind that rejects this, words fail.

Two ways suggest themselves for describing the meaning of 'zowy' in this last case. We can try saying, first, that there's no fact of the matter

---

7. The question isn't how you then fancifully use the inscription 'zowy', but what previous statements using it you now fancifully agree with or disagree with.

whether (i) or (ii) gives the right meaning for 'zowy': the meaning is indeterminate. (This would fit the use of supervaluations as a way of handling vagueness.) It may be better, though, to reject both these candidates, and instead speak of presuppositions.

Consider this assumption, which users of 'zowy' treat as mutually manifest:

Anything that is nakhy is to be sought because it is nakhy.   (1)

Uses of the term 'zowy' take this as a presupposition in the following sense. Suppose a user of the term 'zowy' comes to reject (1). (That is, suppose she plans, in some contingencies, not to seek all that's nakhy.) This user now neither agrees nor disagrees with certain claims couched with the term 'zowy'—and that's not because of uncertainty on substantive matters of how things stand factually or how to live. Friendship, imagine, she thinks to be nakhy but she plans not to seek it. Then she neither agrees nor disagrees with the claim 'Friendship is zowy'. In this sense, 'zowy' is not one of her words.

To agree is to regard as true and to disagree is to regard as false. A user of the term 'zowy', then, accepts this: if condition (1) fails, then the claim 'Friendship is zowy' is neither true nor false. For the user is set, on coming to reject (1), neither to accept nor reject the claim. For the claim to be true or false, then, according to a linguistically competent user of the term 'zowy', condition (1) must obtain. In this sense, (1) is a *presupposition* of this use of the term 'zowy'.[8]

Given presupposition (1), the following are equivalent:

Friendship is zowy.

Friendship is nakhy.

Friendship is to be sought because it is nakhy.

Someone who accepts (1) will accept each of these if he comes to accept any. The claim 'Friendship is zowy', then, we analyze as follows. Its presupposition is (1), and given this presupposition, it holds if and only

8. Talk of presupposition stems from Strawson, "On Referring" (1950), although Strawson doesn't himself use the term there. He says (pp. 330–331) that if there is no king of France, then "The king of France is wise" is neither true nor false. See also Stalnaker, "Assertion" (1978), pp. 84–90.

if friendship is nakhy. Equivalently, given this presupposition, the claim holds if and only if friendship is to be sought because it is nakhy.

Strictly, it is claims or sentences that can have presuppositions in this sense. The presuppostions of a claim are conditions failing which the claim is, by linguistic rules, neither true nor false. We can speak loosely too, though, of a presupposition being "carried" by a term. The term carries a presupposition if claims made using the term carry that presupposition, and do so because they include the term. In this sense, the term 'zowy' carries (1) as a presupposition. Making this loose sense precise, though, would be a tricky matter, to say the least, and I won't attempt to do so. (Take the phrase 'the king of France', for instance. This definite description, we might say, presupposes, in this loose sense, that France has a unique king. We'll say this if we think that because this condition fails, the claim 'The king of France is bald' is neither true nor false. But we may still agree that the claim 'I'm not the king of France' is true.)

Analytic and Synthetic

Suppose we somehow teach our own term 'nakhy' to speakers of Zinglish. They then accept the following as truistic, as mutually manifest:

> Anything that is nakhy is zowy.   (2)

What is the status of this claim? Is it analytic or synthetic? If 'zowy' just means nakhy, then (2) is analytic: it just means, "Everything nakhy is nakhy." Suppose instead that (ii) gives the right meaning, that 'zowy' means "to be sought because it is nakhy." Then (2) isn't analytic; it means, "Anything that is nakhy is to be sought because it is nakhy." Among speakers of Zinglish this is truistic and mutually manifest, but it is not analytic. If this isn't obvious, imagine that Catherine, from outside the community of Zinglish speakers, is an ascetic who plans not always to weigh a thing's being nakhy in favor of bringing it about. She learns Zinglish and interprets 'zowy' as meaning (ii), to be sought because it is nakhy. She therefore rejects (2): she thinks that not everything that is nakhy is to be sought on that account. She's not confused conceptually, and if (ii) indeed does give the meaning of 'zowy', then she's not confused linguistically either. Therefore (2) is non-analytic: it can be rejected by someone who is conceptually and linguistically un-confused.

Suppose alternatively, though, that a presuppositional analysis of 'zowy' is the right one. A wide range of claims couched with the term 'zowy', including claim (2), carry the presupposition

Anything that is nakhy is to be sought because it is nakhy.   (1)

When the term appears in such a context, the resulting claim is neither true nor false unless its presupposition (1) is true, and when (1) is true, then 'zowy' as it figures in the claim is equivalent to 'nakhy': the claim is true only if it is true with 'nakhy' substituted for 'zowy'. Then in an important sense, (2) is neither analytic nor synthetic. For on the one hand, no one can reject it without violating linguistic rules, and so it is not synthetic. Yet linguistic rules don't commit everyone to accepting (2), since they may reject its presuppositions—and so (2), though not synthetic, is also not analytic.

Saying this calls for more care with our definitions and formulations. To be *analytic*, standardly, is to be true in virtue of meanings and logic alone. "Synthetic", then, we might define as non-analytic. Instead, though, consider a stronger sense: a statement is *synthetic*, let us say, if meanings and logic alone neither preclude its being true nor preclude its being false. That allows for a middle ground: that meanings neither guarantee nor preclude truth, but do preclude falsehood. Claim (2) has this status. It can't be false: if its presupposition (1) holds, it amounts to saying that anything nakhy is nakhy, and so is true; if (1) fails, it is neither true nor false; in neither case, then, is it false.

No statement with synthetic presuppositions is analytic. For if a presupposition P is synthetic, then meanings alone don't preclude P's being false. But if a presupposition of a statement is false, we have said, then the statement itself is neither true nor false. Thus the truth of the statement is not guaranteed by meanings alone. Statement (2) in particular, then, is not analytic—and we have seen that it is not synthetic.

Here and elsewhere, I have been making free use of the terms 'true' and 'false'. I can mean these in a minimalist sense, perhaps the one that Horwich presents. Everything I say can also be put in terms of what an observer who learns the language might accept or reject. This indeed is a standpoint that I must take to show that the presupposition (1) is synthetic: it can be rejected by an observer who is unconfused about logic and meanings. Return to Catherine, who plans not always to weigh a thing's being nakhy in favor of seeking it. Nothing about the meanings of descriptive terms constrains the plans one can have; one can coherently plan to take a non-nakhy option when a nakhy one is open. Now Catherine, in so planning, rejects presupposition (1). For the meaning of (1) can be given this way: to accept it is to rule out thinking an X nakhy and yet not seeking X—that is, not weighing an option's leading to X in favor of taking that option. In planning as she does, Catherine goes against this possible commitment, and so she coherently rejects presupposition (1). Since she can reject (1) without logical or linguistic confusion, meanings alone don't guarantee that (1) isn't false. Thus (1) is synthetic.[9]

Now suppose further that the presuppositional analysis of statement (2) is correct, and that Catherine is clear on this; she accepts the analysis. Then since statement (2) presupposes (1) and she rejects (1), she rules out either accepting or rejecting statement (2). Thus (2) is non-analytic: one can be unconfused conceptually and linguistically and still rule out accepting it.

On the other hand, statement (2) is, as I have said, non-synthetic. This too can be put in terms not of truth and falsehood, but in terms of hyperdecided states. Let Hera be a coherent, hyperdecided observer

---

9. On minimal truth, see Horwich, *Truth* (1990, 1998). One question that such a treatment raises is how to frame truth minimalism to allow the truth-value gaps that stem from failure of presuppositions. The deflationary schema has it,

Sex is zowy is true if and only if sex is zowy,

where small caps indicate concepts, so that Sex is zowy is the thought that sex is zowy. We can't read this instance of the deflationary schema as letting us infer by *modus tollens* as follows: Sex is zowy is not true; therefore, sex is not zowy. For perhaps Sex is zowy is neither true nor false; its presuppositions fail. Jason Stanley pointed this out to me. The problem needs more exploration than I can give it here, but we do need to license the following inferences:

From:	To:
Sex is zowy is true.	Sex is zowy.
Sex is zowy is false.	Sex is not zowy.
Sex is zowy.	Sex is zowy is true
	Sex is zowy is not false.
Sex is not zowy.	Sex is zowy is false.
	Sex is zowy is not true.

who accepts the presuppositional analysis of 'zowy'. If she accepts (1), the presupposition of uses of 'zowy' in (2), this commits her to accepting (2). For from (1) it follows that a thing is zowy if and only if it is nakhy. If, on the other hand, she rejects presupposition (1), then she rules out either accepting or rejecting statement (2). No one, then, who is coherent and unconfused conceptually and linguistically can reject (2), and so (2) is non-synthetic. Again, it is neither analytic nor synthetic.

Presuppositional analyses, then, are consistent with one kind of complete rejection of the analytic-synthetic distinction: it could be that no statement with contentful terms is analytic. For all contentful terms, it might be claimed, have presuppositions that are non-analytic. Therefore terms using them are non-analytic. They may be synthetic, in that meanings do not preclude their being false. On the other hand, they may be neither analytic nor synthetic.

This still allows a sharp distinction between synthetic and non-synthetic statements. But even this we might find we should deny. For there might be no sharp fact of the matter whether a term has a presuppositional analysis—and if so, which presuppositional analysis is the right one.

Good and Rational

The very concept of *good* seems to convey that anything that is nakhy is good—or at least that hand-clasping isn't good on its own, for no further reason. Is a limited analytic naturalism for 'good', then, the right view after all, in that naturalistic standards are built into the very concept? I'm not sure. Suppose Juana's plans are so wildly off base as to give no weight to attaining what's nakhy, though they accord great intrinsic weight to hand-clasping. That's crazy, we can say; she is indifferent to all that is really to be sought in life, and yet responsive to something that is not at all to be sought. That said, we have another question to ask: making the sadly mistaken judgments she does, how can she express them? We disagree with her, firmly and entirely; how shall we put this claim of hers with which we disagree? I would say she thinks this: "What's nakhy isn't on that account in any way good in itself, whereas hand-clasping is." That seems to me to formulate what she thinks and what the rest of us reject in her thinking.

You might, however, think this misexpresses her frame of mind. You might think that the concept *good* has built into it certain naturalistic constraints. In that case, you might best put your understanding of her meanings in terms of presuppositions. The term 'good', you might say, carries presuppositions that entail that what's nakhy is to be sought, and that hand-clasping isn't—at least for its own sake, on no further ground. Juana the crazy rejects these presuppositions, and so, to stick to expressing her views correctly, must drop the word 'good' from all her talk. "'Good' is not one of my words," she should say. She misspeaks, then, if she denies that what's nakhy is "good" or if she calls hand-clasping "good" in itself.

This is not, as I say, how to my own mind the term 'good' works. Crazy plans—if formally coherent and not rooted in defective naturalistic beliefs—will stem from crazy views of what, at base, is to be sought in life. A plan can be crazy though the planner's concepts are in good order; we need intact concepts, after all, to specify what's crazy in the plan. To my ear, such plans amount to vastly mistaken views of what, in itself, is good.

Another normative term crucial to philosophy is 'rational'. Man, we all know, is a rational animal; rationality distinguishes us from the beasts. In these dicta, rationality is a property of beings: human beings are rational, whereas beasts are dumb and brutish. The term 'rational', though, applies also to things we can do: in a fix, I may cast around for the rational thing to do, and then do it or shy away. Economists and decision theorists use the term to formulate highly technical questions about courses of action; they sometimes debate which axioms characterize rational action. The term 'rational' applies also to beliefs, and epistemologists—and some probability theorists—debate what makes a belief rational. Controversially, the term even gets applied to emotions.

Many of the basic questions of philosophy and of life can be put as questions of what is rational: How is it rational to live? What is it rational to believe? Is anger ever rational—and is hope? There may, of course, not be any one sharp question that these words convey, but the questions so put do seem to point to central issues in life. It is important to understand what these issues can be, even if traditional words don't precisely capture them.

Now the concept of being the rational thing to do, I might claim, is simply the concept I have been exploring: the rational thing to do is the thing to do; an act is rational if and only if it is okay to do. What, though, should someone say who rejects reason? The Light Brigade reasoned not why; they took as their action guide not rationality, but duty and honor.[10] They thought, we should perhaps say, that riding to an almost sure death was "the thing to do" in their circumstances, but they didn't think it was "rational". If "rational", though, just means "okay to do", then the two thoughts amount to the same thing.[11]

We need, then, a more sensitive treatment of the term 'rational'. Rationality, clearly, has a tie to reasoning—and reasoning, I'll suggest, we can understand naturalistically, as a human activity. Not everything, though, that issues from reasoning is rational: the officer who reasoned what to order and ordered a head-on attack on guns wasn't being rational; he had blundered. The rational thing to do is what you would do on the basis of reasoning that is good or correct. This is the normative mooring of the term.

Could the men of the Light Brigade, if they had the time, give different answers to the two questions, what's rational to do and what to do? What was rational for them to do, I'm saying, is what they would conclude on doing if they reasoned well. Would they think this was different from the thing to do? I don't know. How did they think that good reasoning would come out? Their question wasn't what order to give, but what to do in their own subordinate position, given the order. Individual reasoning on the spot, though, isn't what makes for fearsome cavalry. Ideal soldiers, we may hold, obey orders without thinking it's theirs to reason why. These dispositions don't work well when someone has blundered, but they are why no one wants to be standing in front of these men, in enemy uniform, when their officers do their jobs properly. Now the question of whether it is rational to want to be a fearsome cavalryman seems very much open, unless you don't think life is to be guided by reasoning at all—even good reasoning. But if being fearsome as a cavalryman is rational to want, then it's rational to want to be someone for whom, in the heat of battle, the question of what's rational doesn't arise.

Is the rational thing to do, then, always the thing to do? The thing for light cavalry to *prime* themselves to do, let's agree, is to obey orders

10. See Railton, "Noncognitivism about Rationality" (1993), p. 42.

11. For my treatment of 'rational' as a term that needn't always carry endorsement, see pp. 49–50 in *Wise Choices* (1990).

whatever they turn out to be. Was the thing to do, then, to charge without question? Or was it to balk and face dishonor and decimation? If the latter, and that's what good reasoning would conclude, then this case still displays no contrast between the thing to do and the rational thing to do. The contrast is rather between the thing to do, on the one hand, and the thing to have primed oneself to do, on the other.

What, though, if we think that the thing to do is never to reason, or never to reason in matters of duty and honor? A hard position to work out coherently, perhaps—but suppose we can. Then a contrast may emerge between the thing to do and the rational thing to do. The *rational* thing to do, we can say, is the thing to conclude by reasoning to do, *if* you are to reason on the matter at all. Honor perhaps demands un-questioning obedience, but not, once the question is raised, reasoning to the conclusion to pursue honor and obedience. If this is a coherent position, it seems to allow a contrast between being the thing to do—a matter of honor—and being the rational thing to do.

The concept of being rational, on this account, is still plan-laden, and not purely naturalistic. The concept of reasoning, in contrast, is naturalistic, but what's rational is not what faulty reasoning yields. It is what reasoning yields if you reason in the way that's the way to reason. To conclude how to reason is to plan for how to reason.

'Good' and 'rational', if I am right, are not best analyzed as carrying substantive, naturalistic presuppositions or constraints on what's good or what's rational. The terms 'good' and 'rational' are plan-laden in fairly straightforward ways. In the next chapter, I consider another class of plan-laden concepts, drawing on a theory of "normative kinds" from Geoffrey Sayre-McCord. This theory does turn out to be complexly presuppositional. First, though, concluding this chapter, I take up an-other kind of objection to the claim that our normative concepts are plan-laden.

Planning and Acting

One tenet of expressivism for normative concepts can seem just plain wrong. Expressivism yields "internalism", in one sense of that term of many meanings. It yields a form of what Stephen Darwall labels *judg-ment internalism*: if the term 'ought' works (syntax aside) as does my ar-tificial term 'the thing to do', then a person can't think he ought to do something, right now, and be unmoved to do it.[12] For according to my stipulation, to think something the thing to do is to plan to do it. To think, for instance, that the thing now to do is to defy the bully who torments me is to plan to defy him. And planning right now to defy him right now, to do it at this very moment, amounts to setting out to do it. My theory thus yields internalism in a strong form: if I think that something is now the thing to do, then I do it. My hypothesis about ordinary *ought* judgments is that they are judgments of what to do, of what is the thing to do. I don't, then, think that I ought right now to defy the bully unless I do defy him. If I fail to defy him, then as a matter of the very concept of *ought*, I don't believe I ought to. And for *ought* judgments that seems plain wrong.

It is worth reminding ourselves that this strong form of internalism has long been advocated and seriously debated. Many find it an absurdity, but some instead find it an obvious truth. A full account of *ought* beliefs should explain why this is so. I myself would say this: The notions of plan and belief have their limits. A person often isn't "of one mind" in accepting a plan or not. For a crucial sense of 'ought', I say, the following holds: if you do accept, in every relevant aspect of your mind, that you ought right now to defy the bully, then, you will do it if you can. For if you can do it and don't, then some aspect of your mind accounts for your not doing it—and so you don't now plan with every aspect of your mind to do it right now. Whatever aspect of your motivational system issued in your doing otherwise didn't accept the plan to defy him right now. And so, it seems to me, there's a part of you that doesn't really think you ought to. You are of more than one mind on whether you ought to defy him.

Conflicts among motivational systems were central to my naturalistic discussion, in *Wise Choices*, of "accepting norms"; a motivational system of norm-acceptance, I speculated, competes with other systems of motivation (see especially chapter 4 of *Wise Choices*). Avowedly, though, I developed this speculation not as probable, but as, I hoped, a first approximation to psychological truth. My philosophical question was what to say about normative beliefs if some such psychology obtains.

12. Darwall, "Reasons, Motives" (1997), speaks (pp. 307–308) of "reasons/ motives internalism", one version of which is a form of "judgment internalism". My version might, on this scheme, be called "thing-to-do/motives judgment internalism".

This present book treats not the psychology of oughts, but their logic and epistemology. My conclusions here aren't meant to hinge on the exact truth of any one psychology of planning and acting. But in parallel with my earlier book, I can allow senses in which one can plan to do something, think one ought to do it, but be of two minds on doing it.

What, though, of the weaker, more usual formulation of motivational judgment internalism: that if you think you ought to do it right now, you'll be moved to do it at least to some degree? You may not be of one mind to do it, but you'll be of *some* mind, at least, to do it. Aren't there clear counterexamples to this? I'm convinced that I ought, but cowed and drained as I am, I find no inclination whatsoever to do so. Now again, I'd say, there's no clear, sharp psychological fact of what constitutes accepting a plan, and correspondingly, there's no clear, sharp fact of what constitutes really thinking you ought to do something. A state of mind wouldn't amount to planning if it weren't of a kind that normally plays the right systematic role in leading to action. Otherwise, it's at most going through the motions of planning. It doesn't follow that at every moment, whatever your inhibitions and however abnormal you are in your responses, you tend to do what you plan to do. Like things, I now say, go for ought judgments: a state of mind isn't a judgment of ought all told if it isn't a state of mind that normally issues in action.[13]

Sigrún Svavarsdóttir, though, devises a case to the contrary, where a man indeed does make ought judgments, but is indifferent always and systematically to whether or not he ought to do things ("Moral Cognitivism," 1999, pp. 176–177). Svavarsdóttir's topic is specifically moral obligation, but we should ask whether her argument applies to an ought all things considered, a sense in which, once I've settled what morally speaking I ought to do, I can still ask whether that's what I ought in the end to do. I'll render Svavarsdóttir freely and adapt her case to this kind of ought. Let a man's use of 'ought' match perfectly

13. An internalistic claim this weak, even if it could be established without appeal to a thesis about the nature of normative judgments, cannot, of course, be used as a weapon against analytic naturalism in all forms. Many beliefs in naturalistic fact will share this internalistic feature—belief, for instance, that an action will prevent one's suffering. My arguments against various forms of analytical naturalism have been Moore-like; my thesis that oughts are contingency plans then serves as a diagnosis that explains these Moore-like phenomena.

that of a normal user of the term, she proposes, in every respect apart from motivation. Rachel, imagine, is a normal, rational user of the term 'ought' and of other normative terms. Ira discusses questions of ought and pursues them avidly, speaking in every way as does Rachel—so long as he sticks to questions of what people ought to do, not whether to do it. Ira is irrational only in that he shrugs off his ought conclusions as having no bearing on what to do; he reasons to decisions ignoring his conclusions of what in the end he ought to do, and when he does what he maintains he ought not to do he experiences no dissonance. Rachel and Ira make all the same ought judgments, offering identical arguments and finding the same considerations relevant. Rachel is of course best interpreted as meaning *ought* by 'ought'; that's by stipulation: we're simply specifying the case as one in which every consideration that bears on interpretation supports interpreting her as meaning *ought* by 'ought'. Isn't Ira too, then, best interpreted this way? He makes the same judgments on the same grounds; he argues the same ways and finds the same considerations relevant. He's missing one aspect of the normal use of the concept, true enough, but the overwhelming bulk of considerations support interpreting him this way.

Ira, though, I'll maintain, is only aping having the concept of *ought*. He misinterprets the conversation he is joining. The considerations that Ira adduces, true enough, match perfectly those that Rachel takes to bear on what to do—so we have specified. Rachel, though, acts on her ought judgments, whereas Ira, in thinking what to do, ignores them. Now imagine another man, Roger, who acts on his ought judgments, but disagrees wildly with Rachel on what a person ought to do—and so on what to do. Rachel is a rigorous deontological moralist; Roger is a hedonistic egoist. Ira, whose judgments with the word 'ought' match Rachel's word for word, guides his life exactly as does Roger: his answers to what to do are those of a hedonistic egoist. He thinks that he "ought" to avoid all lies, even when they enhance his prospects for pleasure, but his policy for living is to lie whenever there's the slightest net hedonic advantage in doing so.

Ira does have a term to express his planning judgments, suppose; he uses the term 'should'. What one "ought" to do, he insists, has little or no bearing on what one "should" do—though questions of what one "ought" to do are fun to debate and have great theoretical interest. We now have two candidates for terms that mean *ought* in his mouth—the

two words 'ought' and 'should'. Motivation aside, his 'ought' matches
Rachel's term 'ought', which clearly means *ought*, and his term 'should'
matches Roger's term 'ought'—which also clearly means *ought*. But it
can't follow that 'ought' and 'should' in his mouth both mean *ought*, for
he doesn't treat the terms as equivalent; what you "ought" to do, he
judges, is vastly different from what you "should" do.

Now the interpretive balance in this case, an advocate of Svavarsdóttir's strategy of argument might agree, is swung by his motivation to do what he concludes he "should" do. What, though, if we
change the case back, so that Ira has no term for what to do. He now
just has the term 'ought', which has little to do, he maintains, with
questions of what to do. His term 'ought' in the modified case meant
something vastly different from *ought*. And in the two cases, his use
of 'ought' is just the same. In short, if he has this term 'should' then
his term 'should' means *ought*, and his term 'ought' means something
vastly different. If he doesn't have this term 'should', the advocate is
saying, then his term 'ought' does mean *ought*. If he lacks this term
'should' then he agrees remarkably with Rachel on what people ought
to do; if he acquires this term 'should', then, without changing anything in his use of 'ought', he now vastly disagrees with Rachel, except
in verbal formulation.

I don't know if the advocate would find these consequences welcome; to me they seem strange. The phenomena are these: people can
disagree sharply in the standards that guide their *ought* judgments.
Meaning the same thing, and so being able to dissent, does not depend
on being guided by the same basic standards. That's why Roger can be
a hedonistic egoist in his ought judgments and Rachel a deontological
moralist, and they can engage each other on questions of what a person
ought to do and sharply disagree. Now this, I have been arguing, fits
unhappily with a view that mimicking a person's standards and rationales for *ought* gives one that person's concept of *ought*.

Perhaps we should say, though, that Ira means *ought* by 'ought' just
because his is a term in public language, and so it gets its meaning from
the way the rest of us use the term. Rachel and Roger engage each
other with the term 'ought' because it is a term of our public language,
and the same goes for Roger and Ira: though they agree in every detail
on what to do, they differ vastly on whether one ought to do it. As for
Rachel and Ira, though they differ immensely on what to do, they gen-

uinely agree on what people ought to do. That is because they both use the word 'ought' they draw from our public language. Blackburn (*Ruling Passions*, 1998, pp. 61–66) allows something like this, and it leaves the chief tenets of expressivism unchanged—except that now they apply to the usage of communities, not individuals. For 'ought' to mean *ought* in a linguistic community, internalism must hold for the most part in that community, but not for every odd individual. Such a communitarian view of meaning saves the chief claim of expressivism for 'ought': in my version, that the term gets its meaning from a tie to planning.

I'm not convinced, though, that even this much concession to externalism is tenable. Ira, we're supposing, defers to the community to give the word 'ought' its meaning in his mouth. But Rachel and Roger are both in his linguistic community, and where they disagree—in a substantial range of judgments—Ira can't draw the standards to guide his use from both of them. We've stipulated that, verbally, he matches Rachel and not Roger. His sense of plausibility and relevance for judgments he couches with 'ought' matches hers. What, though, if he's shaken on this score, and begins to be drawn to Roger's way of seeing these matters. Rachel, if she's drawn to Roger's views, is shaken on questions of what to do. Ira is shaken, he says, on what he "ought" to do, but on nothing else. Hasn't this now become an empty word for him?

He can say that he takes a great theoretical interest in what people ought to do, even though settling that he ought to do a thing has no special bearing on whether to do it. But isn't this a theory without a real subject matter? He can say that he is trying to explain our patterns of judgment in a principled way. But "our" judgments seem to follow different patterns, and Rachel and Roger can each perhaps find principles to match their judgments. 'Ought' is a word in our common language, we are trying out saying, and so Ira dissents from Roger when Roger says one ought and Ira says one ought not—but what are they disagreeing *about?* What would make this disagreement genuine, it seems to me, is the normal tie to questions of what to do. Then something would be at stake.

With many terms, to be sure, intuitions on when the term applies may give its meaning. This might be the way to elucidate, for instance, the concept of a cause: tell stories about factor *A* and factor *B*, and see whether we judge that they amount to *A*'s causing *B*. Suppose, though, we find no convergence in these intuitive judgments of ours. Then we don't share a common concept of cause—or at least, not a concept that we can elucidate by these methods. You have your concept and I have mine, perhaps, and our thoughts couched in terms of "cause" just don't engage each other. With questions of ought, in contrast, persistent disagreement doesn't raise a question of whether anything is genuinely at issue. It may call into question our hopes for forming a community of discourse on ought questions. But that is not the same as saying that you have your concept and I have mine.

Ira, of course, can adopt a principled indifference to the kinds of considerations other people treat as bearing on oughts—without drawing too fine a line about what those considerations are and how they legitimately weigh in ought judgments. What he cannot do, in that case, is enter into normative disputes the way other people can. If he applies the term 'ought' to things most people don't, he is then not using the term 'ought' to mean what they do. He can't then have meaningful, fine-grained normative convictions on matters of normative controversy.[14]

We know what 'ought' means, in that we have all learned our language. It is an illusion, though, that we would mean the same thing if we came to be indifferent to questions of what we "ought" to do. Can I settle what I ought to do and still ask what to do? What, then, can you agree with me about or disagree with me about? If we proceed this way, I've been arguing, we have emptied the term 'ought' of all that allows for engagement and inquiry. Sincere the mimic might be, convinced that he is debating something—but he then is mimicking a discourse he misinterprets.

14. See Gibbard, "Reply to Sinnott-Armstrong" (1993), for further discussion along this line.

～ 8

Normative Kinds:
Patterns of Engagement

A TERM CAN REST on plan-laden presuppositions, I have been saying. That might rule out, on grounds of sheer meaning, such outrages as calling hand-clasping "good" for no further reason. It will not, though, render normative concepts straightforwardly naturalistic. Claims with plan-laden presuppositions may instead be neither definitely plan-laden nor definitely naturalistic—for given the presupposition, a naturalistic meaning and a plan-laden meaning may be equivalent. This is one way that a normative claim may qualify neither as clearly plan-laden nor clearly not. A second way, I have said, is sheer vagueness, when there's no fact of the matter which kind of meaning a term has.

Philosophy of science in recent decades suggests another way a term can get its meaning: the term may invoke an explanatory role. In the philosophy of science, Hilary Putnam a few decades ago revived talk of "natural kinds": the kinds that we should treat as "cutting nature at its joints," he proposed, are the kinds that figure centrally in the best natural theory. Geoffrey Sayre-McCord proposes something parallel with norms: he speaks of *moral kinds*, kinds that are to figure in moral thought and language. "The kinds that matter to morals," he says, are "those that are countenanced by the best moral theory" (Sayre-McCord, "'Good' on Twin Earth," 1997, p. 284). Just, then, as it can turn out that with talk of "water," long ago before chemical theory, we

159

were all along talking about H_2O, so it could turn out that all along in our talk of "justice", we were talking about the property that Rawls elucidates in his book *A Theory of Justice*. This could be so, even if there were substantial differences between our old views of what makes something just and the things Rawls's theory says—or even if we badly misunderstood the nature of justice. What would be needed for this is, first, that Rawls's theory of justice is part of the best moral theory. Second, in some way that will need explaining, we would need all along to have best been interpretable as talking about justice as Rawls elucidates it. If all this is so, according to Sayre-McCord, then Rawls will turn out to have discovered "the true nature of justice", of what we have referred to all along with the term (p. 289).

This is a promising start to an account of how a term like 'justice' might get its meaning. It bears a close resemblance to things that Nicholas Sturgeon says, developing a form of naturalism for moral concepts. This chapter explores such a proposal—but because I am studying not just moral concepts but normative concepts in general, I'll often speak of a theory of *normative* kinds. Again I'll explore the ways our thoughts can engage each other or fail to engage each other, how agreement, disagreement, and talking past each other might work with normative kind terms.

Finding Normative Kinds

A theory of normative kind terms requires two major parts. The first is a theory of the kinds themselves: this part tells us what the candidates are for what normative terms might signify. It tells us what makes a property a genuine normative kind. The second part links kinds with terms; it is a theory of interpretation. The question this second part addresses is conditional: given the socio-linguistic facts of a term's use and transmission, which among genuine normative kinds, if any, does the term signify? Which one does it signify in that special manner in which normative kind terms signify normative kinds?

Turn, then, to the first part—the theory of what a normative kind is. The genuine normative kinds, we are saying, are the ones that the best normative theory will countenance. Much will depend, then, on what would qualify a theory as the best normative theory. Perhaps a normative theory is just a naturalistic theory, a scientific (or pre-scientific) theory in a certain realm. It is a naturalistic theory of good, ought, virtue, justice, or something of the sort. And what makes a normative theory good is just what makes any other naturalistic theory good— theories in the social sciences, for instance. If we accepted this set of answers, we'd be regarding justice, if there is such a thing, as a natural kind that figures in the best social science. We'd then defer to social scientists to tell us the true nature of justice, even if we couldn't find much to recommend the thing that has the nature they elucidate. Sayre-McCord rejects this, rightly, I think. We won't defer to causal theory alone to settle what is just or not in social arrangements.

What *are* we doing instead, then, when we create and refine a normative theory and find it good? If the theory we're constructing is specifically moral, then we could say that—in a specially systematic and self-conscious way—we are moralizing. I don't know a term that covers the normative in general as 'moralizing' covers the moral, but I'll speak of our activity as "normative inquiry". I'll read this as including both normative thinking off by oneself and normative conversation, debate, and the like. Normative inquiry, so broadly conceived, is aimed at thinking what to do and how to feel, in various ways, about conduct, character, and the like. Normative theory construction and evaluation is this kind of activity engaged in systematically, with special emphasis on being explicit and consistent, on approaching our questions and contentions critically, and so on refining what we say. Naturalistic thinking too, of course, is directed much of the time at questions of what to do, but strictly naturalistic concepts are shaped by the demands of causal explanation and understanding. Considerations of what to do often guide us in settling what to think about, but never, if we are thinking clearly and purely naturalistically, on what to conclude given the naturalistic questions and the evidence. It was, for example, a question of enormous practical import whether to study nuclear fission, but how we're to think it works depends not at all on what bombs and what power plants, if any, to develop.

In thinking what to do and how to feel, we construct explanations: we explain *why* something is the thing to do in a situation, or why something is the thing to feel about a kind of conduct. We criticize and refine these explanations, and part of doing so will be to refine our accounts of the kinds that figure in these explanations. These explanations are not purely causal, telling why things happen as they do, but something more like *planning* explanations: we settle on what to do and explain why to do it—or we settle on how to feel about something and explain why to feel that way about it. The kinds that figure in these explanations, then, will be special: they will be held not primarily to standards of providing good causal explanations, but rather must bear, in important ways, on questions of what to do and how to feel. This bearing will shape the special, "thick" conceptions that figure in normative discourse.

Take courtship as an example. Sometimes avid courtship turns to harassment. I mean this not in a legal sense, as in employment law, but as the term might figure in moral discussion. What, then, distinguishes courtship turned to harassment from a legitimate, romantically admirable determination to win one's love? The question seems mostly to arise when men pursue women, and surely we recognize some such pursuits as harassment in a morally charged sense—but what does this consist in? She resists his advances, and he's unwilling to take no for an answer. But this description doesn't settle the case as one of harassment. Is a Fred Astaire character engaged in harassment, or is he an avid swain who is admirable in venturing all to win the lady's heart? The answer hinges on whether to respond with outrage or admiration.

This question is broadly moral, and normative discourse is replete with classifications like these. So-called thick concepts like harassing, being gracious, or stinginess are hard to explain, if we confine ourselves to "thin" normative concepts like *ought* or *good* along with concepts that are austerely naturalistic. One approach is to construct presuppositional analyses, as in the previous chapter. Sayre-McCord's proposal, as I'll explain, adds to this approach.

Some kinds, we can say, are more "high grade" than others: they figure centrally in correct explanations and, because they do, are good candidates for what the terms we use in providing such explanations signify. The kind electron is high grade from the point of view of physics, whereas the kind gem is not; the kind pair-bonding might be high grade from the point of view of social theory, whereas other relations people can stand in are lower grade—for example, sitting down at the restaurant table another has recently left. Falling in love explains much, whereas except by some quirk, succession at table explains little. Natural kinds are ones that are high grade from a correct, naturalistic point of view; oxygen, genes, evolutionarily stable strategies, and pleasure are likely examples. Now some kinds count as high grade, Sayre-McCord proposes, not because of the role they play in the best causal explanations of events in the world, but because of their role in explaining what's to be done and what isn't, or what's to be admired and what reprehended—and why. In debates over what constitutes harassment, for instance, classification is responsive to questions of what's not to be done and what's to be reprehended. That is what makes harassment a moral kind and not a purely causal-explanatory kind. If, then, we disagree about what to do or how to feel, or if we disagree on how such conclusions are to be supported and explained, we will disagree about the boundaries of normative kinds.

This means that a normative kind theorist, on the reading I'm offering, should not be a hard-line, metaethical "externalist", who thinks that a "sensible knave" or an "irrationalist" might fully share our normative concepts but not at all be guided in terms of them. Suppose we debate just when avid and determined wooing crosses the line and becomes harassing. Anyone who "doesn't give a damn", for whom no question of action or attitude, actual or hypothetical, hinges on the classification, can't join into the conversation as a full-fledged participant. His use of this kind of language can only be parasitic on the usage of those who do care. Would a serenade be harassing as well as quaint? The sensible cad might predict how people will classify serenades, or role-play at entering the discussion. But it is puzzling what he is doing if he earnestly tries to take sides. There is no such intelligible thing as pure theoretical curiosity in these matters; at stake is how to explain what to do.

Interpreting Normative Kind Terms

If we have settled how to live and why, we have come to a view on what the high-grade normative kinds are. The kinds we treat as high grade are the ones that figure centrally in our planning explanations, in our explanations of why to do things or not, or why to feel certain ways toward things. Settling what these kinds are, though, leaves us short of a full theory of normative language. We still need to know when a term in someone's language signifies a particular normative kind. High-grade normative kinds are good candidates for what a term might signify—but what does it take for a term like 'just' to signify a particular normative kind *K*?

The second part of a normative kind theory, then, must be a theory of linguistic and conceptual interpretation. We have figured out already, imagine, what are the high-grade normative kinds. Interpretation will rest on socio-linguistic facts: what sentences people treat as cogent, for instance. The next part of a theory of normative kind terms, then, must tell us how to go from socio-linguistic facts of the use and transmission of a normative kind term to an ascription of signification—to saying which among high-grade normative kinds, if any, the term signifies.

A preliminary subpart would tell us how to recognize a normative kind term in the first place—but I'll skip over that question, and suppose that we somehow know a normative kind term when we see it. We know too, I'm now supposing, what the high-grade normative kinds are, what are best candidates for what normative kind terms in a language might turn out to signify. We are asking, then, what makes it the case that the term signifies one normative kind as opposed to another, or as opposed to no kind at all.

Sayre-McCord himself has a proposal for what ties kind to term. For the specifically moral case, the question is which normatively significant kind *regulates* our beliefs involving the term—regulates these beliefs causally. "Our use is causally responsive to what are, in fact, instances of the kind and (ii) the use to which the term is put is one of referring to whatever normatively significant kind it is that they are instances of" (p. 270). Suppose that far away, a normative kind term happens to sound like our term 'good'. Whether, by further coincidence, it means *good*, thinks Sayre-McCord, depends on "whether their use of the term 'good' is appropriately regulated by what is in fact good" (p. 285). Suppose, for example, that hedonists are right and good is pleasure. They mean "good" just in case their use is causally regulated by pleasure. Or to take another example, suppose we are right that justice is a high-grade normative kind, and our group far away have a normative kind term that emerged in response to samples of justice. Then justice is what they've been talking about—even if their criteria for what's just differ sharply from ours. "We see their reliance on the criteria as their more or less successful way of picking out instances of what we are referring to" with our own term 'just' (p. 289).

This picture is tempting but, I'll argue, false. Consider a toy example: we have traveled to far climes and encountered a people called the

Bulli. In the Bulli language, we are confronted with a term 'wumpua'. It is a normative kind term, we've somehow established, and our question now is which normative kind, if any, it signifies.

To find what kind this term 'wumpua' signifies, on this false picture, we look to what high-grade normative kind, if any, regulates their use of the term causally. We look at the set of things Bullis apply the term to, or to which they are disposed to apply it. We ask whether this set more or less coincides with any genuine normative kind—justice, say, or brutality. If so, we say that the term signifies that normative kind. If no match is reasonably close, we say that it refers to no kind whatsoever.

I'll put my objection in two ways: by extending the example and by arguing that it doesn't fit the motivations of the rest of the account. First, the general argument: why interpret people? A chief reason is, as I keep saying, to take conversational stances toward them, accepting some things they say, rejecting others, and reasoning with them. If we interpret a term of theirs as a piece of normative language, that should allow us to engage them in normative discourse, to regard them as engaged, incipiently at least, in the same kind of normative theory construction as are we. Now normative theory construction, criticism, and refinement, as Sayre-McCord rightly stresses, isn't pure scientific theorizing—and like things go for normative discourse that is pre-theoretical. In morals, our kinds have to figure in explanations of why to do things and why to feel things. Now the trouble with this proposed interpretive procedure is that it ignores how the Bulli term figures in their own normative discourse. Interpreting this way doesn't even incipiently let us treat the Bulli as like us, able to join us in normative discourse.

Now to extend the example: we ourselves have a normative kind *brutality;* let's suppose that it figures in the best normative theory. The Bulli, I now tell you, apply the term 'wumpua' mostly to acts of brutality; for the most part, they call all and only brutal acts "wumpua". If any normative kind causally regulates their use of the term, it is brutality. Of course this coincidence is rough—but then we ourselves don't all agree what's brutal or not; we dispute child rearing, police methods, criminal penalties, and the like. Our own use is far from perfectly regulated by what's brutal and what isn't. The Bulli too will have their disputes about what's "wumpua" and what isn't, and they tend to deviate from us in a few systematic ways. Still, we all agree, Bullis come close to calling brutal acts and nothing else "wumpua".

I should tell you one more thing about their use of this term: they are enthusiastic for the acts they call "wumpua". They do try to avoid being the objects of these acts, but they give every sign of wanting to perform such acts when they can do so with any safety, and they show every sign of admiring those who perform the acts they call "wumpua". As we interpret the rest of their language, they say, with evident glee, things like "It shows who's boss. It makes people fear you."

Now on this interpretation of normative kind theory, the interpretation I'm opposing, we should say this: their normative kind term 'wumpua' means brutal. Bullis all admire brutality, whereas most of us abhor it. But the property they signify with their term 'wumpua' is that of being brutal.

Now it's not that I utterly rule out translating 'wumpua' as "brutal". If we do, though, I'll argue that we aren't treating the term as a genuine normative kind term, one whose boundaries of application are shaped by genuine normative demands. Suppose 'wumpua' should be translated as "brutal", and that we have developed an otherwise correct translation manual. I have become an expert interpreter, translating according to the manual. Through my mediation, you discuss with the Bulli whether an act is brutal or wumpua—which amount to the same thing, we are now assuming. We discuss an arrest in America: a man was slashing a woman with a knife, and a policeman knocked him unconscious and trussed him. The Bulli say "wumpua!" I translate, and you say, "No, it wasn't brutal. The officer applied the minimal force necessary to put an end to a heinous crime." The Bulli say (as I correctly translate), "So what? The act was wumpua because it hurt the man and showed him the cop was boss."

It seems to me clear that the Bulli and you are here talking past each other, that we have reached a *reductio* of the supposition that I was translating correctly. The acts they label "wumpua" do pretty much coincide with the ones they could recognize as brutal if they had our sensibilities. But the role of the term 'wumpua' in their normative talk isn't at all the role of 'brutal' in ours. We're right, I'm supposing, that the normative kind *the brutal* figures in the best normative theory, and that no genuine normative kind comes closer to regulating the Bulli's application of 'wumpua'—for Bullis themselves are surely wrong in their brutal normative outlook. If any property causally regulates their applications of 'wumpua' to actions, it is the property of being brutal; causally speaking, that property regulates their use of 'wumpua' about as closely as it regulates our own use of 'brutal', with its disputed boundaries of application. But since the boundaries of what they apply the term to are not shaped by anything like the rationales that shape what we ourselves count as brutal, 'wumpua' doesn't mean brutal.

All this assumes that our own term 'brutal' is a normative kind term, that what's brutal and what isn't depends, by linguistic rules that govern the term, on a certain kind of role in explaining what to do and how to feel about actions. As I say, though, I don't object to saying that 'wumpua' roughly means "brutal". In a way it does, and in a way it doesn't. There is some pull to treating both terms, 'brutal' and 'wumpua', as descriptive and naturalistic, and if we do, we'll find their meanings to be close. The point is that on this treatment, you and the Bulli aren't engaged in a classificatory normative dispute, a dispute over shaping boundaries of application to play a role in explaining what to do. On the suspect interpretation of 'wumpua' as meaning precisely "brutal", you and they have a dispute, but it isn't normative. They think the act was "wumpua" and you think it wasn't brutal, but you both approve. Your reasons and theirs don't at all mesh: you favor the act as a minimal necessary use of force and hence not brutal, and they favor it as showing who's boss and hence as "wumpua". You and the Bulli have deep normative disagreements, but the precise issues of whether it was brutal or whether it was wumpua aren't among them. For 'wumpua' doesn't mean brutal exactly but just roughly. They aren't, then, claiming exactly that the arrest was brutal, just that it was of a kind that, we see, roughly coincides with the brutal. They aren't, then, claiming anything that engages your denial.

Likewise, when they dispute whether an act is wumpua and let the question of whether to admire it hinge on the answer, we can't join in and judge who is right among them by thinking whether the act is brutal. The role of 'wumpua' in their normative talk is too far off base for them to join us, using their term, in discussing the boundaries of the brutal. If normative kinds are distinctively responsive to genuine normative considerations and we are at all right on questions of brutality, then nothing in Bulli explanatory practice qualifies 'wumpua' as a successful normative kind term, one that succeeds in picking out a genuine normative kind.

One frequent view of a term like 'brutal' is that it has a descriptive meaning, albeit somewhat vague, and in addition it has an emotive "color". A sensible thug who isn't put off by brutality can tell us when we speak truly or falsely using the term (with some slack for vagueness), but can't sincerely use the term himself, since it carries an emotive color he doesn't share. When we ourselves label a brutal action "brutal", his linguistically proper response is, "You're right, but I wouldn't put it that way."[1] This kind of account applies well, I think, to some terms, such as racial or ethnic epithets. With a term like 'brutal', though, it fails to capture an important feature. Suppose you oppose an act as "brutal", whereas I reluctantly approve of it as a case of justified violence. My response won't be, "You're right, but I wouldn't put it that way"; I'll deny that the act was brutal. Such a case is possible even when we agree on the non-normative facts and when both of us are fully competent in our linguistic mastery of the term. But how can we explain it with the coloring model? If the action we are discussing is in the extension of the descriptive term 'brutal', then you are linguistically incompetent to disagree. If it isn't, then I'm linguistically incompetent in applying the term. If it's in the term's penumbra of vagueness, there's nothing non-normative at issue, and we should both agree that you were sort of right and sort of wrong. The coloring model fails to explain why, when linguistically competent people agree on the non-normative facts but differ in attitude, they can straightforwardly disagree on whether an action is brutal.

An Anatomy of Dissent

I have rejected the coloring model, and earlier I rejected Sayre-McCord's own way of matching a theory of interpretation to a theory of normative kinds. A rough alternative view is this: For a term to signify the brutal as a genuine normative kind term, it must play the right role, more or less, in its users' normative thinking and discourse. It

1. Frege gives this kind of account for a term like 'nag' ("Thought," 1918, p. 331, p. 63 in original). Williams suggests something like this with his analogy of rules in schoolboy tradition concerning who gets to use a term (*Ethics and the Limits*, 1985, pp. 143–145).

must figure, more or less correctly, in explanations of what to do or how to feel about things. When classification under the term bears on these planning questions, the population must treat the way it does as helping to settle what counts as falling under that term. With brutality, for instance, I have been arguing, a tie to what to do is crucial to meaning: an act's being brutal weighs strongly against doing it and in favor of reprehending it, and whether we think an action's properties so weigh helps determine whether we regard the action as brutal. How the term figures in normative reasoning—reasoning about what to do and how to feel about things, and why—bears on its proper interpretation.

This means that when a Bulli favors kicking a captive as "wumpua", he isn't thereby in agreement with us who reprehend the act as brutal. When a Bulli favors clubbing a slasher as "wumpua", he isn't directly denying our claim that this act wasn't brutal. If we are right in our broad views of what to do and why, then on the best interpretation, the Bulli massively fail in their normative presuppositions. Their uses of the term 'wumpua' presuppose that an act's hurting someone to show who's boss explains why to glory in it. Such explanations of how to feel about actions are off base, if we are right, and so in their use of 'wumpua', the Bulli fail to latch onto any normative kind at all. When they dispute whether an action was "wumpua", we can't straightforwardly agree with one side and disagree with the other; we can't say which side is right in their application of the term. We regard what they say as neither true nor false.

When, though, *are* two people in genuine disagreement on normative kinds? This is a general question of how a theory of normative kinds can work as a theory of meanings. In this book, I have proposed a uniform device for representing meanings: identify the meaning with a set of hyperstates, with the set of hyperdecided states of mind in which one would be in agreement. We settle what a statement means when we settle what it is to be hyperdecided and agree or disagree. Can a theory of normative kinds be put in this form—and if so, what does that tell us about meaning, assent, and dissent?

What I'll be saying, in preview, is this: (i) A normative kind theory, if it's precise enough, does lend itself to this form of representation. The theory amounts to a presuppositional account of meaning of a special kind. (ii) Between isolated groups when normative kind terms abound, pure assent or dissent must be rare—and this is a drawback to speaking in such terms. (iii) Still, a close approximation to assent and dissent may often be achieved if two groups are in broad accord in their implicit normative views. Normative kind terms, moreover, have a great advantage: they allow us to work together toward complex normative explanations, and to do so little by little. In view of this advantage, rough assent and dissent may be good enough. Finally, though, I'll allude to Bernard Williams's talk of a "relativism of distance", and argue: (iv) It may be possible to engage with the judgments of people far away, agreeing with them or disagreeing. To do so, think carefully how to live if in their far-away shoes and alien milieu, with their sensibilities. You might then find that your explanations of what to do and why, if in their shoes, mesh with the ones they themselves give. In that case, you can agree or disagree with the judgments they make, coming to speak their language or one that translates into theirs. You might more likely, though, find that even allowing for their vastly different problems and experience, you can't get your planning explanations to mesh with theirs. You will then demur from the judgments they put in thick terms, neither agreeing nor disagreeing.

When, then, will someone hyperdecided like Hera assent to a claim in terms of normative kinds? The account of signifying normative kinds that I have sketched is vague in the extreme, but we can ask how it would look if it were rendered more precise. I'll gesture toward such a rendering, and explore its implications for agreement and disagreement.

Imagine we have achieved the best possible normative theory. It will include a naturalistic theory with its natural kind terms, which are responsive to the needs of purely causal explanation. Imagine the naturalistic part of the theory as understood already, explained by an outside consultant from the philosophy of science. To this naturalistic theory, a normative theory adds two kinds of terms: the planning term 'is okay to do' and normative kind terms—terms which, if the theory is enough on the right track, signify normative kinds.

Now such a theory can in principle be filled out by providing a naturalistic characterization for each normative kind term in the theory. We ourselves cannot do this, at least at present, or we wouldn't have to construct theories with unexplicated normative kind terms. But Hera the hyperdecided could survey the various ways that the normative kind terms of a theory could be rendered naturalistically explicit. Call these *explicitized versions* of the normative theory. An explicitized version of a normative theory contains only thin ingredients: naturalistic terms, the planning term 'okay', and terms definable from these, finitely or infinitely. Hera, then, being hyperdecided, agrees or disagrees with each explicitized version of a normative theory. She'll regard each as correct or incorrect in its claims for what to do, how things stand, and combinations of these.

Sheer correctness isn't the only virtue a theory needs. It must do well at explaining: it must be perspicuous and have other virtues in explaining why to do the things it says to do. The best theory, on Hera's view, will meet two requirements: (i) that it have an explicitized version that is correct on all questions of how things stand and what to do, and (ii) of all theories that meet requirement (i), it scores highest in perspicuity and other explanatory virtues. (Hera's judgments on these explanatory virtues amount to plans for how to understand matters if one has normal human limitations.)

So much for Hera's view of which normative theory is best. How shall we go from this to a theory of meanings in the mouths of ordinary folk. Consider two such folk, Jack and Jill, in the same community. Somehow, what they mean by their normative kind terms depends on the rough normative theory in which those terms figure. Jack, of course, will be no adherent of the very best normative theory; in any highfalutin sense of the term, he will maintain no normative "theory" at all. But he does make normative judgments from time to time, and he has implicit ways of judging acts and feelings in normative terms and of settling what to do. Like things go for Jill, and for others in their community of discourse.

We can now pursue either of two alternatives in developing an account of normative kind meanings. On the one hand, we can attribute an implicit normative theory to Jack himself, and let his meanings depend on his private normative theory. On the other, we can ascribe to Jack meanings that are public, discerning an implicit core of normative theory in the community as a whole, and letting meanings in Jack's own mouth hang on this public theory. Private meanings, after all, have a sharp drawback: for Jill and others to know what Jack means by a term—say, the term 'brutal'—they will have to presume a great deal about Jack's own private thinking. I won't, then, pursue the private alternative, but aim for public meanings. These have another kind of drawback: they require, among the disparate things people assert, deny, assume, and question in their public language, a definite collection of public truisms, a definite background that determines meaning by comprising a public normative theory of sorts. Vagueness in which statements comprise the meaning-setting public normative theory will make for vagueness in what words mean. But perhaps, with enough public consensus, this vagueness can be kept within tolerable bounds.

Interpret the community of Jack and Jill, then, as sharing an ethos, as taking for granted some fragments of normative theory. They implicitly take this theory to be on the right track, and what this theory is determines their public meanings. Our grounds for our attributions are rough and inconclusive, but on these rough grounds we attribute to them a precise normative theory. We can now ask whether this implicit theory matches Hera's, more or less: whether it matches hers in terminology and findings, both normative and naturalistic, and in its conclusions on what to do. If so, we use the best such match to translate their language into the language of Hera's theory. Hera then accepts or rejects a claim of Jack's just in case she accepts its translation. In case there is no close enough match between the theory of Jack's community and Hera's own theory, then Hera neither accepts nor rejects things Jack says; she regards his terminology as failing in its presuppositions.

The result is that Hera either agrees or disagrees, or else she *demurs*, as we can put it, in the sense of neither agreeing nor disagreeing. For any claim that Jack might make, then, we can classify three kinds of hyperstates one could reach: states of agreeing, states of disagreeing, and states of demurring. The meaning of what Jack says, insofar as it bears on questions of assent and dissent, consists of these three sets of hyperstates.

Within a community, on this account, agreement and disagreement are fairly straightforward. There will doubtless be much vagueness as to just what the implicit and partial normative theory is that sets meaning in the community. And given the meaning-setting normative theory and what the best normative theory is, it may be vague whether there is a close enough match to back a determinate translation. But for any one way of resolving these vague matters, it will be definite that when Jack asserts and Jill denies, say, that a clubbing was "brutal," they disagree.

Their disagreement will be plan-laden, in the following sense: two hyperdecided thinker-planners could agree the one with Jack and the other with Jill, and yet agree with each other on all questions naturalistic. Zeus and Hera, we can imagine, are each hyperdecided, and agree on everything naturalistic. Zeus agrees with Jack that the clubbing was "brutal", and Hera agrees with Jill that it was not. That is because their hyperplans are at odds. Hence the explanations that the two think best, explanations of how to live and why, are likewise at odds. Each of their respective putatively best explanations of how to live is close enough to the public one implicitly accepted in Jack's and Jill's community—close enough that this public explanation translates both into Zeus's terms and into Hera's. Jack's claim "The clubbing was brutal," which Jill rejects, translates into Zeus's terms as something that Zeus accepts, and translates into Hera's terms as something that Hera rejects. Sheer difference in plan, then, *could* account for accepting Jack's claim and rejecting Jill's, or the other way around. In this sense, their disagreement over whether the clubbing was "brutal" is plan-laden.

Distance and Engagement

A theory of normative kinds, suitably developed, allows members of a single community with enough consensus to engage each other straightforwardly, agreeing or disagreeing with each other. Community members share a vague presupposition: that a certain publicly accepted set of truisms couched in these terms is translatable into the language of the very best theory of what to do and why. Whether a given claim is true, false, or failing in its presuppositions depends on which theory of what to do is best—and that is itself a question of what to do (and how to feel) and why. Within-community engagement, in short, though infused with vagueness, on each resolution of that vagueness may be straightforward, plan-laden, and rooted in presupposition.

Between linguistic communities, matters will be more complex—and it will of course be vague, in space, time, and networks of social ties, where one community stops and another begins. Possible cases range from isolated communities that are almost alike in ethos to communities that differ vastly. Let us explore how the logic of the situation might work out.

Take first a case of high similarity. Two communities, suppose, set the meanings of their normative kind terms with two slightly different emerging normative theories. For simplicity, imagine the two languages are much like English and the words in the two languages are identical. Ian in one community speaks one variant language, L_i, and Jill in the other speaks another variant, L_j. Background theories T_i and T_j respectively determine meanings in the two languages, and they are close to each other, though not precisely the same.

An analysis of whether Ian and Jill engage each other's thoughts can proceed as follows: for any hyperstate h we might be in, let theory B_h be the one that in that hyperstate we would regard as the best theory of what to do and why. Some such candidate best theories B_h will be in the neighborhood of the public background theories of the two communities, and for some of these, perhaps, the translations from the two languages L_i and L_j into the language of theory B_h will be the same. Hence for some hyperdecided states h we might be in, we'll accept a claim couched in language L_i if and only if we accept its homophone in language L_j. Since, however, the meaning-setting background theories T_i and T_j of the two communities are not exactly the same, there will be exceptions to this pattern. In some hyperstates h, we'll find one meaning-setting theory T_i close enough to the best one B_i to warrant translation, though barely, and the other T_j just far enough away to stymie translation. Which hyperstates are like this will be a vague matter, but any resolution of the vagueness must countenance some such hyperstates.

The result will be not quite to allow straight disagreement, with one person accepting a statement and the other its negation. But Ian and Jill come close to disagreeing in the following sense: Grant either of the two background theories that respectively give their terms meaning; then for *most* ways the truth of what to do might be, Ian would be right just in case Jill were wrong, and vice versa. Moreover, the exceptions lie in a penumbra of vagueness as to whether the presuppositions of their judgments fail. Speakers, then, can engage each other more or less. When one of them denies the homophone of what the other asserts and one of them is right, then the other is wrong—unless the natural and normative truth lies in a narrow and vague range of possibilities, in which case the other's claim is neither right nor wrong.

Ian and Jill, I imagined, differ no more in what they say and do than might two normal members of the same community. Since, however, their two groups have no intercourse or common history, we can't tie their meanings to a single public community ethos; we must treat each group as equipped with its own ethos, though the two are much alike. Of course the phenomena that license attributing a public ethos to a community will be messy and complex—and likewise for treating people as sharing a community or not. The vagueness of these attributions can be resolved in a range of ways, which often means there will be no sharp fact of the matter whether the same public ethos sets the meanings of two people's terms, and what that ethos is. I have been studying the pure case of fully isolated groups speaking, by coincidence, with like-sounding words. From this fantastic case, conclusions will carry over to groups who talk in unlike sounds, but whose talk will seem roughly intertranslatable. In such cases, we observers can attribute rough but not precise engagement.

What, then, when the meaning-setting normative theories of two communities differ vastly? It is of course highly controversial how much ethical systems do differ among humanity, at the level of basic rationale and allowing for different views of how things work in human affairs. Here, though, I'm exploring the logic of engagement and non-engagement, and I want to ask what happens *if* two groups can vary widely and fundamentally in their ethos. It is then that talk of a "relativism of distance" seems plausible, as in the writings of Bernard Williams (*Ethics and the Limits of Philosophy*, 1985, pp. 162–165). What precisely, though, is this "relativism of distance"? Or more to the point, what logical structure of non-engagement results from a wide gap in ethos? One way to approach the question is to ask what emerges from the apparatus of hyperstates and the theory of normative kinds. We can then ask if the resulting analysis is plausible.

Jill and Kalicles, imagine, are from communities vastly far apart in their ethos; Jill's is like ours, and Kalicles's is a Bronze Age chieftaincy. Can they engage each other's thoughts, agreeing or disagreeing in their normative judgments? Each community has its public normative theory—though as always, what theory this is will be vague. The first thing to note is that the theory of Jill's community has somehow developed in response to modern life, and the theory of Kalicles's in response to a Bronze Age life. Normally Jill's judgments concern one set of circumstances and Kalicles's another, and so Jill and Kalicles won't agree or disagree with each other on any one question. Normally we won't need to think about what to do, hypothetically, in surroundings vastly different from any we'll ever meet. This is the chief form that a non-engagement of distance will take: common questions don't arise.

What, though, when Jill dips into the *Iliad?* She then might apply her theory to Bronze Age life, and Kalicles, if fantastically he were told of incidents of modern life, might judge them in his own terms. Neither, though, will have thought seriously about the life of the other. For Jill's thoughts on archaic life to be well founded, she must learn deeply how Kalicles and his fellows experience life and what the social possibilities of his milieu are.

Hera the hyperdecided has a view of what to do and why in Jill's circumstances and what to do and why in Kalicles's. The best normative theory for one set of circumstances, on her view, might be quite different from the best normative theory for the other. True, a common, overarching rationale might cover both and provide the deepest possible explanation of what to do and why—but this might not be the best theory for everyday use. Jill, then, if she does work toward a serious understanding of Bronze Age life and thinks seriously on what to do in those circumstances, may find new terms for couching her normative explanations.

She might then have views enough like Kalicles's and his fellows' that she can simply adopt their language, agreeing and disagreeing with them in their own terms. But more likely, her views on how to cope with hierarchy, war, sex roles, slavery, and the like in their milieu might remain far from theirs, even when she has thought deeply about these questions. Jill and Kalicles are then addressing the very same normative questions and disagreeing in the answers they give.

Jill's views of what to do and why in the Bronze Age milieu may then fail to engage theirs in a further way. They put their views in "thick" terms, and these terms, according to Jill, fail to signify genuine normative kinds—even when applied to their own, archaic way of life. Kalicles's presuppositions fail, she will think. (And Kalicles might say the like of Jill, if somehow he came to master the theory of interpretation we are now devising.) Jill and Kalicles each have a language for thinking what to do if in Kalicles's shoes and why; these languages may each be full of "thick" terms that purport to signify normative kinds that Kalicles's encounters in his life. Thinking in these languages, Jill and Kalicles fail to engage in their "thick" judgments when the following holds: consider those hyperstates that get all natural facts right—

including of course the natural facts of Kalicles's milieu. For no such hyperstate would an observer in that state find that both Jill's and Kalicles's languages translate into the language of the best theory of what to do and why in Kalicles's shoes.

In that case, Jill is committed to demurring to everything that Kalicles couches in local "thick" terms. They can agree or disagree in "thin" terms on what to do in circumstances that Kalicles might encounter, but their explanations of why won't engage each other.

Between the extremes of complete or near-complete engagement and total non-engagement are complex, intermediate cases. With agreement, disagreement, and failure to engage, we are dealing, in effect, with a three-valued logic, and between two propositions in three-valued logic are 2^9 logical relations—512 as opposed to 16 for two-valued logic. Clearly I'd better not try to say much on this subject—though the scheme of hyperdecided states gives us the materials to explore these relations. Vaguely, we can say this: we can hope for a degree of engagement. We'll have it if, on some scheme of interpretation we've found between our two languages, it is plausible, given what we both think so far, that the things we say succeed in being true or false, and what you say is true if and only if corresponding things that I say are true. (Again, all this gets cashed out in terms of the hyperstates in which one would accept it.)

Solving the Frege-Geach problem for a fact-plan language allows normative concept-building, and this will parallel, to a degree, concept-building in science. On the hypothesis that familiar normative language is fact-plan language, such a line of thought accounts for those "thick" normative concepts that seem to break down a strict separation of norms and natural facts. As with the natural kinds countenanced in a science, so with normative kinds: our thoughts on how to live invoke these kinds. In this regard, Sayre-McCord's proposal is right, and an important step forward in the theory of normative concepts. I have offered a different account from his, though, of how a "thick" term can come to signify a normative kind. My story is presuppositional: the ethos of a community offers presuppositions on which thick meanings depend. These presuppositions can fail, and both radicals within a group and alien observers may conclude that they indeed do fail. Whether presuppositions hold or fail is a question of how to live and why—how to live if in a certain community, raised in its ethos.

In a hyperstate one would have a view on all such matters. As before, hyperstates offer a way to analyze meanings. The meaning of a claim is a matter of which hyperstates agree with it, which disagree, and which don't engage. Where "thick" terms purport to signify normative kinds, radicals within and observers without can sometimes agree or disagree with claims couched in those terms. Often, however, they must demur.

The truth in relativism, if I am right, is not quite relativistic. It makes perfect sense, I claim, to agree or disagree on how to live in exotic climes and times. Such questions, though, are immensely hard, and no feasible regimen of thinking oneself into the circumstances of another may be adequate. We should be diffident, then, in such judgments— and that is one truth behind relativism. If we do succeed, though, we'll engage on "thin" questions of what to do if in their shoes; we'll agree or disagree with their views on these questions. We may not engage, however, on questions of why. Explanations of why to act one way and not another will likely be couched in terms thick with plan-laden presupposition. Those who reject the presuppositions can only demur from claims made in those terms. This gives us another truth behind relativism—that often, with the claims of those far away, we must demur. That's nothing special about distance, however, or not invariably. A homegrown normative radical may be in the same position.

All this leaves a deeper question. All I have said supposes that disagreement in plan can span great distances of culture and circumstance. I have argued briefly that there is such a thing as interpersonal disagreement in plan—because we must put our heads together to think how to live. I have not, however, inquired here whether this rationale extends across great cultural distances.[2] I'll argue that it does, but only later. In the meantime, we must note this issue as pointing, perhaps, to the most important truth behind relativism.[3]

2. Participants in my Seminar in Ethics for the fall of 2000, and Nishiten Shah in particular, have pressed me on this.

3. Substantial parts of Part III of my *Wise Choices, Apt Feelings* were devoted to exploring the structure of views one might have on relativism or contentions in its neighborhood. I do not now repudiate anything I said on these matters, but neither have I ever felt confident of my treatment of them.

~ 9

What to Say about the Thing to Do: The Expressivistic Turn and What It Gains Us

$\mathcal{T}$HIS BOOK so far has been chiefly an exploration of possibilities. If my arguments have been correct, then a plan-laden language is at least possible—and indeed everyone who thinks what to do is committed to its concepts. As for our actual normative concepts, the family of concepts that seem somehow "fraught with ought" and hence puzzling, I have sketched a few ways that such concepts might be explained as plan-laden, though complexly. But the biggest possibility, of course, the hypothesis implicit in all this work, is that our actual normative concepts *do* work in some of these ways.

If that were so, it would offer a kind of explanation of these concepts. The explanation would not be straight or direct, for from this hypothesis follows the central thesis of non-naturalists: that straight definitions of normative terms cannot be built entirely of non-normative materials. The hypothesis would, though, explain why planners must have such concepts—or at least are committed to the intelligibility of such concepts. In that sense, it shows these concepts inescapable if we are to live our lives in any way that is even remotely human. It shows how these concepts fit into living a human life, a life of thinking what to do. It shows these concepts intelligible, since questions of what to do are intelligible. The hypothesis explains too the many ways that normative concepts have seemed anomalous: their role lies not in understanding the natural world, but in engaging it.

179

I end this part of the book with some afterthoughts on such a style of explanation. Suppose an account like mine is correct. Does it succeed in explaining the place of *ought*s in nature? Or does it perhaps just amount to plain old non-naturalism in less perspicuous terms? Does it let us engage in normative inquiry and take what we are doing at face value, or is it, despite all I say, a renunciation of all genuine normative thinking?

A look at these questions will leave much unexplored. I have been testing only a few aspects of the hypothesis that familiar normative concepts work as I suggest. Mostly I have asked about logical and epistemological features of our concepts; the hypothesis, I have argued at length, mimics realism for these concepts. I have left unexplored the place of moral sentiments in moral concepts, and of other kinds of feelings in normative concepts more generally. I haven't much considered specific normative terms in English or other natural languages and how they work. These questions interest me immensely, and I have explored some of them in other places—but this is not the book for extensive investigations along these lines.[1]

Truth, Fact, Belief

The expressivist starts with states of mind, and uses these to elucidate normative beliefs or seeming beliefs. Emotivists like Ayer and Stevenson, for instance, start with feelings or attitudes; Hare starts with universal preferences.[2] In *Wise Choices, Apt Feelings*, I myself started, as a first approximation, with states of norm acceptance. In this book I speak of states of contingency planning, along with other states—mixed fact-plan states, as I called them—that can be in agreement or disagreement with straight combinations of planning and naturalistic belief. At the outset, in any expressivist's scheme, the initial states of mind are explained not as beliefs with such-and-such content, but in

1. I discuss moral concepts in "Moral Concepts: Substance and Sentiment" (1992) and "Moral Concepts and Justified Feelings" (1993); see also "Thick Concepts" (1992), and for the concept of good, "Preference and Preferability" (1998).

2. Ayer, *Language, Truth and Logic* (1936), chap. 6; Stevenson, "Emotive Theory" (1937). For Hare, I have in mind especially his formulations in *Moral Thinking* (1981); see my interpretation in "Hare's Analysis" (1988) and Hare's "Comments" (1988).

some other way. They are explained psychologically, as sentiments or attitudes, perhaps, or as universal preferences, states of norm-acceptance—or states of planning.[3] The expressivist then tries to show that these states of mind act much like beliefs: it is as if they were beliefs with a special kind of content. Some expressivists at this point debunk; the story, they say, shows why these seeming beliefs are mere pseudo-beliefs.[4] A quasi-realist like me stresses the vast extent of the parallel between normative convictions, as they emerge in the theory, and the plainest cases of belief in realistic content.

Are normative convictions, then, genuine beliefs, or are they pseudo-beliefs? Are they true or false in any substantial way? Are there genuine normative facts "out there" in the world? At the beginning of the book I evaded these questions. I helped myself to natural facts and naturalistic beliefs, but didn't say if natural facts are the only real facts in the world. I proceeded, I hope, to show a vast parallel between plan-laden judgments and naturalistic beliefs—though plan-laden judgments, I insisted, are not themselves naturalistic beliefs. Are normative judgments, then, beliefs of another kind, beliefs in special, non-natural facts? Or are they states of mind of another kind, similar to beliefs in many ways but not themselves beliefs?[5]

One definite thing I did have to say on this. Once we distinguish properties from concepts, we have no need for non-natural properties to help us explain the special features of normative concepts. Distinguish two families, then, the property family and the concept family. States of affairs are built from properties, relations, and the like, whereas thoughts are built from concepts: property concepts and relation concepts, among others. Only the thoughts and concepts and not states of affairs, I have been saying, need involve anything non-naturalistic. There is no such thing as a specially normative state of affairs; all states of affairs are natural. We do, though, have normative thoughts, and they are distinct from naturalistic thoughts.

3. I think of my shift from norm-acceptance to planning not as a change of position but as a shift of expository purposes. In 1990 in *Wise Choices*, I focused on actual human beings and the psychology of our normative judgments. In this work, I have been looking at ideally coherent planners and exploring concepts that such planners are committed to. Only at the point we have now reached do I ask what all this might have to do with our own, human concepts and the human psyche.

4. Ayer, *Language, Truth and Logic* (1936), chap. 6, is a prime example.

5. Scanlon, for instance, in *What We Owe* (1998), puts the issue this way (p. 58).

Are there, then, normative facts? It depends, in the first place, on what "facts" are meant to be. Is there a fact that water is H_2O, distinct from the trivial fact that water is water? There is just one state of affairs, the trivial one, but two distinct thoughts we can have. (So we can say in the terms I introduced in Chapter 6.) By "facts", then, do we mean states of affairs that obtain—so that there's just one fact here, the fact that water is water? Then clearly, if my quasi-realism is correct, there aren't distinctively normative facts, only naturalistic facts. Or by "facts" do we mean true thoughts, so that it's one fact that water is water and another that water is H_2O? If so, then perhaps we have seen that there are, after all, normative facts distinct from all natural facts. I'll use the term 'fact' in this second sense, so that a "fact" is a true thought, and look to the possibility of normative facts in this sense.

Are these just pseudo-facts, incapable of real truth and falsehood? Are beliefs in them pseudo-beliefs, states of mind distinct from beliefs, which we mistake for genuine beliefs? I took no stand on this at the outset, but what do I now conclude? I still weasel: I say that I need to understand the questions. Explain to me "real facts", "substantial truth", and "genuine belief", and I can think how to answer. You may well succeed, I allow, in explaining these matters. In *Wise Choices, Apt Feelings*, I took it that they could be explained and attempted part of the explanation myself.[6] In this book, though, I haven't supposed either that I got this part of the story right or that I didn't; whether I did would require a thorough reexamination. I do think now, though, that we should at least find these distinctions suspect, and not help ourselves to them until they have been explained and vindicated, to some degree at least. When they are—by someone else or by me—I must then return to these questions of whether normative facts, truth, and belief are pseudo or genuine.

Suppose instead that minimalists are right for truth, for facts, and for belief: there is no more to claiming "It's true that pain is bad" than to claim that pain is bad; the fact that pain is bad just consists in pain's being bad; to believe that pain is bad is just to accept that it is.[7] Then it's

6. In Chapter 6 of *Wise Choices* (1990), I argued that normative judgments are not natural or artificial representations. I also said that according to my theory, "to call something rational is not to state a matter of fact" (p. 8), and I rejected "Platonism" (p. 154).

7. See, for instance, Horwich, *Truth* (1990, 1998).

true that pain is bad and it's a fact that pain is bad—so long as, indeed, pain is bad. I genuinely believe that pain is bad, and my expressivistic theory, filled out, explains what believing this consists in.

Expressivistic quasi-realism, though, if it succeeds, might show something special and important that distinguishes normative facts. We can explain belief in them, it might be said, without helping ourselves to normative facts at the outset, to facts of what's good or bad, or to facts of what is the thing to do. This would contrast with a standard realist's mode of explanation—appropriate, in my view, for naturalistic thoughts. To explain belief in natural fact adequately, we must assume a natural world of which we are a part. We must start with a realm of naturalistic facts. To explain belief in normative facts, in contrast, we need not start with a realm of normative facts—or so it might be claimed. I'll touch later in this chapter on whether such a claim can be made good, and what expressivism looks like if it can't.

Is my theory, then, a form of non-cognitivism? I used to say that it is: it proceeds from materials accepted by classic non-cognitivists like Ayer and Stevenson, and exploits their central explanatory devices. I began to find, though, that when other philosophers declared themselves "cognitivists" or "moral realists", the touchstones they offered were things that I accepted or that my conceptual explanations at least allowed. Normative claims can be true or false, independent of our accepting them. To accept this is, roughly, to restrict your plans to ones that are not contingent on which plans, in the contingencies you plan for, you would accept if that contingency obtained.[8] Normative questions have a right answer (Dworkin, "Objectivity and Truth," 1996, p. 89): where the question has definite plan-laden content, this doctrine of a right answer follows from my device of hyperdecided states of mind. In any such state, after all, you would be convinced of what the right answer was, and so think that the question does have a right answer. "Morality," says Ronald Dworkin, "is a distinct, independent dimension of our experience, and it exercises its own sovereignty" ("Objectivity and Truth," 1996, p. 128). Not quite "of our experience", I would quibble: moral claims involve *oughts* that aren't just a matter of how our experience goes; we can experience fervor and conviction and

8. See Blackburn, "Errors" (1985), p. 9, and my *Wise Choices* (1990), pp. 164–166.

be wrong. Dworkin's words, though, presumably make Hume's point, that moral conclusions don't follow analytically from non-normative premises—along with the claim that we can know morality or some of it. Like other expressivists, I began with Hume's point and developed a theory to explain it. I spend the final chapters of this book exploring claims to normative knowledge. We can't consistently plan, I claim, and deny that in some important senses, normative knowledge can be had. In one sense, then, I am a "non-cognitivist": I draw from central aspects of that tradition. This may not lead me, though, to anything that staunch "cognitivists" deny.

What's to Dispute?

If cognitivists won't deny my contentions, then I'm left with a di-lemma—or so a number of writers claim. So is any quasi-realistic ex-pressivist. Starting as expressivists, we mimic normative realism, or try to. We're then damned if we fail, of course, but we're damned too, the claim goes, if we succeed. For if we succeed, then where is any dis-tinctive metanormative position? What's new? What are we rejecting? Ronald Dworkin, for instance, tells us that if expressivists succeed in reinterpreting claims to normative objectivity, they cannot then stop the process, "before it embraces and therefore destroys their own non-cognitivism" (p. 110). For in that case we expressivists can't deny any-thing in the realism we attack.

This seems a strange worry. After all, a single pattern can be ex-plained in more than one way, and one such explanation may be better than another. My own theory explains much that non-naturalism takes as brute features of the non-natural realm. If the good exercises its own sovereignty, why does goodness depend on natural fact? That's just the way the concept works, the non-naturalist must be reduced to saying: it just does. Or if he defines 'good' in terms of something like 'ought' or 'a reason', he must then rest his answers on some other brute finding: say, that oughts or reasons supervene on the natural. And why, as I keep asking, does what we ought to do matter for what to do? Non-natural-ism lets us ask this question but offers no answer; I say that the concept of ought just *is* the concept of what to do. Why do we, in a natural world, have non-naturalistic concepts? Because we think what to do, I explain. Many claims of non-naturalists I can interpret as correct on my theory or meaningful on my theory—but that doesn't make my theory and theirs equivalent in what they explain and how they explain it.

The bulk of explanations non-naturalists offer, to be sure, are left untouched by my quasi-realism. Mostly non-naturalists explain, like the rest of us, why we ought to do some things and not do others, why some acts are vicious and others admirable, and other such substantive normative puzzles. Expressivism, I keep stressing, is not a substantive theory of what's right and wrong, what's good and bad, and what makes it that way. It leaves us to treat substantive matters in their own terms and explain them in their own terms.

Does an expressivist, then, deny anything that other normative theorists maintain? I am of course denying that normative concepts are naturalistic concepts, explainable in the same way as psychological concepts, sociological concepts, or the like. What, though, of normative realists who join me in this denial? I've been using the old-fashioned term 'non-naturalist' to sweep in a wide range of current normative theorists—many of whom might repudiate the label. Non-naturalists, as I mean the term, join me in denying that normative concepts are naturalistic concepts. They think, though, unlike me, that explanations of normative concepts come to an end with basic normative concepts that we must leave unexplained, or explain just in terms of each other. All we can do, by way of explaining, is to rely on our prior mastery of these concepts and clarify and refine this mastery. Now I myself agree with this for *straight* analyses of normative concepts. I claim too, though, that we can explain much obliquely, characterizing normative concepts by describing independently the states of mind that employ them. We can of course also characterize normative beliefs, as do non-naturalists, in terms of their content. We can identify a normative judgment as the belief that such-and-such—say, as the belief that one ought to shun pain, or that politicians are all sleazy. But this, I am saying, is not the only way to characterize normative beliefs; we can also explain them as plan-laden judgments, or as carrying plan-laden presuppositions. This yields further insight.

What, then, is at issue between me and a theorist who treats oughts or reasons as primitive? Perhaps nothing. I can accept much of what such a theorist says, and this theorist, I'm claiming, can go on saying pretty much what he does and accept all that I say. If he agrees too that I have offered a further kind of explanation of normative concepts, from a different angle, then our views have converged. Such a convergence is a happy ending, not a worry: if thinkers with different starting points arrive at like conclusions, that lends support to the conclusions.

Non-naturalists, though, as I mean the term, also deny that the expressivist's mode of explanation works, that it provides a correct explanation of normative concepts. In this, of course, they and I disagree. Our disagreement, though, might be on either or both of two distinct issues. My central proposal we might call the *internal adequacy thesis.* Divide claims on normative matters and claims about normative concepts into those which are *internal* to normative thinking, on the one hand, and, on the other hand, *external* claims, commentary on normative thinking, concepts, and their truth-makers that aren't part of normative thinking itself or equivalent to it. The hypothesis of this book then counts as external. It is part of my quasi-realism, though, to contend that many claims that might seem external can be interpreted as internal—and that my hypothesis explains them as intelligible. "Normative facts are out there, subsisting independently of us" might just be a fancy way of putting an aspect of a plan for living. Return to a specific instance of this claim, "It's a normative fact, out there independent of us, that one ought not to kick dogs for fun."[9] Accepting this might amount to planning to avoid kicking dogs for fun, planning this even for the contingency of being someone who approves of such fun, and who is surrounded by people who approve. The claim of independence, then, turns out to be internal to normative thinking—though arrayed in sumptuous rhetoric.[10]

A theory of normative concepts, let us say, is *internally adequate* if it accounts for everything internal to normative thinking, or everything internal that is intelligible. Now I don't, of course, think that my theory of normative concepts as I've developed it is internally adequate, entirely and completely. The theory is work in progress. I do, though, propose that my theory of plan-laden concepts is on the right track to explaining normative concepts, that some explanation along these lines would be internally adequate. Let the *internal adequacy thesis* be this claim.

9. Again, the example is Blackburn's, "Errors" (1985), p. 9.
10. Dworkin maintains this strongly; see "Objectivity and Truth" (1996), p. 109. On this point, then, he, Blackburn, and I agree—as we do on many other points. See Blackburn, "Blackburn Reviews Dworkin" (1996).

A non-naturalist may reject the internal adequacy thesis; in that case, I tentatively disagree. Non-naturalists, though, may divide on a further, hypothetical issue. Suppose the internal adequacy thesis is correct, and some version of expressivistic theory is internally adequate to normative thinking. Still, some non-naturalists might say, an expressivistic theory must leave something out. Others might say that internal adequacy is all that a theory of normative concepts needs.

Ronald Dworkin formulates a set of contentions in terms much like these. He thinks that if the internal adequacy thesis is correct, then expressivism fails to constitute an independent metanormative position. This contention I have already laid forth and answered. Dworkin bases his contention, though, on a thesis that merits examination on its own. An expressivist like Blackburn, says Dworkin, "has no way of separating the supposedly external mistakes the projectivist corrects in the name of naturalism from the internal convictions he embraces as part of the 'business' of morality" ("Objectivity and Truth," 1996, p. 112). Internal claims, then, are the only claims that non-naturalists have ever made that expressivists could intelligibly find problematic. It follows that if the expressivist accepts the non-naturalist's internal claims on normative matters, then there is nothing left in non-naturalism for an expressivist to deny. Internal adequacy itself is, to be sure, a genuine issue—though in Dworkin's view, inconsequential. (For again, if the internal adequacy thesis is false, then expressivism is wrong, and if it is true, thinks Dworkin, then expressivism destroys itself.) But he denies that, apart from this, expressivists can object to anything in non-naturalism. No non-naturalist has ever maintained an external thesis at odds with expressivism, and no non-naturalist could. There is nothing in non-naturalism, then, for an expressivist to deny.

Now it matters little for my purposes whether this is so. I am in any case offering a different kind of explanation from what the non-naturalist offers. Clearly, though, there is a further, non-internal claim that a non-naturalist *could* make, an intelligible claim that I do deny. This claim is hypothetical: that even if the internal adequacy thesis is right, even if some form of expressivism is adequate internally to normative concepts, it leaves something out. Call this the *external inadequacy thesis*. It is an existential claim and as such, clearly intelligible, whether right or wrong—and it is intelligible for me to reject it. This isn't a claim that Dworkin himself makes; he stoutly rejects any external inadequacy thesis. But it is a claim that a non-naturalist at least *might* make, and it's worth taking the trouble to reject it.

Has any non-naturalist ever maintained the external inadequacy thesis, this thesis that I reject? Perhaps not. The thesis is subtle; to understand it one must conceive of the internal adequacy thesis and ask what happens if it is correct. Older non-naturalists had never heard of expressivism, and so couldn't formulate the internal adequacy thesis. Current non-naturalists are often most concerned to attack the internal adequacy thesis, not to inquire what to think if we find it true. Few if any non-naturalists beyond Dworkin, then, have conceived the external inadequacy thesis and taken a stand on it. But if they did, I would guess, some would find it plausible. Dworkin and I both reject it, but that doesn't mean there's nothing to reject.

I have been asking whether, when expressivism so mimics non-naturalism, anything is at issue between a non-naturalist and an expressivist. I have found three points of contention. First there is the internal adequacy thesis: it is a live question whether any form of expressivism can be internally adequate to normative concepts. Second, if the internal adequacy thesis is right, there is the issue of best explanation: what best explains the internal phenomena on which non-naturalists and expressivists agree? Third there is the issue of external inadequacy: if the internal adequacy thesis is right, does expressivism still leave something out? On the right track or not, this book makes claims that others might deny.

Non-Naturalism by Theft

Another way that expressivism might fail to be a genuine alternative to non-naturalism would be if it pilfers the materials of non-naturalism at the start. T. M. Scanlon (*What We Owe*, 1998, pp. 58–59) suggests that I may have done something like this. As his own basic normative notion he takes being a *reason*, which is "counting in favor" of something. The term 'counting' may be a little misleading, I'd think, since it suggests a kind of arbitrariness, as what "counts" as a city, say, is a matter of stipulation. We might say that a reason "weighs" in favor of something— though that could be taken as carrying another suggestion that Scanlon rejects, that reasons always operate as a kind of resolution of forces pushing for one course of action or another. I myself welcome the concept of a reason as counting or weighing in favor. In this book, I have instead used the notions of being *okay* to do or being *the thing* to do as the basic planning notions to be explained. Clearly, though, along with these we need the concept of being a *reason*. Being the thing to do, after all, is a matter of how reasons work out, of what a person has reason all told to do. Contingency planning—planning what to do—involves, often or always, weighing factors for or against various courses of action in various contingencies. To do so is to regard these factors as reasons, and so we can run the expressivist's stratagems of explanation on the notion of being a reason.

Scanlon obliquely raises the question, though, of whether this gains us any independent understanding.[11] To say that R is a reason to do X, I said in *Wise Choices*, is to "say to treat R as weighing in favor of doing X".[12] Notes Scanlon, "This analysis does not avoid reliance on the idea of being a reason, or 'counting in favor of,' since that very notion, in the form of 'weighing in favor of,' appears in the characterization of the attitude he describes." That isn't a fault, thinks Scanlon, "but it is relevant to an assessment of exactly what that account is supposed to accomplish" (*What We Owe*, 1998, p. 58).

To understand the state of mind, "treating R as weighing in favor of doing X", Scanlon is saying, we must already understand what it is for R *really* to weigh in favor of doing X—and that is just for R to be a reason to do X. We thus haven't explained the concept of being a reason; we have simply helped ourselves to it. The expressivist helps himself to all that a non-naturalistic realist needs.

Now all this would be true enough if "treating R as weighing in favor of doing X" were explained as, somehow, acting as if one believed that R really does weigh in favor of X. But whether or not the phrase I used lends itself to that reading, another reading is also available—one that suits the expressivist's direction of explanation. To "treat R as weighing in favor of doing X" is to plan in a certain way, to figure what to do in a

11. Part of the issue, as Scanlon presents it, is whether "taking X to count in favor of doing A" is a belief, as opposed to "a special judgment-sensitive attitude" that is not a belief (p. 58). That, as I have said, did fit my own understanding of the issues in *Wise Choices, Apt Feelings*, but doesn't do so in this book. Here I address a different strain in Scanlon's commentary.

12. Quoted by Scanlon (p. 58) from my *Wise Choices* (p. 163). In *Wise Choices* I speak of "accepting norms"; I skip that aspect of my formulation in this discussion, since I'm not using it in the present book.

certain way, a way we can describe without helping ourselves to the notion of being a reason. It is to weigh consideration R toward doing X.
We start, then, with a psychological notion, a person's weighing a consideration toward taking a course of action. This contrasts with a notion that sounds much the same but is normative: Suppose, in deciding,
I say to myself, "R weighs toward doing X." I'm not then describing my
process of deliberation; I'm deliberating. I'm saying, in effect, that R is
a reason to do X. This latter, normative notion is the one I seek to explain. I explain it, obliquely, in terms of the psychological notion of a
person's weighing R in favor of doing X. That it counts in favor is a
normative thought, a thought that I can have in deliberating; that I
count it in favor is, in contrast, a psychological thought about the kind
of state of mind with which an expressivist's analysis starts.

What, then, is this purported state of mind, weighing factor R in favor of doing X? It is calculating what to do on a certain pattern, a pattern we could program a robot to mimic. Let the robot code aspects of
its circumstances (factors), and code alternative movements that it is
wired up to have emerge from its calculations (acts). This talk of "cod-
ing" ascribes content to configurations of electric charge and the like in
the robot's circuitry, but let's take this much interpretation as already
accomplished; our question is how to go from these ascriptions to ascriptions of its weighing factors in favor of alternatives. The robot,
imagine, attaches number representations (call them "indices"), posi-
tive and negative, to factor-act pairs. It then totals up the indices for
each act, and performs the act with the highest resulting sum. If the robot is set up in this way, then the index it attaches to factor-act pair R,X
then constitutes the degree to which it weighs factor R toward doing X.

We ourselves can settle what to do in a like way, not toting up num-
bers explicitly perhaps, but proceeding as if we did. When we do, say I,
we are *weighing* considerations. Regarding features of our situation as
reasons to do one act as opposed to another, my theory is, consists in
such weighing. Two distinct notions are thus in play: the psychological
notion of weighing a factor in one's planning, and the normative one of
something's being a reason. An expressivistic style of explanation can
start with the psychological notion, and explain the normative one in
terms of it. It explains the concept of being a reason to do X via the
state of mind, in effect, of believing it to be a reason to do X. This state

of mind is explained as one's weighing that factor in favor of doing X—and to do this is to form contingency plans on a certain pattern.

It is also possible, of course, just to start with the concept of being a reason, and explain other normative concepts in terms of it. That is what Scanlon does: he proceeds as a non-naturalist (in my terminology) who takes the concept of being a reason as primitive. (As Scanlon recognizes, he also needs the concept of there being most reason all told to do X; that amounts to my primitive concept of X's being the thing to do.) Proceeding this way must be possible, if my own account of normative judgment is right, for on my theory, the concept of being a reason is one to which we are all committed. Again, though, by proceeding in the reverse direction, the expressivist explains phenomena that non-naturalism, on its own, treats just as unexplained normative facts.

Normative Meanings

What kind of explanation of meanings is the expressivist offering? What, according to me, is the place of *ought*s in a world of natural fact? I've had complex things to say on this broad question, but mostly I've answered obliquely—looking to normative thoughts and normative meanings. That raises a question in turn: what of the place of these? What, in a world of natural fact, is the place of thought and meaning? On this question hinges a great deal for the kind of explanation of normative concepts that I hypothesize in this book.

One kind of response I might attempt is strictly naturalistic. The states of affairs in which thoughts and meanings figure are strictly natural states of affairs. Moreover, when it comes to our concepts of these states of affairs—to thoughts and meanings conceived as thoughts and meanings—these concepts are strictly naturalistic. Although oughts and values, I've been stressing, aren't to be explained naturalistically, thoughts and claims about oughts indeed are to be so explained. That's one possibility.

A major current of philosophical thought, however, maintains that this won't do. "Meaning is normative," as a slogan goes. I interpret this as meaning things like the following: the concept of what a term means is itself a normative concept, "fraught with ought". Claims about meaning are thus covert *ought* claims. Meaning is a matter not of what people do say, or what they are disposed to say, but of what they *ought* to say—or perhaps, of what it would be *correct* to say, or what *commitments* saying it carries. Likewise for mental content: the concept of what a person is thinking is itself a normative concept.

Much theorizing along these lines has stemmed, during the past two decades or so, from Saul Kripke's presentation of Wittgenstein on following a rule (Kripke, *Wittgenstein*, 1982). The issues involved in this debate have proved daunting, and there is as of yet no consensus on whether meaning is normative and if so in what sense.[13] I myself have written on the subject ("Meaning and Normativity," 1994; "Thought, Norms," 1996), but have not discovered a position on the subject that convinces me. In this book I'll say very little on this subject; I won't try to explain the issues involved, or say why some philosophers are drawn to the view that meaning is in some important sense normative and others reject any such view. Still, what if some claim that "meaning is normative" is correct? Where would that leave the explanatory project in this book?

One aspect of the naturalism that I've been advocating survives unchanged. There are no peculiarly normative, non-natural properties, I've insisted—though there are natural properties of special normative interest. That was part of my emendation of Moore in Chapter 2: Moore, I said, had no need of non-natural properties to explain what's at issue in normative disputes; what he needed was non-naturalistic concepts. If the concepts of meaning and of mental content are normative concepts, still the *properties* of meaning or thinking that such-and-such can be natural properties.

Expressivism, though, is supposed to explain what's special about normative concepts. The expressivist's stratagems are meant to obviate the need for non-naturalistic mumbo-jumbo. Now, though, we find that to talk in terms of meanings at all, we've got to help ourselves to *ought* concepts. The concept of meaning itself, after all, we are now supposing, is infused with the concept of *ought*. What has the expres-

---

13. Among those who accept some version of a "normativity of meaning" thesis are McDowell, "Wittgenstein" (1984), Boghossian, "Rule-Following" (1989), Brandom, *Making It Explicit* (1994), and Lance and O'Leary-Hawthorne, *Grammar of Meaning* (1997), pp. 55–65. For critiques of the thesis, see Horwich, *Meaning* (1998), chap. 8, and Millar, "Normativity of Meaning" (2002).

sivistic turn now gained us? Normative concepts can't be given a straight analysis in naturalistic terms, expressivists have always insisted. If concepts of meaning and mental content are normative, it follows that they, like any other normative concept, thwart any straight naturalistic analysis. The expressivist now turns to oblique analysis: we elucidate the concepts of ought, meaning, and mental content by saying what it is to *judge* or *believe* that a person ought to do something, or that he means such-and-such or that he is thinking that such-and-such. But this oblique analysis itself, it is now said, helps itself to *oughts*—and *ought* was the very concept we initially found mysterious. What has been gained?

The structure of an expressivist's explanations, if all this is right, will have to be much like that set forth by Robert Brandom in his book *Making It Explicit* (1994).[14] It must be expressivism with a regress: according to Brandom, "It's norms all the way down" (p. 44). In the terms I have developed in this book, Brandom's regress-style expressivism may amount to the following (though how much of what I say here fits Brandom's theses and intentions I won't try to assess). First, as I've been saying all along, for any normative claim *C*, there is a natural state of affairs that *C*'s obtaining would consist in. And as I've been maintaining, we can't translate claim *C* into naturalistic terms, but we can elucidate the claim by taking an expressivistic turn, saying what psychic state *P* would amount to accepting claim *C*. (This state *P* is a state of planning, according to me.) Now, though, comes the regress: to specify state *P* as a psychic state, we must employ normative terms—and so we are now left with a new normative characterization to explain; call it *C**. Now the process starts again: there's a natural state of affairs that *C**'s obtaining would consist in, and a psychic state *P** that would amount to accepting claim *C**. State *P** gets a normative characterization *C***, to which the same kind of analysis applies. And so on.

14. For my interpretation of Brandom, see "Thought, Norms" (1996). Brandom tries to work without an analytic-synthetic distinction, which makes it difficult to see what the thesis that "meaning is normative" could come to. I myself don't find an analytic-synthetic distinction unproblematic; that's central to the matters that puzzle me as I try to come to a view on whether "meaning is normative". I'll present Brandom, though, as if he did find claims about what a concept consists in intelligible. Brandom also maintains that mental content is somehow a social matter; I'll ignore this thesis, which I claim is independent of what Brandom has to say about the normativity of meaning. (See my "Thought, Norms," 1996.)

This regress never strikes non-normative bedrock. One kind of claim that a naturalistic expressivist makes, then, a regress-style expressivist can't make. In a sense, says the naturalistic expressivist, the world is an entirely natural world. True, there are normative truths, and those truths aren't naturalistic. But when we explain their meaning obliquely, we specify—recognizing only naturalistic truths—what believing normative truths consists in. Naturalistic truths are the only ones we must start out recognizing in order to explain, in one way or another, everything. In that sense, the basic fabric of the world is naturalistic. The regress-style expressivist can't say this: by this test for what the basic fabric of the world includes, *ought*s and naturalistic *is*s qualify equally.

I talk more in the next section about what the expressivistic turn gains us. For now, my question is how plan and naturalistic fact interact, if the regress-style expressivist is right. Here is the picture for my own version of expressivism: we start our thinking both with naturalistic beliefs and with plans—including plans for what to believe and when. When we think of ourselves and others as thinkers, we're not purely conceiving of ourselves in naturalistic terms; we're also planning our thinking. To believe that we are planning our thinking is in turn not only to conceive ourselves naturalistically but also to plan our thinking. We can say in naturalistic terms what planning consists in, but to conceive planning as planning is, among other things, to plan. Conceiving ourselves as thinkers and planners, then, intertwines naturalistic belief and plan.

What plans of mine are involved in thinking of you as a thinker and planner? I don't have a story along these lines worked out, and I'm quite unsure whether any such story will turn out to be cogent. In this book, I've taken the key to meaning to lie not in oughts but in agreement and disagreement: we know what a thought is when we know what it would be to agree with it or disagree with it. That leaves us to ask about the place of agreement and disagreement in a world of natural fact—and I leave this as a problem for other occasions.

Explaining with States of Mind

Expressivism, as I keep saying, consists in a pattern of explanation. The explanation starts with a state of mind, which is described in some way other than in terms of its content as a belief; it then identifies that state of mind with normative belief. The state of mind may perhaps be characterized naturalistically, as I tried to do in *Wise Choices, Apt Feelings* when I sketched a speculative psychological theory of accepting norms. It hasn't been part of this book to explore further this naturalistic project. Mostly I accept what I said in that earlier work, and I haven't much been exploring what modifications, if any, I should make to what I then said. I have argued in this chapter that weighing considerations is naturalistically recognizable: we can identify thoughts about reasons by their role in leading to action. I have also touched on how the account might look if "meaning is normative," so that claims about planning states of mind can't be put in purely naturalistic terms. These questions, however, have not been a major topic of this book. Instead, I have developed my starting slogan, "Thinking what one ought to do is thinking what to do." I have explained one kind of thinking in terms of another. Thinking what to do I have treated as something we recognize "from the inside"; I address us as beings who do the sort of thing I'm describing. True, we can recognize planning naturalistically, in that we could recognize a robot that was in effect engaged in planning. It's also true that a major unsettled issue is whether thoughts about thought can be purely naturalistic. For the most part, though, I have passed over these matters, and appealed to an understanding of planning that we have as planners ourselves.

What, viewed in these terms, does the expressivist's direction of explanation gain us? A kind of vindication for our normative concepts, say I—but why do they need vindicating? We wouldn't, after all, give them up if no vindication were to be had. We couldn't manage without them, and many of our normative judgments—that suffering is worth avoiding, that seeing supports believing—are far more credible than any view could be that they are all nonsense. As Ronald Dworkin says, "If you can't help believing something, steadily and wholeheartedly, you'd better believe it" ("Objectivity and Truth," 1996, p. 118). (And if we after all did shed all our normative concepts, we'd no longer even be equipped to judge that we ought not to embrace them; that itself would be a normative judgment.) Why not, then, forgo the twists and turns of expressivism, and just start with the normative concepts we have. Apply them, refine them, debate and theorize in terms of them, to be sure, but don't attempt to see them "from the outside".

Yes, I agree, you'd better believe that torture is wrong and children are to be cherished and nurtured, with or without the kind of story of normative concepts I attempt in this book. But to say this and only this is to live with anomaly. Why conceive of the world in any but naturalistic terms, when science tells us how to be strictly naturalistic in our conceptions? Because, say I, we are actors and planners, and not just observers and explainers of what we observe—and because we can agree or disagree in plan. On this modest base rests my whole story of how these concepts work, and what we are thinking when we think in normative terms. We are thinking what to do and why—and anyone who acts must find such thinking intelligible. Normative concepts, then, aren't hocus-pocus, even of a kind we find we just can't shed. We can't do without them, true enough, but the reasons we can't stem from what I have been saying. Expressivism explains *why* we can't do without normative concepts. It thus vindicates concepts that we might otherwise find raise an inescapable anomaly. We vindicate these concepts not by rendering their content in naturalistic terms, but by assimilating their use to a kind of thinking that needs no vindication: thinking what to do.

How, then, should we think of the many concepts we use to guide our choices and feelings, when these concepts aren't on their way to a role in our uniform, naturalistic rendition of the world and our place in it? We can stubbornly refuse to be puzzled, since these aren't, after all, concepts we could give up *en masse*. Finding concepts puzzling, though, can lead to new understanding. (As a parallel, think of Einstein's critiques of the concepts of time and length, and how these critiques led, among other things, to $e = mc^2$.) I myself have been stubbornly puzzled by normative concepts, and I have offered a kind of account of these concepts and why we have them. We are beings who think together how to live, what to do and how to feel about one thing or another. Such a being, I have been arguing at length, is committed to concepts much like these normative concepts that puzzle a naturalist. These concepts fit into the world not as ways to conceive of nature as nature, but as concepts that a natural being must have if it acts and thinks what to do.

~ IV
Knowing What to Do

~ 10

Explaining with Plans

CAN GOODNESS AND BADNESS and the like explain things that happen? It was the evil of the tsarist regime, a student might think, that provoked its overthrow. Historically oversimple this may be, but it does seem on the right track. In any case, it doesn't seem downright incoherent; it doesn't seem a conceptual impossibility. Could we tell, after all, from a sheer study of the meaning of the term 'evil' that this wasn't the right story?

Disputes over whether morals explain happenings—and if so, how—have figured crucially in debates between "moral realists" and their opponents. A claim that morals are somehow unexplanatory appears in arguments that moral terms are special—that they don't just describe things in terms of their properties. It appears in the debate between moral realists, on the one side, and expressivists like me. Moral realists, in counterattack, argue that moral claims can figure in causal explanations, and use this finding to argue against expressivism.[1]

1. Harman—who is not precisely what I am calling an "expressivist"—gave such an antirealist argument in *Nature of Morality* (1977), pp. 6–7; see also Blackburn, "Reply" (1981), pp. 164–165, 185–186, and *Spreading the Word* (1984), pp. 182, 247, and Williams, *Ethics* (1985), pp. 132–155 for similar arguments. These arguments have given rise to much debate: Sturgeon attacks Harman's argument in "Moral Explanations" (1985). An exchange between Sturgeon and Harman consists in Sturgeon, "What Difference" (1986), Harman, "Moral Explanations" (1986), and Sturgeon, "Harman" (1986). An exchange between Blackburn and

On my own view, evil can give rise to opposition, sure enough—but the claim that it does passes beyond sheer causal/historical explanation. Others could agree on all the causes and yet disagree as to what is evil and what is not. These conclusions I share with other expressivists who have debated the issue at length, in particular with R. M. Hare and Simon Blackburn. We all think that evil supervenes on natural properties, and that this has much to do with the sense in which the evil of a regime might explain its downfall.

In this final part of the book, however, I steer clear of entering these debates directly. I return to speaking not directly of morals, or even of normative issues more broadly. I ask again about the content of planning, about such plan-laden conclusions as that an act is "the thing to do" or that it is "okay to do". I ask how such judgments would have to work.

Assume with me, then, that judgments with plan-laden content—judgments laden with *to-be-done*ness and okayness—work in the ways I have developed. Can plan-laden content figure in explanations of why things happen? And if so, would this mean that there are plan-laden facts in a more robust way than I have allowed? Would this vitiate a distinction I have been maintaining between plan-laden terms and "descriptive" terms? In the final four chapters to come in the book, I ask how far we could push the parallel between plan-laden and naturalistic judgments. Plan-laden judgments aren't naturalistic, I take it, but once we say that, is there any informative sense in which natural facts are part of the fabric of the world and plan-laden quasi-facts are not? If *to-be-done*ness operated fully and fundamentally as cause and effect, just as do natural qualities, then in what sense could *to-be-done*ness not be part of the real structure of the world? On the other hand, suppose *to-be-done*ness failed to explain things that happen, whereas goodness and badness did so explain. That might then refute my proposal that good and bad are plan-laden concepts.

In this chapter I offer an account of how plan-laden explanations of happenings might work. Call these "practical explanations"—in paral-

Sturgeon consists in Blackburn, "Just Causes" (1991), Sturgeon, "Contents" (1991), and Blackburn, "Reply" (1991). I argue in a somewhat parallel way from an evolutionary hypothesis in "Human Evolution" (1982), pp. 40–43, and *Wise Choices* (1990), pp. 107–125. Sturgeon criticizes these arguments in "Nonmoral Explanations" (1992). See also Cohen, "The Arc of the Moral Universe" (1997).

lel with "moral explanations" (and drawing on standard practice in translating Aristotle). Later, I explore whether this reading perhaps misses something. That leads, in the next chapter, to the question whether there's any such thing as plan-laden knowledge.

A Practical Explanation

Joe is reading *War and Peace*, along with a bit of auxiliary Russian history, and he puzzles over General Kutuzov's decision to retreat from the French invaders. Kutuzov retreated, Joe eventually concludes, because retreating, in his situation, was indeed the thing to do. (For a general to "retreat" is, of course, for him to be in effective command and successfully order a retreat.) Other generals might not have retreated in Kutuzov's situation, but Kutuzov was rational, in that he strongly tended to do whatever was the thing to do in his circumstance. This and the fact that retreat was the thing to do explain his decision to retreat. Something's being the thing to do thus explains the movements of a vast army.

This amounts to an explanation in terms of being okay. To be the thing to do is to be uniquely okay among one's alternatives. Joe thinks that among Kutuzov's grim alternatives, ordering retreat was okay and nothing else was—and that that explains why Kutuzov ordered retreat. ('Okay' in our technical sense, remember, does not mean satisfactory; it means something closer to "not inadvisable in the circumstances". Even when no alternative is at all satisfactory, at least one will be okay.)

This is what Joe thinks. Whether or not he is right, are his thoughts at least coherent? One issue we can set aside: Tolstoy, Joe is aware, denies that the decision of one man can explain the movements of a million, and so concludes that the movements were inevitable. Joe is clearly coherent in rejecting such a sweeping historical inevitabilism: he agrees that in the full explanation of the movements of vast armies, much more enters in than the decision of one man. The explanation must include the causal structure that constitutes that man's being in effective command. Still, Joe insists on the side of common sense, one man's decision can be crucial. Had the decision been different, so would have been the movements of armies.

Is it incoherent, though, for Joe to think that being okay enters into the causal story? Can retreat's being the thing to do causally explain

Kutuzov's decision—and hence the movements of armies? Or since facts are one thing and plans another, must truly causal explanations stick to the facts? In expanded form, Joe's explanation goes as follows:

   (i) Kutuzov strongly tended to act in okay ways (or ways that were close to okay).
  (ii) In his situation, retreat was okay, and nothing else came close to being okay.
 (iii) Because of (i) and (ii), Kutuzov retreated—that is, ordered retreat.
 (iv) Because he ordered a retreat, vast armies moved.

What might be fishy in Joe's thinking is its practical-causal core. Claim (iv) is no part of this core, since it is in no way a practical claim. I include it only to remind us of the scale of an event that might plausibly have a good practical-causal explanation. Claim (iii) is crucial to our issue. If we move Kutuzov's rationality into the background, we get the following as the rough practical-causal core of Joe's explanatory thinking, a thought that is at once practical and causal-explanatory:

Kutuzov retreated because retreating was the thing to do. $(\mathcal{B})$

This involves accepting the impurely practical claim (ii)—roughly, that retreat was the thing to do—and that Kutuzov retreated because (ii) obtained.

Claim $(\mathcal{B})$, though, suggests two claims that may behave differently. One is a matter of what caused what:

Retreat's being the thing to do caused Kutuzov to retreat. (C)

The other is a matter of explanation, of what explains an event, causally speaking. This is the crux of what I have labeled a "practical explanation":

Retreat's being the thing to do explains why Kutuzov retreated. $(\mathcal{E})$

(Sometimes I'll speak more explicitly of a "practical-causal explanation".) We need to explore whether this could be an intelligible and coherent thing to accept.

Accepting the Causal Claim

The solution of the Frege-Geach problem in Chapter 5 offered a general way to interpret claims like (*C*) that mix plan with fact. How does this solution apply to Joe's causal claim (*C*), that retreat's being the thing to do caused Kutuzov to retreat? As with any claim, we can try saying its content will be a matter of which hyperdecided states one could be in and accept it. In a hyperstate one has a hyperplan, and one has a hyperdecided view of the facts of the universe. By "facts" in this chapter I'll continue to mean facts that are not plan-laden. "Facts", then, are true thoughts that are not plan-laden. They do include psychological facts of how one does plan, but they don't include what's okay to do or not. (I speak, to be sure, with an eye to asking later whether plan-laden findings should be called "facts", but for now I distinguish sharply between decisions and other deliverances of planning and "factual" beliefs.)

Start as before, then, with hyperdecided Hera. Hera suffers no factual uncertainty, and she has a hyperplan: for any possible circumstance whatsoever, she is fully decided on what to do if in that circumstance. She has a fully decided view, then, of what Kutuzov's situation was, and a plan for what to do if in such a situation. She accepts Joe's claim (ii)— that in Kutuzov's situation, retreat was the thing to do—just in case she plans to retreat if in Kutuzov's situation as she thinks it to have been. Suppose again, for the sake of example, that she is a hedonistic egoist: her plan is always, in any situation hypothetical or practical, to do something egohedonic. Then she accepts (ii), that retreat was the thing to do, if and only if she thinks that in Kutuzov's situation, retreat and retreat alone was egohedonic.

Hera, imagine, thinks that Kutuzov had strong evidence that if he retreated, he would be relieved of his command, Russia would be defeated, and he would be forced into a highly pleasant retirement with his family under French dominion. This, she thinks, would be egohedonic in his situation: a peaceful forced retirement offers more pleasure, on balance, than the long, slow victory Kutuzov could achieve by ordering his army to stand its ground. Hera's plan is to go for comfort, not victory.

Hera then accepts claim (ii), that in Kutuzov's situation ordering retreat is the thing to do. What, then, of Joe's claim (*C*), that this caused him to order retreat? Hera thinks that ordering retreat was uniquely egohedonic, and that this caused Kutuzov to order retreat. She thinks too that being egohedonic is what constitutes being okay to do, and so being uniquely egohedonic constitutes being uniquely okay—which is to say, being the thing to do. In accepting all this, she accepts (C). This is far from the only way for a hyperdecided planner to accept (C), but it is one way of doing so—and it is Hera's way, we are imagining.

Another hyperdecided thinker might narrowly agree with Hera on (ii) and (C), while agreeing with her on little else. Diana too, imagine, is hyperdecided in fact and plan. She holds that always the thing to do is to do one's duty—whatever one's duty is and whatever the hedonic prospects it offers. She has firm views on the duties of a general: the general's duty, she holds, is always to maximize chances of eventual victory, whatever the cost to himself or anyone else. She has, then, a universal plan, and for cases of being a general, her plan is always to maximize chances of victory in the end. She thinks that in Kutuzov's situation, ordering retreat maximized his prospects of victory. That, she thinks, is why he retreated. Diana agrees with Hera, slow and exhausting victory stands to be far more painful for him, on balance, than quick and luxurious surrender—but she plans for victory, not for comfort.

Hera and Diana both accept (ii), that retreat was the thing to do, and they both accept (C), that this caused Kutuzov to retreat. Both are hyperdecided, but in sharply different ways. They differ, first, on the prospects retreat offered. Hera thinks it offered a pleasant retirement in defeat, whereas Diana thinks it offered a slow and painful victory. They disagree, second, on what to pursue in life: Hera plans for her own pleasure, whereas Diana plans for duty (on a conception of duty that she has). Their goals are at odds, and their factual beliefs are at odds. Nevertheless, they both accept the two things we are scrutinizing: (ii) that in Kutuzov's situation, retreating was the thing to do, and (C) that its being the thing to do caused him to retreat.

What, then, of Joe, who unlike Hera and Diana, is far from hyperdecided? His impressions of Russian history are hazy. He rejects Hera's egoism, let's imagine, but is undecided on the hypothetical question of what public goal to pursue if one is a general. Nevertheless, he accepts (C)—and this he has in common with Hera and Diana. What is the content of what he accepts, and what might be his grounds?

He disagrees with Hera about what to pursue in life: he rejects, for the case of being a general, planning solely to advance his own net pleasure. He rejects Hera's views of Russian history: he doesn't think that Kutuzov was responding as an opportunist and defeatist when he ordered retreat. Still, I am saying, on the narrow questions of (ii) and (*C*), Joe and Hera agree: they both accept (ii) and they both accept (*C*).

As for Diana, Joe perhaps doesn't reject any of her views of how to live or of how things were for Kutuzov—but he doesn't accept them all either. He's far from decided on many of these matters. Nevertheless, on the questions of (ii) and (*C*), Joe and Diana agree: they both accept these claims.

The Content of the Causal Claim

What, then, is the content of Joe's explanatory claim (*C*), that retreat's being the thing to do caused Kutuzov to retreat? The claim must be something that Joe, Hera, and Diana all accept. I have proposed understanding it by thinking of Hera, Diana, and others who are like them in being hyperdecided. The content of (*C*) is a matter of the range of ways one could be hyperdecided and accept it.

Alternatively, we can speak in plan-laden terms, and put the matter as follows: join me now in speaking practically, and accepting those things to which anyone who plans anything is committed. There is a property, we can now say, that constitutes being the thing to do. (*C*) now just means this:

> Retreat's having the property that constitutes being the thing to do caused Kutuzov to retreat. (C^*)

Hera, who thinks that this property is being uniquely egohedonic, will accept this when and only when she accepts the purely factual causal claim

> Retreat's being uniquely egohedonic to do caused Kutuzov to retreat. (C_b)

Diana, who has other decided convictions as to what this property is, accepts (C^*) and hence (*C*), but rejects (C_b).

Since Hera is hyperdecided, the basis of her accepting (C) can be factored into a purely causal part and a purely practical part. So can Diana's. Hera has a hyperplan P_h always to do what is egohedonic, and she has the causal-historical belief F_h that retreat's being uniquely egohedonic caused Kutuzov to retreat. Diana's basis likewise factors into a purely practical part P_d and a purely factual part F_d—though each is quite at odds with what Hera accepts. Claim (C) isn't equivalent to either the conjunction of P_h and F_h or to the conjunction of P_d and F_d. For one can accept (C) and reject both these conjunctions. (C), though, is equivalent to a grand disjunction of such conjunctions. It amounts to the disjunction of all conjunctions of this form:

> Property F constitutes being the thing to do, and retreat's having
> property F caused Kutuzov to retreat.   (1)

Each statement of form (1) conjoins a purely practical statement—a pure matter of contingency planning—with a purely factual statement. To accept (C) or (C^*) is not to accept any one such conjunction, but rather, to accept the disjunction of all such conjunctions.

Joe, who is far from hyperdecided, accepts the plan-laden causal claim (C), that retreat's being the thing to do caused Kutuzov to retreat. He accepts no single one of the conjunctions in (1), but he does accept the grand disjunction of all such conjunctions. Some of the conjunctions in this grand disjunction he rejects; for instance, he rejects the conjunction of P_h and F_h that Hera accepts. On others—Diana's, for instance—he is agnostic.

Joe, then, can accept (C) without the kind of basis that Hera and Diana have. Hera's basis for accepting (C) factors into two parts P_h and F_h, one purely practical and the other purely factual. Diana's basis likewise factors. Joe, in contrast, has no such factorable basis for accepting (C). Retreat's being the thing to do, he's convinced, caused Kutuzov to retreat. But he's not fully decided as to what it was that made retreat the thing to do in Kutuzov's situation.

Why, then, might he accept (C)? He might accept it on authority, because his guru accepts it or because Tolstoy accepts it—even though he doesn't know what their bases are. Alternatively, he might have come to trust Kutuzov's judgment from long experience. He has thought hard about Kutuzov's decisions in many other cases and, on reflection, has always agreed with them. He has come to agree with them on close scrutiny, even when he was initially unclear what would be the thing to do in such a situation. By now, he trusts Kutuzov to do only what's okay to do. Joe's trust is far from blind, but he extends it even when he hasn't refined his plans for how to live enough to settle what it's okay to do in Kutuzov's circumstances.

What I am saying about plan-laden causal claims fits a somewhat vague proposal that Simon Blackburn makes on "moral explanations"—explaining, for instance, a revolution by the injustice of the old regime. I'll paraphrase what Blackburn says, using my own technical vocabulary. Some such explanations, he says, really explain in terms of beliefs about injustice: the widespread belief that the regime was unjust caused its downfall. Sometimes too, a person accepts an explanation in terms of injustice because, like Hera and Diana, he has a view as to what property constitutes being unjust, and thinks that the regime's having that property caused the revolution. (This doesn't require his being hyperdecided, but does require being decided sufficiently: say, thinking that being undemocratic is a way of being unjust, and that the old regime's being undemocratic caused its downfall.) Blackburn, though, thinks there may be a third way for an expressivist to treat moral explanations. The first step, he says, "is to allow propositional forms of discourse"—as I have been doing with my semantics of fact-plan worlds. "Once that is done we have the moral predicate, and features are simply abstractions from predicates." We then "explain how such a feature might be causally relevant" (Blackburn, "Just Causes," 1991, p. 206). This strategy he calls "more speculative" than the two other strategies he has proposed, and concedes that "it is not obvious that this position will be available to" an expressivist. I have been showing that an analogue of his position is available for plan-laden causal claims—and indeed, is required by things that I claimed in earlier chapters. I have been doing, then, for plan-laden causal claims what Blackburn proposes for "moral explanations" (pp. 206–207).

A Hypothesis

Hera accepts two claims:

Retreat's being uniquely egohedonic caused Kutuzov to retreat,

$$(C_b)$$

which is purely factual, and

Being the thing to do = being uniquely egohedonic.   (2)

This identity statement (2) is to be read as a claim of property identity: the property of being the thing to do is the property of being uniquely egohedonic. From these two statements, I have been assuming, follows the plan-laden causal claim,

Retreat's being the thing to do caused Kutuzov to retreat.   (C)

Indeed the causal claim (C), I have been saying, amounts to a grand disjunction of combinations like (C_b) and (2). Claim (C) follows from (C_b) and (2), I have taken it, by a simple principle of substitutivity: terms that signify (or quasi-signify) the same property can be substituted for each other, preserving truth. ('Truth' here is minimal truth, and the principle can be put in terms of what someone who is coherent and hyperdecided can accept.) We might ask, however, whether this logical principle applies to causal contexts. Being water and being H_2O are the same property; do they play the same causal role? The answer to this qualm seems to be that they do: if water causes a plant to revive, then so does H_2O. The assumptions I have been making, then, do seem to work for causal claims like (C). We can reasonably take it that they still obtain in the special case of a causal claim that is plan-laden.

Turn now, though, to explanatory claims, to claims of what, causally speaking, explains what. Our example of a plan-laden causal explanation (a "practical explanation" or "practical-causal explanation") was this:

Retreat's being the thing to do explains why Kutuzov retreated. $(\mathcal{E})$

We show this to be intelligible if we characterize the hyperstates in which it is accepted and those in which it is rejected. Now our Hera accepts claim (2) of property identity, and she accepts the purely factual causal explanation,

Retreat's being uniquely egohedonic explains why Kutuzov retreated. $(\mathcal{E}_b)$

Does she then accept practical explanation $(\mathcal{E})$? We obtain $(\mathcal{E})$ from $(\mathcal{E}_b)$ by substituting a term that, according to Hera, signifies the same property: we substitute 'thing to do' for 'uniquely egohedonic'. Can we substitute terms that signify the same property in a causal-explanatory context like $(\mathcal{E}_b)$ and preserve truth? It seems not. The terms 'water' and 'H_2O' signify the same property. But water's being H_2O explains much, whereas water's being water explains almost nothing. The treatment I have given to plan-laden causal claims like (C), then, may well not apply to practical explanations like $(\mathcal{E})$.

Perhaps, though, the style of argument I have been using still applies, with modifications. Hera accepts a claim that is much stronger than claim (2) of property identity. Her hyperplan always to do what's egohedonic is couched not in terms of the property of being egohedonic, but in terms of the factual concept of being egohedonic. In Chapter 6 I dubbed the concept expressed by a one-place predicate like 'is egohedonic' an attribute. Hera's hyperplan is always to do what's egohedonic, and so she accepts the claim that I'll put as follows: being okay to do consists in being egohedonic. For any situation she might be in, Hera plans to do whatever is egohedonic.[2] For purposes of forming a hyperplan, she conceives of any situation in factual terms. Two attributes, we can say, are factually equivalent if and only if they apply to the same things in every factually conceived situation. So according to Hera,

> The attribute of being the thing to do is factually equivalent to the attribute of being uniquely egohedonic. (3)

The term 'consists' is defined on this pattern: being okay consists in being egohedonic if and only if (i) being okay is a plan-laden attribute, (ii) being egohedonic is a factual attribute, and (iii) being okay is factually equivalent to being egohedonic.

We can now tentatively argue that Hera accepts practical explanation $(\mathcal{E})$. The principle we need is one of the indiscernibility of factual equivalents in causal-explanatory contexts:

PRINCIPLE $(\mathcal{I})$: If two attributes are factually equivalent, then in causal-explanatory contexts, a term that expresses one can be sub-

---

2. That is, she permits herself an act just in case it is egohedonic, and requires it of herself just in case it is uniquely egohedonic.

stituted for a term that expresses another without change of minimal truth value.

This cashes out in what someone like Hera, who is hyperdecided, will accept. If her hyperplan is always to do what's egohedonic, then she will accept practical explanation ($\mathcal{E}$) if and only if she accepts purely factual explanation ($\mathcal{E}_b$).

Is the indiscernibility principle ($\mathcal{I}$) correct? We could make it correct by fiat: As before, interpret practical explanation ($\mathcal{E}$), that retreat's being the thing to do caused Kutuzov to retreat, as a grand disjunction of conjunctions like that of (3) and ($\mathcal{E}_b$). Then just by the meaning of disjunction, a hyperdecided thinker-planner accepts ($\mathcal{E}$) if and only if she accepts one of these disjuncts. What we set out to explain at the outset, however, was not a theoretical construct like this grand disjunction, but rather such claims as that the badness of the old regime explains the revolution—practical explanations as they appear in ordinary thought. Whether the kind of analysis I have offered applies to ordinary practical explanations I haven't established.

We can take the kind of analysis I have offered, though, as a hypothesis. The hypothesis is that a practical explanation amounts to the kind of grand disjunction that I have been presenting. I'll ask in the next section what follows if this hypothesis is correct. Later in the chapter, I'll examine reasons to doubt the hypothesis, and move to a further interpretation of what a practical explanation might amount to.

How Only Facts Explain What Happens

Hera thinks that retreat's being the thing to do explains why Kutuzov retreated. She doesn't take anything plan-laden, though, to be what really, at base, does the causal explaining. Kutuzov retreated because retreat and retreat alone was egohedonic: that's the causal explanation, she's convinced. So put, of course, the explanation is abbreviated; it needs to be filled out. But what fills it out will be more facts. Hera, we are imagining, has a full view as to what those additional facts are; she can tell us a complete causal-explanatory story, in fully factual terms. That, on her view, is the full explanation of why Kutuzov retreated. The explanation contains nothing plan-laden. Hera can then adjoin a pure planning claim: that being okay consists in being egohedonic.

This commits her to a practical-causal explanation as well, the explanation (ℰ) that Joe accepts: that retreat's being the thing to do explains why Kutuzov retreated. But this, on her view, adds nothing causal-explanatory to what she already has said. She accepts Joe's explanation (ℰ), but the real causal-explanatory work, she maintains, has been done by facts alone—facts that, however relevant to planning they may be, are in no way themselves plan-laden.

This gives sense to Harman's claim that wrongness and the like don't explain things that happen—or more precisely, to an analogue of this claim for plan-laden concepts. In a sense, *to-be-done*ness doesn't explain anything that happens. In another sense, to be sure, it may: Hera, Diana, and Joe all agree that retreat's being the thing to do explains why Kutuzov retreated. But Hera, at least, thinks that this is by virtue of another, purely non-plan matter: that retreat's being uniquely egohedonic explains why Kutuzov retreated. Being the thing to do, on her view, explains nothing beyond what is explained by the facts alone.

What of Joe, then? And what of the rest of us who are likewise not hyperdecided? Joe thinks that retreat's being the thing to do explains why Kutuzov retreated. Unlike Hera, he has no purely factual explanation of Kutuzov's retreating to offer. Still, in a sense, he thinks that a purely factual explanation is the full causal explanation. He can't say what it is—but he is committed to there being such an explanation. And so, I claim, are the rest of us, when we accept a practical-causal explanation.

This we can argue in our canonical way. Joe is committed to anything that he would accept in every hyperdecided state he could reach without changing his mind. But anyone who is hyperdecided and accepts the practical explanation (ℰ), that retreat's being the thing to do explains why Kutuzov retreated, accepts that some purely factual, non-plan explanation does all the real causal explaining. A hyperdecided thinker-planner accepts, in this sense, that the full causal explanation of a happening can't be plan-laden. Therefore Joe too is committed to the claim that, in this sense, only non-plan facts really explain what happens.

And so are we all. Shift, then, to speaking in plan-laden terms, saying things to which anyone who plans is committed. Causal explanations can perhaps be couched in plan-laden terms, in terms of being okay to do. Such explanations may be correct, for anything we have established, and they may be genuinely explanatory, so far as they go. But all the causal-explanatory work there is to be done can proceed in terms of facts alone, in terms that are not plan-laden. That doesn't mean that we know how to give such an explanation; we may be in Joe's predicament. A practical-causal explanation may be the only one we have. Still, if some practical-causal explanation of an event is correct, that is because some purely factual, non-plan explanation is correct. The factual explanation does all the explaining there is to do. To that we are all committed, if my argument has been right.

Loose Ends: Levels and Ghosts

Isn't what I have been saying just a familiar matter of levels of explanation? Higher-level explanations are a staple of philosophy of science. Storms explain damage, but if the explanation is correct, then so is an explanation in terms of elementary particles and quantum theory—an explanation we can't give. The quantum explanation operates at a more basic level, and does all the explaining there is to do. Thoughts and goals explain only what neural goings-on explain more basically.

Such higher-level explanations, though, are quite different from practical explanations. If an event is explained at two different levels, one more basic than the other, then anyone who really understands both explanations could see—limitations of insight aside—that if the more basic explanation is right, then so is the higher-level explanation. Statistical mechanics explains, at a molecular level, what classical thermodynamics explains at a higher level: heat flows and the like. Understand what goes on at a molecular level and the statistical patterns that govern it, acquire the concepts of heat and temperature, and you have the materials for understanding what, at the higher, thermodynamic level, explains the heat flows in the system. For you don't really understand what the "molecules" of statistical mechanics are until you know what they have to do with the familiar world around us. (Imagine a theory of ghost molecules that bounce around like regular molecules, but don't interact with us. Positivists think such a theory meaningless, and in any case, whether or not they are right, this ghost mechanics is missing a crucial aspect of statistical mechanics. It includes the same mathematics, but what explains familiar happenings is not the pure mathematics alone.)

Suppose now, in contrast, that Hera is right about everything, and consider the two explanations she accepts of why Kutuzov retreated. A hyperdecided perfectionist Poseidon could understand both explanations perfectly, accept Hera's factual explanation of why Kutuzov retreated, but reject her practical explanation. Kutuzov retreated because doing so was uniquely egohedonic, he can agree, but not, he'll insist, because it was the thing to do—for it wasn't: being the thing to do consists in nothing remotely hedonic. This is a coherent view for Poseidon to take, even if wrong; taking it reveals no conceptual limitations or confusions on his part. Indeed, it is the view he is committed to take, since he accepts Hera's factual explanation of why Kutuzov retreated and he plans his life as a perfectionist.

We could put the contrast in terms of bridge principles. When two explanations of the same thing are correct at different levels, the concepts that figure in the respective explanations are connected by bridge principles. Heat, for instance, is mean molecular kinetic energy per degree of freedom. Now imagine you understand statistical mechanics, and you understand temperature, specific heat, and the like at the gross, thermodynamic level. But say you don't see the connection: you fully understand what explains a rise in mean kinetic energy per degree of freedom, but you don't see what it has to do with a rise in temperature. Is such a thing possible? If you don't see these ties, you don't fully have the concepts that figure in statistical mechanics: molecule, motion, and the like. You are missing, in your concepts of these things, anything about how they tie in with the world we experience around us. Hera's bridge principle, we might say, is that being okay consists in being egohedonic. A perfectionist can reject this, however, and doing so doesn't impugn his grasp of the concepts involved. If Hera is right, what it impugns is his plan for living. The bridge principles that tie higher- and lower-level factual explanations together enter into the concepts involved, whereas the principle that ties a practical explanation to the factual explanation that exhausts the purely causal part of the explaining is a matter of how to live.

We might now ask a further question: are the facts that causally explain why things happen, at base, all natural facts? The answer depends on what 'natural' means. In a very broad sense, all facts that figure in plans are natural; they are constructible, though perhaps only infinitely, from recognitional concepts. But the term 'natural' might be given a narrower reading, one that excludes such things as ghosts and magic, demons and gods, vibes and auras. Call these things "extra-natural"; it won't greatly matter, for what I have to say, precisely where we draw the line between the natural and the extra-natural. Extra-natural properties aren't what Moore meant by "non-natural" properties; he insisted that his attack on "naturalistic definitions" applied as well to theological and metaphysical definitions.

Extra-natural properties, if anything has them, belong to the causal order: when a ghost haunts a house, according to lore, it causes creaks and bumps in the night. Abstract, *a priori* arguments of the kind I have been giving, it follows, won't demonstrate that natural as opposed to extra-natural facts explain all that happens. If things in the world do have extra-natural properties, then their having these properties may well help explain happenings—and my arguments don't by themselves rule out extra-natural properties. (They do show that we don't have to believe in extra-natural properties to accept ethical and other normative claims—but that should be no surprise.)

Worries over extra-natural properties are a quibble, and responding to them comprises a fine point in the argument I have been giving. My arguments do not rule out such properties, I have conceded, and so if we don't count such properties as "natural", I have not proved that only natural properties explain happenings. Many of us, though, stoutly believe on other grounds that no extra-natural properties are exemplified. Once we are convinced that only plan-free facts explain why things happen, we'll accept that only natural facts do such explaining—natural facts as opposed to extra-natural ones.

Let us take stock. Practical explanations are sometimes correct, perhaps. But if they are, that is no reason to reject expressivism. For an expressivist can account for why it might be coherent to accept a practical explanation of a happening. If he does accept such a practical-causal explanation, he can account for what he is thereby doing. Moreover, the expressivist can maintain, facts explain what happens in a way that plan-laden concepts don't. The point isn't that plan-laden explanations of what happens must all be mistaken. Rather, if such a plan-laden causal explanation is correct, then the real explaining is done by natural facts. Plan-laden concepts figure correctly in causal explanations only because some naturalistic explanation is correct. The full, true story factors into a planning part and a naturalistic part, and the naturalistic part then contains the full causal explanation. Such an account is consistent with expressivism, and allows that for all our concepts dictate, practical explanations may be correct.

Responding to a Non-Fact of Constitution

Do correct practical explanations really factor as I have described? There may be grounds for doubt that they do. Take a prime kind of practical explanation, namely, explanations of decisions. Decisions we are treating as plans of a special kind. A judgment that a particular course of action is now the one to take, that it is one's uniquely okay course of action, amounts to a decision. That's how I've defined the terms 'okay' and 'thing to do'. Why, then, did Kutuzov retreat? Because he judged retreat to be the thing to do. Why did he so judge? Because retreat was the thing to do in his circumstances—and crafty general that he was, he realized that it was. Another general, to be sure, might have retreated for bad reasons—say, because his astrologer demanded it. He then would not be retreating because it was the thing to do, but because he was superstitious. But if all was right with Kutuzov's deliberating, then he retreated because retreat was the thing to do and he realized it. Of course, this explanation is schematic and abbreviated. Still, we can say, if the full explanation of Kutuzov's judging as he did vindicates his judgment, then this sketchy explanation must be right as far as it goes. A vindicating explanation of a decision will show it to be responsive to what was okay to do and what wasn't.

Now on the view I have been sketching, this has a clear gloss. We are to gloss the claim

Retreat's being the thing to do explains why Kutuzov retreated. ($\mathcal{E}$)

And this gloss we have already in hand. There is a factual attribute F, we've been saying, that being okay consists in. ($\mathcal{E}$) obtains, then, just in case retreat and retreat alone has attribute F and this explains why Kutuzov retreated. Suppose, for instance, that theorist Hedda is right and F is being egohedonic. Then ($\mathcal{E}$) is so just in case the following holds:

Retreat's being uniquely egohedonic explains why Kutuzov retreated. ($\mathcal{E}_h$)

Of course if egohedonism is wrong, then ($\mathcal{E}$) might be correct though ($\mathcal{E}_b$) were incorrect. Percy the perfectionist might accept ($\mathcal{E}_b$) and still reject ($\mathcal{E}$), and be conceptually coherent in doing so. Claim ($\mathcal{E}$), then, doesn't mean the same thing as ($\mathcal{E}_b$). But if Hedda is right in her egoistic hedonism, then ($\mathcal{E}$) and ($\mathcal{E}_b$) are both correct or both incorrect. In that case, all there is causally to ($\mathcal{E}$)'s obtaining is ($\mathcal{E}_b$)'s obtaining: Kutuzov's planning must be responsive to retreat's being uniquely egohedonic.

Isn't there more, though, to vindicating Kutuzov's practical judgment? Suppose still that Hedda is right. For Kutuzov to "realize" that retreat is the thing to do, his plans must respond to retreat's uniquely being egohedonic. It's his plans that must respond, not just his factual judgments of what's egohedonic—that we're already saying. Still, isn't something additional too required for vindication? For Kutuzov to "realize" that retreat is the thing to do, mustn't his judgments respond to its being the thing to do not just *qua* being uniquely egohedonic, but *qua* just that—*qua* being the thing to do?

Imagine first that Kutuzov's practical views, his views on what to do, factor into a factual part and a pure planning part. He judges retreat and retreat alone to be egohedonic, and also judges that being okay consists in being egohedonic. His plans are responsive to retreat's uniquely being egohedonic, then, in two steps: an apprehension of natural fact, plus a pure planning judgment of what being okay consists in. To vindicate this whole package, then, don't we have to vindicate both steps? Kutuzov has the right view of what being okay consists in—so thinks Hera. But wouldn't it spoil things if this were just by good luck or happenstance?

In the parallel case of a naturalistic judgment, we do require vindicating two steps. Jill, imagine, starts to study chemistry and judges that the lake is filled with H_2O. She so judges because she knows that it is filled with water, and thinks that water is H_2O. But imagine that she thinks this last by happenstance. Her friend Jack copied some chemical formulas and matched them to common substances at random: wood with H_2SO_4 and the like. Water he happened to match with H_2O. Jill was trusting, and she studied Jack's formulas. Her judgment about the lake is correct, but the story of how she came to make it doesn't vindicate her judgment.

Suppose, then, that Kutuzov had formed his practical views by hiring a consultant whose advertisement he had run across. The consultant, buffaloed by the task of discerning what being okay consists in, wrote out the leading theories on slips of paper, put them in a hat after attaching each one to a dog biscuit, and called for his dog to draw one out. Wouldn't a view formed this way be defective even if correct? Kutuzov's judgment wouldn't in this case constitute "realizing" that being okay consists in being egohedonic—even if his judgment is correct. And so his decision to retreat wouldn't be a matter of "realizing" that retreat was the thing to do. He would realize that retreat was egohedonic, and correctly judge it to be the thing to do. But this would be fortuitous in a way that discredits the judgment.

A vindicating explanation of a naturalistic judgment presents the judgment as knowledge; it presents it as somehow "tracking" the fact judged. Isn't vindicating a decision, then—vindicating a judgment of what to do—a matter of displaying it as a case of plan-laden knowledge? Genuine plan-laden knowledge would be something more than sheer naturalistic knowledge joined to a correct way of going from naturalistic judgment to plan-laden judgment. This last, pure planning part of one's propensities to decide, after all, might be correct just fortuitously. What we need, it seems, is not just that one's plans track the natural facts that constitute being okay, but that they somehow track being okay itself.

So far, we have considered the case where Kutuzov's judgment factors: he has a view as to what being okay consists in and a view as to what course of action has this attribute. We need also to ponder a case where they don't so factor. Being okay consists in being egohedonic, suppose; one's own pleasure is the thing to seek. And Kutuzov's plans do "track" expected pleasure for him. They don't, however, do this via explicit assessments of pleasure. Enough evidence that a course of action is egohedonic reliably leads Kutuzov to plan on it, but not because he thinks about pleasure as such. It might even be that his explicit beliefs about pleasure are distorted; that his plans reliably track evidence of the long-term pleasure a course of action holds for him, but he rationalizes his choices as noble sacrifices of pleasure. If that is what Hera thinks is going on, she may still say the following: that although Kutuzov doesn't explicitly know what's egohedonic or that being okay consists in being egohedonic, he does indeed know what to do. He knows what to do, but offers faulty rationalizations. In such a case, Kutuzov's planning might very well, as Hera thinks, constitute knowledge. This would be "practical" knowledge, a "tracking" of okayness.

Again, though, for Kutuzov to apprehend what is okay and what isn't, must it not be more than fortuitous that it's pleasure his planning tracks? Must he not somehow be tacitly appreciating that one's pleasure is the thing to pursue? Being okay consists in being egohedonic; must he not somehow be acting as he does because of this? He must, it seems, be somehow responsive to what being the thing to do consists in, even if he doesn't make explicit judgments on this score. That one's own pleasure is the thing to pursue in life is not a "fact", as we have been using the term—even if, as I've been imagining for the sake of illustration, pleasure indeed is the thing to pursue. Still, that it is the thing to pursue must, it seems, somehow explain Kutuzov's acting as he does, if he acts from real knowledge of what to do.

Choices for Expressivists

Can an expressivist countenance plan-laden explanations of things that happen? Plan-laden content is non-factual, in a sense; can such non-facts explain events? In particular, can they explain how people plan? Is what to do something that we can know in the way that we know facts?

Answers to these questions might be thought to mark a divide between practical "realism" and practical "anti-realism". An anti-realist, it might seem, must deny that any sense could be made of such responsiveness. Talk of "realizing" or "apprehending" what's to be sought in life must be rejected—or at least, on an overliteral understanding of such talk. Nothing much like factual apprehending or knowledge is involved, the non-realist seems driven to say. Or more precisely, we do apprehend facts of the normal, prosaic kind, and our plans respond to these facts, correctly or incorrectly. But there is no such thing as being "responsive" to a non-fact of what being okay consists in. This isn't something that could have causal effects, and so it isn't something we could respond to. So the non-realist seems forced to contend.

It seems that we do think about what to do, and sometimes get it right. It seems that it's not just happenstance that we "track" the right attribute in our planning, to the degree that we do. We seem, then, not just to be responding to prosaic facts, but to the truth about the end in life, about what being okay to do consists in. A "practical intuitionism"—a view modeled on old-fashioned moral intuitionism—might best seem to account for these abilities that we claim for ourselves. A practical intuitionist of this stripe would hold that being okay is an attribute of a singular kind, and that we are somehow equipped to apprehend this attribute and things about it in a way akin to a kind of inner seeing. Kutuzov, then, apprehends not just that retreat and retreat alone is egohedonic, but that retreat is the thing to do. This last is a fact, the fact of retreat's having an attribute that goes beyond its being uniquely egohedonic. Kutuzov apprehends this further fact. And deciding what to do—when it goes beyond just choosing out of indifference—just is apprehending or misapprehending this fact of what to do.

Notoriously, though, classical intuitionists offered us no explanation of how such a faculty could work and no grounds for thinking that these seeming apprehensions are veridical, beyond a visual metaphor and an analogy with mathematics. All this offers no explanation of how what went on with Kutuzov might constitute a veridical apprehension. We might find intuitionists vindicated in their claims, but only if we work to interpret and explain what intuitionists can only proclaim.

Another form of moral realism has been the naturalistic form of the "Cornell" school.[3] Philosophers of this school, however, avowedly are not treating plan-laden concepts of the kind I am examining. For they deny "motivational judgment internalism" for the concepts they study: they deny that to accept, say, that cheating is wrong is to be motivated, to some degree, not to cheat.[4] We cannot correspondingly deny that to accept that retreat is the thing to do is to be motivated to retreat. Internalism applies to plan-laden concepts by definition—whether or not it applies to any concepts we really have. There remains the question I touched on in Part III of this book, "Normative Concepts," whether familiar normative concepts are plan-laden. Whether we can "apprehend" plan-laden matters might well bear on this question. Our hypothesis, after all, is that familiar normative concepts are plan-laden, and we do seem to apprehend normative matters. If this seeming apprehension cannot be accounted for or explained away on the hypothesis, then the hypothesis may be in trouble.

What, then, can expressivists say about "knowing what to do"? One available tack is just to deny that there is anything more to this than I have already described: that one's plans "track" the factual attribute that being okay consists in. Another way to approach these questions,

3. Prime expositions are Boyd, "How to Be a Moral Realist" (1988), and Sturgeon, "Moral Explanations" (1985).
4. See, for instance, Boyd, "How to Be a Moral Realist" (1988), pp. 214–216.

though, would be to soften further the differences between a "practical realism" and the quasi-realism I have been expounding. Claim that expressivism allows that we indeed can have knowledge of what to do—or at least, something that acts very much like knowledge. Claim that this includes knowledge of what, ultimately, to go for in life, of what being okay consists in. These things will not be matters entirely of what I have been calling "fact", ordinary prosaic facts of what would cause what and the like. Still, perhaps the expressivist can find such non-facts explaining things that happen, explaining them in much the way that facts can. In particular, perhaps the expressivist can depict one aspect of wisdom as knowing or apprehending what to do in a way that parallels apprehending everyday facts around us. And if some of this apprehension is immediate, that might count as intuiting what to do.

In the next chapter, I'll explore these possibilities—though the exploration will be inconclusive, I should warn. There is much to be said for a position that denies that "knowing what to do" fully parallels knowing prosaic facts. Plans can be right or wrong, and they can be warranted or not; these may be all the distinctions we need to account for phenomena of planning and plan-laden judgment. I'll ask, though, whether an expressivist can allow "knowledge" of plan-laden non-facts in a stronger sense than I have so far allowed. I don't think the answer is crucial, either to our lives as planners or to the merits of expressivism. We can be legitimately confident of our plans, under favorable circumstances, whatever the answer to this question turns out to be. And I doubt that there are things we believe about our plans that the less conciliatory expressivist doesn't accommodate. Still, we can ask how far, in this further regard, expressivism could mimic intuitionism.

~ 11

Knowing What to Do

$\mathcal{J}$OE COULD HAVE BEEN a superb jazz trumpeter. But this highly competitive pursuit in the public eye he found threatening. He has now laid down his trumpet, forever as he intends it, and has turned full time to the active but relaxing cultivation of his garden. He is competent at gardening and finds a quiet satisfaction in it, but still, his aptitude for gardening is nothing special.

Joe, then, works his garden when he could be practicing trumpet, and rejects the option of practicing instead. He thereby makes planning judgments, judgments of what to do. We now want to ask whether these judgments constitute something like knowledge. Does he know what to do and so act on this knowledge?

We might reframe the question as follows: Take as a parallel knowledge of prosaic fact. Naturalistic facts are prime instances of these, such facts, for example, as what would lead to pleasure or torment for oneself or others, and what would lead to trumpet playing that draws applause and is a source of pride. These are things that Joe might come to know, or that others wiser than Joe might already know. Mathematical facts are another prime instance of the facts I am calling prosaic; Joe surely knows that $5 + 7 = 12$. We speak of *knowing* such prosaic facts, and epistemologists try to analyze what this consists in. Suppose we succeeded with an account of knowing prosaic facts, so that we could say what kinds of judgments of prosaic fact are cases of knowledge. How much parallel might there be with judgments of what to do?

221

Suppose a parallel is fairly complete: just as in the realm of prosaic fact we distinguish some judgments as knowledge, so with judgments of what to do, we can make a distinction that is much the same. The distinction isn't, suppose, just a fetish or a matter of idle classification, but has some importance; marking this distinction has a like rationale with prosaic fact and with matters of what to do. Then, we might conclude, there is such a thing as knowing what to do—or at least "quasi-knowing", which might as well for most purposes be knowing.

How full a parallel might there be, then, between Joe's state of mind in planning to garden and his knowledge of prosaic facts? To answer this kind of question, I have time after time exploited the idea of a hyperdecided state. What does it take for a hyperdecided observer to be one who concludes that Joe knows—that he knows, for instance, where his spade is? A hyperdecided judge like Hera has a view on every prosaic fact and a plan for every contingency. The totality of these beliefs and plans is coherent. The content of any claim, I keep saying, is a matter of the set of hyperdecided states the claim allows. That should go for Hera's claims as to what Joe knows and what he doesn't know. Turn then from Joe's judgment that his spade is in the shed to his judgments of what to do. Consider Joe's judgment that, in his own case, gardening is okay to pursue and trumpeting isn't. Is there a stance that Hera can take toward this that parallels her stance toward Joe's judgment that the spade is in the shed?

Joe, in short, judges that his spade is in the shed—and observer Hera regards his judgment as an instance of knowledge. What, then, if Joe makes a judgment not of prosaic fact, but of plan-laden "non-fact"? He judges that spadework and not trumpet runs is now the thing to do. A parallel set of beliefs and plans on Hera's part would constitute her thinking Joe's judgment to be a case at least of "quasi-knowledge". In this chapter, I explore this program.

Spurious Judgment

One way to deny that Joe "knows" what to do, of course, is to claim that he has it wrong. Knowledge requires true belief, and so one cannot disagree and attribute knowledge. (More precisely, one cannot disagree with a belief one attributes to Joe and yet coherently think it knowledge.) Athena, imagine, is a perfectionist: she stresses developing one's highest and rarest talents, even at the cost of psychic torment. She disagrees with Joe, then, on what to do if in Joe's shoes. This isn't a matter of disagreement on natural fact, or disagreement as to how to assess Joe's evidence: Athena rejects none of Joe's factual beliefs or assessments of the evidence. Rather, whereas Joe has planned for the pleasures of Epicurean tranquillity, Athena plans—for the case of being Joe and in Joe's shoes—for high achievement. (Specifying her principles of planning fully would, of course, have to include specifying her standards for levels of achievement; imagine that we have somehow done this.)

Athena, then, thinks that Joe doesn't know what to aim for ultimately in life because his view of what to aim for in life is wrong. Her disagreement with Joe isn't naturalistic: she agrees with all his judgments of prosaic fact. Rather, their disagreement is *purely practical*; it is a difference over what ultimately to aim for in life. Joe plans for modest and satisfying achievements in gardening, when he might instead have planned for high achievement in music, but in a life of struggling with fearsome standards and the terror of constant public scrutiny.

Joe may, of course, form his plans still having not worked out views of what, ultimately, to aim for in life. In the case I have been imagining, his views of the natural facts agree with Athena's, and any way he could become hyperdecided without changing his mind would involve his disagreeing with Athena as to what, ultimately, to pursue in life. In a more likely kind of case, Athena rejects Joe's plans, though there is no way of pinning down the disagreement as purely naturalistic or purely practical (or in both pure forms at once): some ways of filling out Joe's judgments would include naturalistic judgments that Athena rejects but that chime with her views of what's to be sought in life, whereas others would involve no naturalistic disagreement with her, but include views she rejects of what, ultimately, to live for.

A second way to deny that Joe knows what to do is to agree with him on what to do if in his shoes, but think he has it right by sheer fluke. His correct judgment of what to do, an observer may think, is not a result of any general tendency of his plans to "track" the property that constitutes being the thing to do.[1] That might be because his plans

---

1. In the vast philosophical literature on knowledge, talk of "tracking" stems from Nozick, *Philosophical Explanations* (1981), p. 178.

don't track this property in general, or it might be because something in this particular case gets in the way of the tracking. The writings of epistemologists provide many instances of such singular failure to "track" a property amidst general reliability—thinking correctly, say, that cows are on the hill in front of one because one sees models of cows that have been set up on this side of the hill, and not because of the real cows hidden on the other side. In ways like this, plans too might fail to "track" the property that constitutes being okay to do.

We have established, then, two ways in which Joe can plan what to do, and yet fail to "know" what to do: (i) he judges wrongly, planning to do something it is not okay to do, or (ii) his plans fail, in this instance at least, to "track" the property that constitutes being okay to do. The puzzle raised in the previous chapter, though, was whether there are other ways not to "know" besides these two. Hera, imagine, agrees with Joe's decision to give up the trumpet for the garden spade. She even thinks that, in general, his plans respond properly to the facts, and that this particular decision is a case of his plans "tracking" the property that constitutes being okay to do. She is an egoistic hedonist, and she thinks that, whether or not he thought in these terms, Joe decided for the spade because doing so was egohedonic. Can she still think that his tracking pleasure in his planning is somehow fortuitous—fortuitous in a way that defeats a parallel with knowledge?

In one of the Kutuzov cases of the preceding chapter, the answer was yes. Kutuzov, I imagined at one point, chose his guide to life on the advice of a consultant who determined what to advise by drawing lots— and who happened to draw the right guide. Kutuzov thus "tracked" the right property, but didn't genuinely *know* what to do. This example shows that the requirements we have considered so far were insufficient by themselves. For Hera to think that Joe knows what to do, she must think not only that in choosing as he did, Joe was tracking pleasure for himself, the property that constitutes being the thing to do. She must think that this tracking itself is somehow a matter of genuine insight—that he knows, in practice, what to live for.

Reliance

One aspect of planning for life is planning reliance on others: planning to take some things on authority, to defer to other people in some of one's judgments. I defer to scientists, say, in my judgments on quarks, and on the chemistry of benzene: I myself haven't mastered the evidence, and so I use their informed judgment as proxy for my own. Even more so, we might say, I defer to myself: I defer to my past self when I rely on my past conclusions without rethinking them, and I defer to my future self, myself as I will be after further inquiry, when I think further inquiry worthwhile for the further knowledge and insight it will yield. Simon Blackburn proposes these considerations as a key to the concept of knowing. If I am to defer to someone as a source of information, mere truth is not enough. "His position may not deserve respect as the *kind* of position from which one may safely accept information" (Blackburn, "Knowledge," 1984, p. 37).

These considerations offer a possible answer to the question we have been puzzling over: what is there to "knowing what to do" beyond "tracking" the right property in one's decisions? I can defer to others, after all, in my judgments not only of how things stand, but of what to do. If I regard you as wiser than I, then I may rely on your judgment of what to do if in my shoes. I might then, in effect, be deferring not only to your naturalistic judgments, but to an implicit judgment you make as to what being okay to do consists in. I may rely, in effect, on your judgment of what to pursue in life, of what to live for. I don't, presumably, treat you as my utter guru and master, and so my deference to you will be only partial. Still, some degree of deference to the judgment of others is normal and well advised. Why, after all, should only I be able to judge in fundamental matters of how to live? As with judgments of plain fact, moreover, so with plans, I must defer to judgments of my own—past, future, and hypothetical. I rely on past planning without rethinking questions of final end. If I set out to think further and more deeply on life, without having already come to a firm view as to what constitutes being okay to do, I am deferring—no doubt in a limited way—to myself as I will be when I think further. Sometimes I will even defer to judgments that are hypothetical, to judgments that I might make in certain conditions: as I consider alternative courses of inquiry I might pursue, I find one promising only in that I defer to my judgment as it would be as a result of that course of inquiry.

When I defer, I attribute knowledge. Or at least, I go some way toward attributing knowledge: my deferral may be tentative and reserved, in which case I am tentative and reserved in attributing knowledge. We might understand my reservations in two ways: First, I may suspect but not be certain that the person I defer to "really knows", because I don't know enough about the position he's in. Second, my standards for "knowing" may be tighter or looser. I can say that you pretty much know what to do if in my shoes, and since I don't know at all, I must place tentative reliance on your judgment. These two kinds of reservations are not entirely separable; the higher my standards for "knowing", the less certain I may be that you are in the kind of position I count as "knowing".

How could we go from these vague considerations to a characterization of "knowing what to do" that parallels knowledge of plain fact? Defining knowledge has been a heavy philosophical industry, and no clear account of knowledge emerges as an established, widely accepted philosophical finding. If reliance plays the role that Blackburn proposes, that suggests why success would be elusive. Whom to rely on— and when, and how much? That depends very much on the alternatives, on the other ways one has of coming to a judgment on the matter. If we ask what Joe knows, we abstract away from questions of who is to rely on him, with what alternatives. We can hope, then, not to take a clear, successful account of knowledge of plain fact and apply it to plans, but only to gesture toward what might be a promising account of knowledge, and sketch a recipe for going from such an account to an account of knowing what to live for.

One kind of account of knowledge is the "no defeater" family. For Joe to know there are cows on the hill, according to such an account, requires two things: general *reliability* and absence of *defeaters*. Take the case of knowing by seeing. Joe uses his eyes, and judges that there are cows on the hill in front of him. What is needed for this to be knowledge? The first requirement is for him to be a reliable judge of such matters in general. He needs capabilities of vision to recognize what he sees, abilities generally sufficient for the kind of task at hand. This might be normal vision; it might be subnormal but sufficient given how close these cows are. Or he might be an expert cow-spotter, able to recognize cows even from a distance that would stymie the rest of us. The second requirement is for there to be no *defeaters:* there must be nothing quirky getting in the way in this particular case. Joe might judge incorrectly despite his general abilities of visual judgment: the cows he thinks he sees are in fact clever models, robots being tested for a movie.

That he judges incorrectly is a prime kind of defeater. Or he might judge correctly, but on the basis of being misled: there are cows on the hill, but on the other side where he can't see them; he judges correctly that there are cows on the hill, but only because he takes fake cows for real.

We speak of Joe's knowing or not with an eye to reliance; the concept of knowing serves to guide us in relying on some kinds of judgments and not on others. Whether Joe knows, though, depends not on us but on him. We focus on Joe alone, shifting those of us who might rely on him into the background and abstracting away from our features. We place two kinds of conditions on him that bear centrally on questions of whether to rely on him: his general reliability, and an absence of defeaters in this particular case.

Knowledge Claims as Plan-Laden

The vague sketch I have been offering suggests that attributions of knowledge are plan-laden. Joe knows there are cows on the hill, we say; he knows because he sees them. This means very roughly, the proposal is that judgments like his are to be relied on. Concluding that Joe knows, then, amounts to planning to rely on his judgment.

Perhaps instead, though, his knowing is a plain fact of some sort, a special kind of fact we find especially relevant to questions of reliance. Is there some fact, then, that every linguistically competent speaker subscribes to when she claims that Joe knows where he left his spade? Suppose two speakers agree on all the prosaic facts, but disagree on whether to rely on people like Joe to find where they have left their spades. They agree that Joe has a true belief on this score, but disagree on whether to rely on beliefs like Joe's. Don't they thereby disagree on whether Joe knows where he left his spade? If so, what's at issue between them isn't some question of fact, but a question of what sorts of beliefs to rely on. The question of what Joe knows is plan-laden.

As with any other plan-laden concept, to be sure, knowing that so-and-so will consist in something factual. The by now familiar argument shows that we are all committed to this claim. As always with content, the content of a judgment of knowledge is a matter of the kinds of hyperdecided observers who would agree with it and the kinds who would disagree. To a first approximation, the argument is this: Hera has plans for reliance on another person's judgment that Φ, and her plans take the form of deferring to judgments that have a certain factual attribute—call it F. She thus regards F as what knowing that Φ consists in. She therefore thinks that there is a factual attribute that knowing that Φ consists in. Since every hyperdecided judge accepts this, even we with all our doubts about the world are committed to it. Now I change roles and voice what I am committed to. There is a factual attribute that knowing that Φ consists in.

The argument is a first approximation because Hera's plans for deferring to Joe depend not only on what he and his situation are like. They depend on what she herself is like in the situations she plans for: if she regards herself as having other sources of information, she need not depend on Joe. (We cash out what information she regards herself as having in terms of other features of her plans, in terms of her plans for similar situations for which she doesn't plan to accept that Joe judges as he does.) Attributions of knowledge, though, abstract away from these variations in those who might defer. To the degree that the notion of knowing that Hera employs is clear, she regards Joe's knowing as entirely a matter of what Joe and his situation are like. It is a matter, she thinks, of his having a certain property P, and so she regards P as constituting knowing that Φ.

Still, the concept of knowing that Φ is plan-laden. Hera and Heracles may agree on all the facts of Joe's situation, but if they differ enough on whether to defer to his judgment, they differ on whether he knows. Coherence and agreement on the plain facts doesn't guarantee agreement on whether Joe knows that Φ. When Hera attributes knowledge and when she doesn't depends on her plans—and in this sense, the concept of knowing is plan-laden. (Theists, for instance, may disagree whether faith brings knowledge: they disagree in plan for whether to rely on faith-driven convictions.)

What I have said falls far short of fully mapping the interplay of plan and fact in judgments of knowledge, but I shall take up only a few features of this kind of account. One delicate matter is that Hera, though opinionated in the extreme, plans for situations in which, by her present lights, she will be ignorant. Hyperdecided Hera has views on everything, and she doesn't agonize about her actual grounds for these views. She plans, though, for situations where her evidence will be limited and where she will find herself puzzled about what to think. Is this paradoxical? If she thinks she knows everything about the situation she plans for, why not just plan to believe the truth? For knowledge of cows on hills, the answer might be that her plans must be couched subjectively, in terms of what is available in the situations she plans for. Her plans for being in Joe's shoes, then, cover all situations that are subjectively like Joe's, whether or not the cows are real. Otherwise the plan is not implementable: a plan to believe there are cows on the hill if and only if there really are is, for example, no plan at all. We must examine later, though, whether hyperdecided observers can illuminate the purest of planning claims: claims to know what at base to aim for in life.

Another delicate matter will be how to abstract from variations in those who might rely on Joe's judgment. Hold Joe's own situation constant in the situations Hera plans for. Very roughly, she plans to defer to Joe's judgment in situations E of the following sort that one might be in: First, her plans to judge in E that there are cows on the hill are grounded in plans to judge in E that Joe so judges. Second, in the objective situation one plans to attribute to Joe if one is in E, there is no feature that Hera treats as a defeater. For her to regard feature D as a defeater is for her plans for deferring judgment to contain a proviso: if her plan for E is to judge that he has feature D, then her plan is not to rely on his judgment—and so not to judge that there are cows on the hill, but to suspend judgment.

Knowing What to Live For

All I have been saying is rough and inexact, despite its complexity. Drawing lessons from cases like Joe's is a daunting part of epistemology. An account like the one I am sketching may or may not be on the right track, and we are far from having a guarantee that the complexities I have broached soon come to an end. My aim, though, is not to refine such an account further, but to suppose that we had one along these broad lines. For a hyperdecided observer to attribute knowledge, on this kind of account, is for her plans for deferring in judgment to combine with her factual beliefs in a certain kind of pattern. Thinking along these lines, I am assuming, is a promising way of approaching questions of knowledge—and so we can now ask how it extends to knowing what to do. Suppose, I want to ask, an account like this were well developed. Would it extend not only to Joe's naturalistic beliefs, but to his plans and to his plan-laden judgments? Given that Joe can know where his spade is, would anything parallel apply to Joe's planning what to do, his planning to take up the spade and not the trumpet?

In her plans for situations one might be in, Hera will plan sometimes to defer to Joe's planning and sometimes not. Roughly, she will say that Joe knows what to do if her plans are to defer to his judgment on the matter. When, then, will Hera regard Joe as not merely happening to track the right property in his plans, but displaying, in his planning, a "knowledge" of what ultimately to live for? She will do this, we might venture, when she plans to defer to his judgment of what to do, and this is not just a matter of her planning to defer to his naturalistic judgments.

Contrast, then, two kinds of cases that Hera can plan for. For case F, she just plans to defer to Joe's powers to apprehend natural facts, such as that gardening will be pleasant. She plans to judge independently that one's own pleasure and freedom from suffering are the things to live for, and to judge independently that Joe's planning tracks his own pleasure. She then plans to rely on Joe's plan-laden judgments as indicators of how to track one's own pleasure in one's planning. Her plan for case F, then, is to credit Joe with tracking the right end in his planning, but not in any way to defer to Joe in her own choice of end.

For case G, in contrast, she plans to defer to Joe in her very choice of final end. Not that she need think that Joe has an explicit doctrine of what to live for. She plans, though, to credit him with planning that tracks his own pleasure, and she plans no independent judgment of her own as to what to live for. Rather, her plans for case G are this: if in G, then track one's own pleasure in one's planning, and do so *on the basis of* Joe's tracking pleasure in his planning. In that sense, she plans to defer to Joe on the question of ultimate end. That is the contingency plan she makes for case G.

Hera's plans for case G are a part of what constitutes her thinking that Joe knows what to live for. Her plans for case F are not. Her plans for F, to be sure, do not *exclude* thinking that Joe knows what to live for. But since her plans for this case are to make an independent judgment of what to live for, no question of whether or not to defer to Joe on this arises. To determine if she thinks Joe knows what to do, then, look not to cases like F, which are irrelevant. Look rather to a pattern of cases like G, cases for which she plans no judgment of what to live for unless in reliance on Joe.

At this point I should raise a possible worry—though I'll argue that with due consideration, the worry disappears. Hera is hyperdecided, and so she herself has a view of what to live for. (Perhaps she's a hedonistic egoist.) Trivially, she regards her own view as correct. How can she plan, for some circumstances, to defer to Joe on what to live for? Why not simply plan, for any epistemic circumstance that might arise, to take the view which she, in her hyperdecided state, thinks true? (If Hera is a hedonistic egoist, why won't she plan always to accept hedonistic egoism?)

For the question of where Joe's spade is, in contrast, Hera could not possibly plan always to take the right view. For she must have the same plan for any two situations that are subjectively indistinguishable, and although Joe's spade is often where he remembers putting it, in subjectively indistinguishable situations it isn't there: someone has moved it, say, without yet perturbing Joe's own experience. The question of what most basically to live for, in contrast, has the same true answer for every possible circumstance. To be sure, whether to go for wealth or love, for insight or benefactions to others, might differ from person to person and from time to time. The fundamental question in living, though, the purely practical component of how to live, is one of dependence: *how* does what specifically to seek depend on one's circumstance? You differ from me in natural qualities, suppose, and in consequence, whereas the thing for me to seek is wealth, the thing for you to seek is mitigating the sufferings of others. How, the purely practical question is, does this difference in what to seek depend on our differences in nature, in natural circumstance? Hera's single hyperplan implies an answer to this question of dependence; we discern Hera's answer by seeing how her plan makes what to seek depend on what one is like.

And so the worry remains this: when Hera plans how to plan, why not plan always to adopt her very own actual hyperplan—her own plan for what to seek as a function of what one is like? She thinks this plan correct, after all. Why plan ever not to accept it?

This worry misconceives the role of hyperstates and hyperdecided observers. Hera is not a self-aware participant in human inquiry; she is a dramatic representation of a complete and consistent set of plans and opinions. We human inquirers can entertain various aspects of her state of mind, sometimes agreeing or disagreeing, sometimes suspending judgment. Two components of a hyperstate are a hyperplan for action, and a hyperplan for coming to plan-laden convictions. This latter hyperplan we could call *epistemic;* it is a plan for what to believe. (Or if it is best to regard planning as a matter not of belief but of "quasi-be-lief", we can call plans for how to plan *quasi-epistemic*—but I'll omit the "quasi".) Now one consistent epistemic hyperplan is, to be sure, always to adopt hedonistic egoism as one's hyperplan for what to do. That means adopting hedonistic egoism no matter how wildly implausible it seems to you or anyone else, and would go on seeming to you as you thought more, and as you vividly pictured the consequences and con-sulted others. That's a logically possible hyperplan, sure enough—but of no plausibility to Joe or to me.

We mortals ask how to plan what to do when we are uncertain what to do and on what basis, and we need to plan our inquiries. Or perhaps we are each settled on a policy for acting, but we disagree, and seek to agree on how to settle our dispute. To plan to settle, no matter what, on hedonistic egoism is idle. We would accept it only if we were so com-placently settled on pure questions of what to seek in life that we had no need of epistemology. Alternative plans speak better to our condi-tion. Prominent attempts to define normative concepts often can be seen as appealing, implicitly, to such plans for how to plan. Ideal ob-server definitions specify an epistemic state and in effect treat it as au-thoritative. The ideal observer, perhaps, is one who has thought mat-ters through, vividly and repeatedly, in an otherwise normal frame of mind. Joe's epistemic plan might be, among other things, to defer to the ways he would plan what to do if he were in such an ideal state.[2]

Joe, in short, will have partial views on how to live. He may also have views on when to discount his own judgments and when to defer to the judgments of others. These amount to plans for how to plan, and his views on who knows what, I am venturing, are contained in aspects of these metaplans, the ones I am calling epistemic. You and I can have epistemic plans for when to defer to Joe, and these amount to opinions about what Joe knows and what he's ignorant of. All this goes both for Joe's views on where his spade is and his views on how to live. Hyperdecided observers, fictional as they are, themselves harbor no

---

2. Ideal observer definitions have most often been directed at moral concepts. See Firth, "Ethical Absolutism" (1952); Brandt's qualified attitude method, *Ethical Theory* (1959); and Smith, *Moral Problem* (1994). Brandt adopts such a strategy for a reforming definition of 'rational' in *A Theory* (1979). Railton offers such a defini-tion of a person's good in "Moral Realism" (1986).

doubts on what to live for. But they plan what to believe and what to plan given evidence. Keeping track of their hyperstates can be a way of studying the logic of claims to planning knowledge.

Reliability and Knowledge

In effect, then, Hera's plans include judgments of what it takes to be a reliable judge of what to live for. Being reliable is a matter of being someone to rely on, and so thinking someone reliable amounts to planning to rely on such people. On what basis, then, might Hera find Joe or his like reliable on questions of what to live for? She treats some kinds of people as more reliable than others on such questions, and so her plans for deferring amount to embracing standards for reliability. She accepts, in effect, an epistemology of the end of life, a view of what makes for reliability in the way one's planning responds to the facts.

Planners to trust, Hera might well think, are those whose planning issues from vivid and repeated awareness of available relevant facts in an alert and dispassionate frame of mind.[3] Call these conditions *K*. To this she must add another requirement, a normal constitution as it affects planning judgments. She won't, after all, defer to just any possible being who meets the other conditions. For any judgment one could make, no matter how bizarre, there must surely be a *possible* kind of being who would make that judgment if he met conditions *K*—if his planning issued from vivid and repeated awareness of available relevant facts, an alert and dispassionate frame of mind, and a normal constitution as it affects planning judgments. What Hera can plausibly think, then, is this: that planners to trust are those who not only meet conditions *K*, but also have normal planning constitutions.

What could normality be as it figures in Hera's planning? She may stipulate some of its elements, but mostly she will have to rely on normality's being prevalent. Normality, in a situation that Hera plans for, must be a matter of what the bulk of *actual* judges are like in that situation. Consider her planning for being in situation *G*. She plans, suppose, to be opinionated in *G* on all matters of fact—including all matters of Joe's constitution that underlie his intellectual, emotional, and

---

3. Brandt, in *A Theory* (1979), speaks of vivid and repeated awareness of relevant facts (pp. 110–113). Firth, in "Ethical Absolutism" (1952), requires the ideal observer to be dispassionate.

planning propensities, and all matters of the constitutions of others who exist in G. Her plan for G is to defer to Joe on questions of how to live, in part on the grounds that his constitution in that situation is normal.

Hera plans also for situations where she knows much less about Joe, where she knows only that he is normal. Imagine another situation G^* for which she plans to be less than opinionated. For G^* she plans to attribute to Joe the following natural properties: (i) his general situation, (ii) that he decides to lay down the trumpet for the spade, and (iii) that his so planning issues from vivid and repeated awareness of available relevant facts in an alert and dispassionate frame of mind, and (iv) that his constitution as it affects planning judgments is normal. (Being normal in G^* is a matter of how features of constitution are distributed among people who exist if one is in situation G^*.) She plans to suspend judgment on what Joe's constitution is and how features of his constitution are distributed in the population. Her plan for G^* is likewise to defer to Joe on questions of how to live, again, in part, on the grounds that his constitution in that situation is normal. She needn't settle entirely, in her planning, what properties normality consists in; she can rely on taking what is common to be normal.

So much for Hera, who is hyperdecided; what of the rest of us? We lack detailed views on anyone's psychic constitution, but we do have somewhat vague views on what sorts of judges to trust: roughly, perhaps, the ones that meet conditions K, the conditions that Hera sets down for most trusting judgments of what to do. We don't plan to defer to the judgments that any *conceivable* being that met conditions K would make. Nor do we embrace much by way of specifications of the constitutions that qualify a planner as reliable. Rather, our plan, for any situation S, is to defer to the judgments that people—or most people, perhaps—who inhabit S would make if they met conditions K. This is an impure planning matter, one that mixes plan with fact. Specify exactly what a constitution C consists in—dopamine levels and all—and I have no idea whether to defer in my planning judgments to a person with such a constitution. For I don't know if constitution C is typical of human beings or something bizarre and alien to us. My plan, rather, is to trust *us*. With many qualifications, I plan to trust us as we are, whatever our range of constitutions may be. I treat the typical human constitution as trustworthy given certain vague conditions, and know that this commits me to taking certain other kinds of constitutions as untrustworthy. I don't judge which constitutions are which, except that the ones we in fact have are at least to some degree to be relied on.

This seems the only coherent stance we could take in our planning, the only stance that would not undermine its own acceptance. Otherwise, how could I trust my own planning from one moment to the next, without reviewing all its grounds again? I survey the considerations and confidently decide what to do, but as soon as I stop surveying the considerations, I must trust my judgment of a moment ago. If we plan at all, then, we are committed to attributing to ourselves, in this sense, some knowledge of what to do. This is knowledge that goes beyond just happening to track the right property in our planning, just happening to track the property that constitutes being the thing to do. We fasten on the right things to live for because we are in a condition to be trusted on such matters—so we judge.

Can we, then, sometimes know what to do? When we do, is this real knowledge; is it knowledge in the same sense as with natural features of our surroundings? Knowledge or quasi-knowledge—which it is I won't try saying. In crucial respects, though, plan-laden judgments can at least parallel the clearest and most literal cases of knowledge. Plan-laden judgments may be true, in a minimal sense, and they can be formed in a way to rely on. The finding that a judgment meets these conditions is plan-laden. This holds too for knowledge of natural facts: it holds for the finding that, say, a scientist's belief in natural selection is reliable. If planning judgments to trust are still not fully cases of knowing, they share many features with full knowing. The parallels extend far.

~ 12

Ideal Response Concepts

$\mathcal{W}$HAT CONSTITUTES being okay to do? It is, we might try answering, whatever I would settle on as my guide to living if I thought about the matter in a way that was ideal. That's truistic, perhaps—and to a number of philosophers, such thoughts have suggested a way out of Moore's problem. (Michael Smith gives the final chapter of his 1994 book *The Moral Problem* the title "How to Solve the Moral Problem".) These thoughts suggest a broad strategy for constructing definitions of ethical terms and of other normative terms. The definitions can be descriptive and naturalistic, and still the upshot may be proof against Moore's bundle of refutations.

The strategy is this: first, find a response tied to the concept we want to define—as, for instance, moral disapproval is tied to the concept of being morally wrong. Next, formulate what makes for ideal responses. (The ideal observer, says Roderick Firth, "Ethical Absolutism," 1952), is omniscient, omnipercipient, disinterested, dispassionate, and in other respects normal.) Finally, define the term in question ('wrong', for instance) as eliciting the response from an ideal responder. (An act is *wrong*, the definition might go, if it would elicit disapproval from any observer who was omniscient, omnipercipient, disinterested, dispassionate, and in other respects normal.) I'll call any definition in this broad form an *ideal response definition*.

Such definitions for normative concepts offer an alternative to expressivism. These analyses are straight and naturalistic, unlike the oblique analyses of an expressivist: such a definition says straight out what a term means, so that we could, at the cost of being wordy, substitute the new analysis for the old term. Even if we don't bother, we know that we always could. Alternatively, such a definition may be proposed as a reform or precisification: give up the old term, with its old, vague and confused meaning, we can urge, and substitute this new, straightforward understanding.

An expressivist like me, in contrast, thinks that normative terms have their own kind of meaning, and that such meanings are indispensable. Normative concepts are not naturalistic, and no naturalistic analysis captures a normative meaning. Moreover, no naturalistic concept can substitute adequately for a normative concept—at least in contexts that raise fundamental questions of how to live and how to respond to acts, states of affairs, and the like.

In this chapter, I look at ideal response definitions and argue that they fail—at least in their fullest ambitions. More precisely, they fail in any naturalistic form. Being *ideal* as a responder, I say, is itself a plan-laden concept, and so if 'wrong' means, by definition, disapproved of by an ideal observer, the definition is not naturalistic but plan-laden. This line of thought leaves the way clear, however, for ideal response concepts that are themselves plan-laden. Such concepts are important, and I scrutinize their behavior.

Descriptive Ideal Response Definitions

Turn again to plans. Hyperdecided Hera will have plans not only for whose judgments to defer to, barring more reliable grounds for judgment. She will have plans for which kinds of judges to give more deference to and which to give less. Given the total network of her plans, we could discern which kinds of judgments she plans maximally to defer to. Her plans contain a conception of what kinds of beings are *ideal planners*, ideal judges in matters of what to live for.

She might draw on this conception to devise an ideal response definition of being the thing to do. The response, in this case, is to plan to do; an act is okay, she can say, just in case an ideal planner would plan to do it. (That is, he rules out ruling out doing it.)

Our discussion now ties in, as I have indicated, with an important class of theories in moral philosophy, with ideal response definitions of normative terms, as I am calling them.[1] For being okay to do, start with the thought that what's okay is what I'd plan to do were I an ideal planner. As for what natural property it is that being okay consists in, it is whatever property the acts I plan would all share if I pondered how to live in an ideal way. What, then, makes a way of thinking ideal? In the spirit of ideal response definitions in the literature, we might answer along lines like the following: one must be in a dispassionate frame of mind, vividly imagining the alternatives, and considering all relevant thought experiments and philosophical arguments—those whose consideration would affect one's plans for life. A philosopher can refine such a characterization and make it precise, and then propose it as a definition. A way of thinking counts as *ideal*$_d$ (descriptively ideal), he can stipulate, iff it has descriptive properties A, B, C, and D. Define an act, then, as i_d-*okay* if and only if it has whatever property I would settle on as my guide to living if I thought about the matter in a way that was ideal$_d$.

Imagine we have these concepts adequately defined. As the concept of being ideal$_d$ is descriptive and naturalistic, so is the concept of being i_d-okay: it is a descriptive concept of some property P that acts can have. The concept is subjective and response-invoking, in that it appeals to the planning response one would have to thinking about things in a certain way. Other descriptive concepts of this same property P will also be available. One, an objective one, will be the concept by which I would think of P if I planned in an ideal$_d$ way and took P as my guide to living. Perhaps if I considered matters in an ideal$_d$ way, I would become a hedonistic egoist in my planning, deciding always to do what is egohedonic. I would have, then, an objective concept H of being egohedonic, offering maximal prospects for net pleasure in one's life. The concepts of being i_d-okay and of being H will then be alternative descriptive concepts of the same property—the one concept subjective and response-invoking, the other objective.

Such an ideal response definition might be put forth as a sheer stipu-

---

1. Prime examples of definitions in this spirit are Firth's ideal observer theory, "Ethical Absolutism" (1952); Brandt's qualified attitude method and quasi-naturalistic definition, *Ethical Theory* (1959); Brandt's reforming definition of 'rational', *A Theory* (1979); Railton's definition of a person's good, "Moral Realism" (1986); and Smith, *The Moral Problem* (1994).

lation, allowing the speaker to abbreviate complicated things she will be going on to say. At another extreme, it could be claimed as giving what we already mean by a term—I'll comment on this ambition shortly; I think it cannot be achieved. A most promising status to accord to such a definition is a third one, that of a reform: a proposed substitute for a meaning that, in our thoughts as they stand, is unclear.

A reform must aim for *relevance*. Choose the wrong conditions as "ideal", and an ideal response definition is of no help. It would be no endorsement of happiness as one's sole end in life to find, say, that under brainwashing in a mad hedonist's reeducation camp, I would track it as my aim. The proponent of the concept of being i_d-okay hopes for something like this: that although we cannot agree, initially, on whether H is what constitutes being okay to do, we can agree that whatever is i_d-okay is okay—that whatever property constitutes being i_d-okay also constitutes being okay to do. If we agree on this, we reduce the question of what, ultimately, to live for to a descriptive question: what property constitutes being i_d-okay.

Relevance need not be uncontroversial. If a descriptive, response-invoking concept is proposed to substitute for a plan-laden concept, controversies over its relevance will be plan-laden: they will involve questions of what to live for. Imagine, for example, that upbringing affects one's judgments of what to live for: those brought up with kindness and gentleness pursue happiness, fulfillment, and warm relations with others, whereas those raised with a firm hand that doesn't spare the rod give more weight to order, status, achievement, and avenging slights. (An adequate psychology of upbringing must no doubt be far less simplistic than this, but imagine that this pop caricature of human development were the truth.) You, suppose, defer only to the planning of someone who, along with other characteristics, has been brought up with kindness and gentleness, whereas I defer only if the planner has been raised with a firm hand that didn't spare the rod. We will disagree, in consequence, as to what constitutes being the thing to do, and so we will find different proposed substitutes to be relevant. No appeal to a response-invoking descriptive concept will settle our differences, for we each would appeal to a different one.

We might, to be sure, do better, and find a response-invoking descriptive concept that was relevant uncontroversially—or discover that nothing turned out to hinge on whose candidate for ideal planner one defers to. Then again, even if no one reform is found relevant by all humanity, some group of us may be able to take a reform as settled. We cannot, though, take it as settled in advance, on sheer grounds of meaning, that some such concept will serve the purposes for which we need the concept of being okay to do. Moreover, suppose we had found such a universal substitute: that so unproblematically as no longer to need any thought or discussion, a particular descriptive concept i_d-*okay* had been found relevant to all purposes of planning. Even then, philosophers would still need the plan-laden concepts I have been expounding, concepts of being the thing to do and of being okay to do. For philosophers, along with various others of our jobs, labor to identify the uncontroversial presuppositions of our thinking. That job would remain even when the reform had become unproblematical. And at that point, a crucial presupposition of our thinking would be that being i_d-okay constitutes being okay.

Plan-Laden Ideal Response Definitions

Part of the appeal of ideal response definitions, if I am right, lies not in their strict sense, but in the suggestions of the term 'ideal'. Any coherent planner will think that the thing to do in a situation is whatever she would now opt for, in her plans, on an ideal view of the matter. For we can understand "ideal" qualifications for planning just as the ones to defer to. That is to say, characteristics D make one an *ideal* planner just in case the way to plan if one lacks these characteristics is to defer the judgments one would make if one had them. Let me use the term 'ideal' (as opposed to 'ideal$_d$') to express this plan-laden concept of ideal response. An act is *i-okay*, we can then say, just in case it has whatever property I would now settle on as my guide to living if I thought about the matter in a way that was ideal.

The concept of being i-okay is response-invoking, but it is not purely descriptive and naturalistic; it is plan-laden. You and I may agree on all facts, and yet disagree on what is i-okay. For we may disagree only in our plans for whom to defer to in our planning judgments. Cases where planning judgments depend heavily on upbringing will provide examples: your ideal of a judge, say, was raised kindly and gently; mine with a rod in a firm hand. What is i-okay according to you may then not be i-okay according to me.

The concept of being i-okay is not the concept of being okay. For the concept of being i-okay is indexical in a way that the concept of being okay is not. You and I might, if rendered ideal, make different plans for the same exact plight, the same exact hypothetical contingency. We might plan differently for the plight of Socrates, who must choose between hemlock and exile: perhaps you, if idealized, would plan death by hemlock for Socrates's plight, whereas I, if idealized, would plan flight into exile for that same exact plight. In that case, Socrates's taking the hemlock is i-okay with respect to you but not with respect to me.

Still, a requirement of pragmatic coherence ties the two concepts together. If I am coherent and have views on these matters, I'll think Socrates's drinking the hemlock okay just in case I think it i-okay with respect to me now. For by definition, a state is ideal if and only if it is one to defer to, and an act is i-okay (with respect to me now) if and only if I'd judge it okay if I were ideal. Deferring, I judge hemlock okay just in case I think my ideal self would so judge it—that is, just in case I think it i-okay. More precisely, characteristics D render anyone *ideal* just in case the following holds: for any possible person i at time t and any hypothetical contingency s, the thing for i to plan to do in contingency s is whatever i *would* plan to do in s if i had characteristics D. It is a requirement of coherence in planning that, for any contingency s, one accept the following (where I^+ is myself as I would now be if I were ideal)[2]: the thing to do in s is whatever I^+ would plan for contingency s.

Let me illustrate further with an example that has enough structure to display the contrasts we need. Young Plato, imagine, has thought matters through and embraced a descriptive concept of being ideal$_d$. To be ideal$_d$ is, by definition, to be dispassionate and maximally engaged in dialectic. Plato treats this as a fully relevant substitute for the plan-laden concept of being ideal: he thinks that being ideal consists in being ideal$_d$, in being dispassionate and maximally engaged in dialectic. He plans, then, always to defer to what his ideal$_d$ planning would be, when he knows what this is and when he is not himself in an ideal$_d$ state.

Plato now sits with Socrates in the prison cell as the time approaches when Socrates must either take the hemlock or flee. Xanthippe has been sent away so that the men can shoot the dialectic undisturbed. (I'll call them 'Soc' and 'Xanti', as their close friends do.) Xanti now asks

---

2. Railton uses the '+' notation in roughly this way in "Moral Realism" (1986).

herself whether, if faced with Soc's plight, it is okay to take the hemlock. In other words, she is planning what to do, when the time for the hemlock comes, if in Soc's plight.

Plato, in turn, asks himself how Xanti is to judge; he plans for the case of being Xanti. Call Xanti's situation X: in X she is wrought up, brooding, and bitter over philosophy. Let S be Soc's situation when handed the hemlock; Xanti in situation X, then, is deciding what to do in contingency S. Wrought up and embittered over philosophy as she is, she decides if in S to take the hemlock. A reliable soothsayer, however, has told her that if she were ideal$_d$, her plans for S would be to flee: she would then find continuing philosophical inquiry to be of overriding importance.[3]

Plato's plan for the case of being Xanti in X is to *think* the following: that in S, whatever act is i-okay with respect to herself is okay. Let X^+ be Xanti's situation as it would be were she ideal$_d$: not wrought up and embittered, but dispassionate and maximally engaged in dialectic. Plato plans to think, if in X, the following: that were one in X^+, one's plan for being in S would be to flee. He plans to defer to such planning. He thus plans, if in X, to *plan* to flee if in S.

Soc's fleeing, Plato thinks, is i-okay with respect to Xanti, in the sense that if *she* were ideal, her plans for being in S would be to flee. It is not i-okay, he thinks, with respect to himself: were Plato himself ideal, he is convinced, he would find civic duty to be of overriding importance, and his plans for being in S would be to take the hemlock. He thus (i) judges that the thing for Soc to do is to take the hemlock, but (ii) plans to judge, if in Xanti's shoes, that the thing for Soc to do is to flee.

This shows a kind of split attitude toward Xanti's judgments: he plans if in her shoes to judge, as he sees it, incorrectly.[4] Why, though, should his plan for being in state X not be to judge correctly—and so, as he sees it, to plan not to flee but to take the hemlock? Viewing certain characteristics of a planner as ideal, we have been saying, is a matter of planning when and how to defer, in one's planning, to the judgments one would make if one had those characteristics. One plans to

3. More precisely, Plato regards the soothsayer as reliable: his plans for situation X are to accept what one remembers the soothsayer as saying.

4. I puzzle over such situations in *Wise Choices* (1990), chap. 11; see esp. pp. 214–217.

rely, in certain kinds of situations, not on one's own present judgment but on the judgments one would make in circumstances that don't obtain. The basic way to plan is not this, but to think directly about the relevant considerations and make one's plans accordingly. Plans to defer in one's judgments address situations in which such direct planning is somehow unavailable; it is planning for when to distrust one's own current powers of direct judgment.

To capture planning judgments of both kinds, then, we should let hyperdecided planners like Hera make plans on at least two different levels: plans directly for what to do in each possible situation, and plans for how to plan. These latter plans we might call *quasi-epistemic:* just as one's *epistemic* plans are plans for what beliefs to form in hypothetical circumstances, in light of ensembles of evidence one might have, so these quasi-epistemic plans are plans for what plans to form in hypothetical circumstances—and plans, I have been arguing, act much like beliefs; they are "quasi-beliefs". One's quasi-epistemic plans, then, abstract away from direct, first-order questions of what to do. Hera, then, can consistently ponder the situation S of Soc, and both (i) plan to take the hemlock if in S, and also (ii) for the case of being Xanti in X, plan to *plan* to flee if in S. Hera's plan for X is a plan for how to plan, and so it brackets her answer to the first-order question of what to do if in S.

Absolutist Alternatives

Hera thinks that Soc's taking hemlock is okay but not, with respect to Xanti, i-okay. Should we allow being i-okay to come apart, in this way, from being okay? The culprit seems to be the indexicality of being i-okay—the way, for instance, that fleeing if one is Socrates can be i-okay with Xanti but not with Plato. To say that *fleeing in S is i-okay with respect to X* is to say this: a person in X^+ would plan to flee if in S. Xanti's ideal situation for planning, X^+, is characterized in terms of what Xanti is actually like; in X^+ one has the mental constitution of Xanti in X, but transformed and idealized in certain ways. Xanti idealized, alas, may plan differently from Plato idealized: they may have different plans for the contingency of being in Socrates's shoes. Why settle, though, for this indexicality? Matters would be far more straightforward—they would be coherent far less problematically—if we could achieve a non-indexical, absolute notion of being i-okay.

I think, though, that some such indexicality is unavoidable. How might one render i-okayness (or a suitable variant) absolute? One possible strategy would be to specify what constitutes being an ideal planner so tightly as to guarantee that all possible ideal planners would agree. Plato might be convinced that all possible observers, were they rendered ideal, would agree in their judgments. In other words, he might accept a principle of *quasi-epistemic absolutism* as follows:

> The property that constitutes being ideal is such that for any two possible beings x and y, if they both had that property, then they would agree in all their planning judgments.   (Abs)

That would rule out the complex scenario above, in which Plato plans to plan one way if himself and a different way if Xanti.[5]

What property, though, could satisfy this condition? Consider a hyperdecided way of agreeing with Plato and accepting principle (Abs). Hera has a descriptive conception of what constitutes being an ideal judge; she thinks, let us say, that to be ideal is to be *H-ideal*, where the concept of being H-ideal is descriptive. She accepts the following:

> Being H-ideal constitutes being ideal, and for any two possible beings x and y, if they were each H-ideal, then they would agree in all their planning judgments.   (Abs_H)

Planning, though, is a matter of judgment and plausibility, of finding it plausible that some things matter more than others, that certain considerations outweigh various opposing considerations. The concept of being H-ideal must be a quasi-epistemic concept, formulated in a way that doesn't simply specify all the planning judgments that one must make to count as H-ideal. The content of one's plans isn't necessitated by such general, quasi-epistemic properties as dispassionate judgment, vivid awareness of all considerations, attending to all relevant arguments, and the like. How one would judge if one met conditions like these is a matter of temperament, of a mental constitution that underlies one's dispositions to find some things plausible and others not

---

5. Firth offers an absolutist ideal response definition in "Ethical Absolutism" (1952). Smith may be offering a similar theory in *The Moral Problem* (1994), chap. 6, suggesting that there might be "a convergence in the desires that fully rational creatures would have" (p. 187).

in H-ideal conditions. How could the right kind of temperament be specified in a way that settles how one would judge if one had certain quasi-epistemic properties, and doesn't just specify the content of the judgments one would make? I don't quite know how to prove this impossible, but I don't see what such a specification could look like.

One possibility remains: defer to the ideal judgments of the agent herself, of the person whose choice of acts one is planning. In planning what to plan for the contingency of being Socrates, Plato might defer not to an idealized Xanti, or even to himself idealized, but only to Socrates himself idealized. Plato might hold that only in situation S^+ is one an ideal judge of what to do in S: that to be an ideal judge, one must possess an idealization of the mental constitution of the agent—one must be as the agent himself would be if, say, he were dispassionate and maximally engaged by dialectic.

Many will find such a standard entirely plausible. It avoids, after all, the logical difficulties that have been vexing us, and it doesn't require "cooking" one's descriptive specification of what makes one ideal to guarantee particular substantive results. The standard, moreover, seems especially non-alienating: it tells us not to plan, for the case of being Socrates, to act on a standard that is alien to Socrates, but instead to act on what one's own best judgment would be. This may all seem a happy confluence of virtues, both forced on us if we are to avoid a kind of epistemic incoherence, and welcome as embracing a non-alienating standard of decision.

Accepting this form of non-alienating absolutism, though, would be alienating in a worse way still—or so I shall argue. Accepting it would be incompatible with a kind of trust one needs in one's direct thinking about what to do in a situation. As I think what to do, I respond primarily to first-order considerations. I also have second-order views of what constitutes better or worse judgment in one's planning. When considerations of the two orders conflict, I face a kind of pragmatic contradiction: I must revise either my first-order views on how the considerations stack up and weigh against each other, or revise my second-order views of what judgments of mine to defer to. Adjustments will presumably go both ways, or sometimes one way and sometimes the other: in making these revisions, I won't always accord my second-order judgments hegemony; they will be under pressure for revision, just as are my first-order views.

Turn, though, from deciding what to do right now to contingency planning for circumstances one is not now in: planning for what to do if someone else, or if oneself in different circumstances. The "non-alienating" absolutism that is being proposed then has one's second-order views dominating entirely. Think of Xanti planning what to do if Socrates, who must choose to flee or die. To judge what it's okay for Soc to do is to plan for the contingency of being him, with all of his characteristics. Xanti can't slip into thinking that, in this contingency, she has any of her actual deep convictions, projects, attitudes, or sources of fulfillment—apart from those few she shares with Socrates in actuality. Serious planning for the case of being him will require immense insight and sensitivity to all the ways that being him is not like being her.

Still, Xanti has pondered much on how to live (though when she expresses any of these views to the men in her life, they give no heed, so that she soon finds herself venting her frustration with their conceits, and they dismiss her as a shrew). Two considerations rank high in her estimation: pursuing those projects one finds consuming and which give shape to one's life, and giving play to one's spontaneous desires so as not to mortify them. She allows civic duty some role in her planning, but conditioned on a polis that is a system of cooperation with mutual respect. Socrates's consuming, life-shaping passion is philosophy, and to take the hemlock cuts short his philosophizing. In deciding not to flee, he mortifies his spontaneous desire to live. In the polis as it stands in this post-defeat hysteria, mutual respect has disappeared. If, though, she is to plan as an anti-alienation absolutist, she must think that these aren't the things that ultimately matter. She must think, in effect, that nothing ultimately matters except in mattering *to* someone, in striking someone as mattering. What matters, ultimately, for her own life, she must think, is not the pursuit of life-shaping, consuming projects like raising her children, not giving play to one's spontaneous desires—but that these are the things that strike her as mattering.

To think such a thing is itself alienating: Certain things seem to Xanti to matter in themselves. Now, though, she must think that they matter only in *seeming* to her to matter—and so wouldn't matter if one didn't recognize that they do. Now to be sure, some degree of alienation from one's thinking is a part of being self-critical and open to re-thinking: one must draw back from one's direct view of matters and see it as a view that might be wrong. But our "non-alienating" absolutism requires Xanti to reject her direct view entirely, except as a subjective happening in virtue of which some things come to matter. Indeed, even in her planning for the contingency of being Socrates, she doesn't accept Soc's own view of the matter, or the view an idealized Socrates would have. She now must plan to take the hemlock not on the ground Socrates accepts—that, in the circumstances, civic duty is overriding—but on a ground Socrates would find alien: that civic duty presents a subjective appearance to him of being overriding. (He does often defer to the voice of his daimon, to be sure, but as he might want to convince Euthyphro, his daimon prescribes the hemlock because taking the hemlock is the thing to do. The "non-alienating" view he rejects: that taking the hemlock is the thing to do because his daimon prescribes it.)

Alienation, then, cuts two ways. I can think that in no possible situation would one experience the thing to do as alien to one's way of judging, if only certain of one's quasi-epistemic defects were remedied. But then I must think that all that matters is non-alienation—and that is a very alien thing for any of us to think.

What, though, of the logical difficulties in rejecting the absolutist principle (Abs)? They cannot be decisive. For the same kinds of conflict that arise when (Abs) fails for planning also arise for judgments of natural fact or of mathematical fact. Imagine a principle of absolutism in mathematical judgments:

> The property that constitutes being ideal is such that for any two possible beings x and y, if they both had that property, then they would agree in all their mathematical judgments.　　　(Mabs)

Isn't there always a possible being who would respond to mathematical considerations in a way different from the rest of us, even if given all the epistemic virtues that don't just amount to being disposed to give the right mathematical answers?[6] That does not in itself refute the view that there are mathematical truths; it just shows that a conceivable perverse mental constitution could lead one to getting things wrong, even if endowed with all the virtues of a mathematician that don't amount just to cooking the books. If such epistemically innocent mistakes are

---

6. Wittgenstein's late treatments of mathematics stress the problems that this possibility raises; see *Philosophical Investigations* (1953), esp. pp. 53–88.

possible in mathematics, then there is no logical contradiction in sup-posing it possible. A like structure in planning for life, it will follow, can't be ruled out on grounds of logic.

The End of Inquiry

In the preceding chapter on knowing what to do, I treated knowledge as reliability: to regard Joe as knowing is to plan to defer, in certain conditions, to judgments like his. I attempted no precise definition along such lines. In part, I suspect that the concept of knowing is not precise in the first place. More important, the pattern of willingness to defer that constitutes attributing knowledge is likely to be intractably complex.

Ideal response definitions, though, suggest a more precise character-ization of what it is to attribute knowledge. Ideal judges presumably *know*, when they get matters right as a result of being ideal and other-wise having the right kind of mental constitution. At least tacitly, we can say, they know what to live for; they don't just get matters right for-tuitously.

Truth, on one view, is what we would accept "at the end of inquiry". This need not be a definition of truth; something more along a defla-tionist line might better give the meaning of 'true'. Still, it has an air of truism—in ethics, at any rate. At the same time it is baffling: surely some kinds of inquiry would come to an end in the wrong place, leav-ing us with false answers. How shall we characterize these kinds of in-quiry to rule them out? We have some inkling, of course, of what would qualify as the right kind of inquiry in the limit, but surely our ideas on this are vague and themselves need refinement; we can't now formulate a precise and serviceable naturalistic definition of "the end of inquiry". As we proceed in our inquiries, we expect we can refine our ideas of what kind of inquiry is reliable. But still, it seems that we could get refining wrong. Perhaps in the next half century, we'll talk our-selves into a racial and sexual characterization of ideal inquiry and come to a firm rejection of all "scientism" and "rationality worship" in inquiry. The put-down with a pun that appeals to audience prejudice, perhaps, will come to be regarded as the most telling form of argu-ment. Modernism will come, until the end of inquiry, to be seen as a brief mistaken interlude in human history, an interruption of the true

unfolding of the human spirit. Perhaps we will think all these things—
and if so, perhaps we will be wrong.

The logic that looks to hyperdecided observers, though, offers an interpretation of "the end of inquiry", an interpretation that avoids these
pitfalls. "At the end of inquiry" simply means this: as a result of ideal
inquiry. Suppose an anti-hedonist Aunty says, "At the end of inquiry,
we would conclude that pleasure is not the only thing that has intrinsic
value." This means the following: that ideal inquiry would lead us to
conclude that not only pleasure has intrinsic value. To say this is to
make a claim that is plan-laden. To make this claim, Aunty need have
no worked-out theory of what constitutes ideal inquiry. We analyze the
content of the claim she makes by asking what sorts of hyperdecided
judges would agree and what sorts would disagree. A hyperdecided
judge Hero has plans to defer to the judgment of others or not in each
possible situation, and also has plans for what to do and views on how
things stand. From his plans to defer we can glean the kind of judge he
plans maximally to defer to in his judgments. He agrees with Aunty if
he thinks that *that* kind of judge will conclude that not only pleasure
has intrinsic value.

Aunty of course will have *some* views about what kinds of inquiry are
valid and what kinds spurious. Hero, then, may agree with her claim
that ethical hedonism would be rejected at the end of inquiry, but disagree with other things that Aunty accepts. This particular claim of
Aunty's, like most of the other things she accepts, derives its force from
its potential to combine with other things she might accept, and so to
yield conclusions as to how things stand, what to do, and how to judge.

In this chapter, I have explored a special class of plan-laden concepts,
ones that pick out a property via trustworthy responses. For a single
property, we now find multiple concepts. Four of these concepts are
now salient. Before, we had (i) the planning concept of being okay, and
(ii) the naturalistic concept that answers how to live. What this second,
naturalistic concept is, we said, is a question of how to live; egoistic hedonists think it is the concept of being egohedonic. These are concepts
of a single property; call it P^*. Now, with responses in play, we have two
further concepts of this same property P^*. There's a plan-laden ideal
response concept: (iii) the concept of being i-okay, of being what one
would plan to do were one an ideal planner. Finally from the concept of
an ideal planner, we get a further, descriptive concept of the same prop-

erty P^*, the property of being okay to do. Some natural property of planners constitutes being ideal as a planner. Which property this is will be a question of how to plan one's planning. Some naturalistic concept of this property, though, answers how to plan one's planning. Let the adjective 'ideal*' express this naturalistic concept. With this concept of being ideal*, we can now construct a descriptive, naturalistic ideal response concept of the property P^*: (iv) the concept of being what an ideal* planner would plan to do.

Philosophers sometimes speak of "response-dependent properties". Such talk is misleading, if I am right; we might better speak of "response-invoking concepts". For being okay to do, we have many concepts of a single property. Two of the four I have listed are response-invoking: (iii) is a plan-laden response-invoking concept, and (iv) is a descriptive, naturalistic response-invoking concept. I myself am quite uncertain which concept (iv) is, and if I were certain, my view would be controversial: it is a question of how to plan one's planning.

An ideal response definition, in short, invokes ideal conditions for a response—conditions, we might try saying, under which the response could amount to knowledge. Any such definition, I argued, will fail to capture the *concept* of being okay to do, though it may signify the *property* of being okay to do. An ideal response definition may be naturalistic, specifying conditions for being ideal in naturalistic terms. Whether it gets these conditions right is not a conceptual question alone; it is a plan-laden question. The concept it formulates, then, will not be the concept of being okay to do. An ideal response definition, on the other hand, may be plan-laden. It replaces *to-be-done*ness with *to-be-planned-to-be-done*ness. Such indirect plan-laden concepts are useful; we may be able to settle on one and use it to settle what to live for. Even then, however, an ideal response concept cannot serve as a full replacement for the simpler concept of being okay to do. Neither indexical versions nor their absolutist alternatives, I argued, answer all calls for plan-laden thinking. Like conclusions went for "the end of inquiry". This too is a plan-laden notion, and as we refine our plan-laden thinking, we refine our views on just what it is to refine our thinking.

～ 13

Deep Vindication and Practical Confidence

*U*P TO NOW, I have been claiming triumph after triumph for a program of quasi-realism for planning. Plans, and plan-laden judgments more generally, turn out in remarkable ways to mimic prosaic descriptive judgments. The predicates 'is okay to do' and 'is the thing to do' act much like ordinary, descriptive predicates, in a multitude of ways: judgments in terms of these predicates can be correct or incorrect. Standard logic applies. There is a natural property that constitutes being okay to do, and a naturalistic attribute that being okay consists in. Being okay to do can figure in causal explanations. We can even speak of a person's "knowing" what to do, and of epistemic (or "quasi-epistemic") virtues in planning and plan-laden judgment.

At this point in our argument, though, the two kinds of judgments may diverge. Unless one has the right kind of mental constitution, I have been arguing, all the epistemic virtues in the world won't lead to judgments that are correct. There is, moreover, no satisfactory way to specify what makes for the right kind of mental constitution that doesn't, in effect, settle by fiat basic controversies over how to plan. Perhaps this lends practical inquiry—thinking what to do—features that don't entirely parallel inquiry into how things are. Such possible divergences are the topic of this chapter: limitations on quasi-realism for plans. I explore ways in which a plausible view of plans might lack certain parallels with a realism for how things stand.

251

Young Plato, in the last chapter, had a view of what constitutes the epistemic virtues. He planned, for the case of being Xanti, to defer to ways Xanti *would* judge if she had all these virtues: he planned, if in her situation X, to judge as one knows one would judge in idealized situation X^+. But he doesn't himself, in his own situation, defer to the idealized Xanti—to Xanti$^+$, as we can call her. Xanti's mental constitution is different from his own, Plato realizes. Xanti$^+$, then, would judge differently from Plato$^+$, and he defers to the judgments of Plato$^+$, the judgments he himself would make if he had all the epistemic virtues.

In that sense, he doesn't attribute to Xanti even the potential for knowing what to do. Or at least he denies that someone like her can know what to do for one particular contingency, that of being in the shoes of Socrates, though he may still think her competent to judge a womanly sphere of life. All this means that in an important sense, Plato thinks that he and Xanti can't form a community of inquiry on questions of what to do if Socrates. Even ideal discussion, he thinks, wouldn't lead to a meeting of minds. He also thinks that on this question, even epistemic virtues without limit would not be enough to turn Xanti into a knower: the judgments of Xanti$^+$ can't be relied on, young Plato is convinced.

Perhaps the same pattern obtains, though, with scientific judgments. Some people take the layout of fossils in rock layers to support Darwinian theory. Others take fossils as a test of faith, a pattern designed by the creator to cull faithful, believing sheep from intellectually hubristic goats. I myself am convinced that if I had all the epistemic virtues and knew all about fossils, rock layers, and the like, I would accept an account of the descent of humanity along Darwinian lines. Who is to say, though, that some people don't have a mental constitution that, even in the face of all this evidence, would lead them instead to accept the doctrine of special creation meant to mislead the unfaithful? Fossils are to the earth what his navel was to Adam, some may conclude, put there by the Creator to make it *look* as though natural processes had been at work for a long time already.[1]

In neither planning nor science, then, do the epistemic virtues logically guarantee reasonable judgment. Can any real contrast be drawn,

---

1. I owe this way of putting the doctrine to Chad Hanson.

then, between science and plans? Or is this scientific impasse on all fours with the impasse of Plato and Xanti?

Deep Vindication

One way to examine these matters would be to turn to a paradigm of knowledge, namely, sensory apprehension. How is "seeing" what to do like seeing with the eyes, and how are they different? In particular, does literal seeing yield knowledge in a way that "seeing" what to do fails to parallel?

Metaphorical seeing may be a good place to start our inquiries. Any judgment whatsoever, after all, must rest on a kind of "seeing". Take planning again: Joe may often settle what to do by reasoning. At times, though, he may just "see" or "realize" what to do. And even when he reasons what to do, we can ask about the starting points of his reasoning and the various steps he takes in his reasoning. These do not involve further reasoning—though on demand Joe could, perhaps, provide some further reasoning to back them up. He seems, then, just to "see" or "appreciate" where to start in his thinking and how to proceed from there. Every case of judging what to do, we can say, rests on somehow "seeing" aspects of how the facts bear on what to do.

Back, then, to seeing with the eyes. Joe sees cattle on the hill up ahead of him. He thereby *apprehends* that there are cattle on the hill. He uses his eyes and exercises his capacities for visual apprehension. Truisms all—but what stands behind them? What *vindicates* our visual capacities, so that we can be said to apprehend facts and acquire knowledge by means of them?

Joe himself may have no view on this matter—or he might just say, "God gave us eyes to see." This last, if it were the full and plain truth of the matter, would vindicate seeing as a perceptual capacity. That is to say, it would show why we are the sort of beings who could be expected often to get things right when we use our eyes. It would show why beings like us wouldn't be hopeless judges of what's what on the basis of vision.

Darwin offers another kind of explanation of our perceptual capacities: they stem from a long history of natural selection that shaped the human genetic plan. To this we must add histories of invention and cultural transmission, in virtue of which, for instance, most of us can read, and some of us can interpret microscope slides.[2]

Let's give Hera, then, plausible views about the nature of a human being like Joe, and about what explains this nature. We want, after all, to examine attributions we ourselves could share. Hera is no believer in special creation *ex nihilo*, with evidence manufactured to fool unbelievers. She accepts Darwin—perhaps as an atheist, or perhaps thinking that the gods work their will through those natural processes of the universe that they have ordained. In particular, she accepts a Darwinian vindication for vision as a perceptual capacity. Reproductive success in ancestral populations depended on many of one's judgments being correct. This produced strong selection pressures for shaping mechanisms to judge ever more accurately. Vision, as a result, is a highly refined system "for" yielding correct judgments of the layout and activity of things and organisms around us. We might call such a vindication, fully worked out, a *deep vindication* of our visual capacities.

This points to an important feature of factual apprehension. Joe sees cattle, and has knowledge on that basis, though he can't spell out a satisfactory vindication for his judgment. He has no vindication beyond "I see them," or a simple theistic vindication that doesn't square with the evidence, or perhaps a garbled "good of the species" version of Darwin. But a correct vindication is to be had—perhaps the one that Hera accepts. In coherently claiming to know that cattle are on the hill, and in claiming to see them, Joe commits himself to *there being* a deep vindication of the capacities he exercises in making the judgment. He doesn't know what this vindication is, and he may never even have thought about vindications. Still, he couldn't coherently claim that he sees cattle on the hill, and yet deny that there exists a deep vindication of his visual capacities.

A deep vindication is not a vindication from an Archimedian point outside everything. We rely on our senses and our powers of thinking to explain why the senses of beings like us would be generally reliable. The "depth" of the vindication is not a matter of evading this inescap-

2. This is not to say that culture is separate from genes: it is because of our specifically human genetic plan that we, as infants growing to adulthood, respond as we do to our surroundings, human and otherwise, and interact with others in ways that go to make up the history of culture. For one view of this, see Tooby and Cosmides, "Psychological Foundations of Culture" (1992).

able kind of circularity, of lifting oneself by one's bootstraps. The point is that the circle is non-trivial. It is not just a matter of determining with the senses that things are so-and-so, and then noting that the senses tell us that things are that way, and therefore speak correctly. The view of the world we establish with our senses tells us why beings such as we have senses that mostly work.

Such a deep, Darwinian vindication of vision appeals to vision's usefulness, to the ways it promotes reproduction. Clearly those who were hopeless at getting everyday, surrounding facts right would tend not to reproduce. They would bump into things; they would fall over cliffs and get killed. Such an explanation of usefulness fits a general schema that is crucial to many kinds of factual knowledge. Call this the *contingency detection schema*. Many courses of action are advantageous under some contingencies and not under others. In the simplest kind of case, the most advantageous scheme of action takes the form: "Do A if contingency C obtains, and B otherwise." A way to fit this scheme with high reliability combines two mechanisms. The first (the detecting mechanism) reliably ensures that one *believe* that C just in case C obtains. The second (the acting mechanism) ensures that one do A if one believes that C, and do B otherwise. Call these together the *detecting-acting complex*.

Other ways might obtain the same result. Consider an "anti-schema" that works as follows: First, an "anti-detecting" mechanism ensures that one believe falsely—that one believe that C just in case C does *not* obtain. Then combine this with a "perverse" acting mechanism, which ensures that one do A if one *dis*believes C, and do B if one believes that C. At this point, a second feature of the schema comes into play: charity. It may be up for grabs what's to count as "belief that C". Playing the right role in the contingency detection schema is what makes us *count* the state as belief that C. In the description of the anti-schema, a state was called "disbelief that C", but by a principle of charity, that's the wrong label. It should be called "belief that C", and the relabeling turns the anti-schema into the standard contingency detection schema.

The contingency detection schema explains, for a wide range of judgments, why we wouldn't be hopeless at getting things right. It does so in a broadly uniform way, appealing to selection pressures, to what promoted reproduction in the course of human evolution. It cites (i) the importance of responding in certain ways to contingencies, (ii) the usefulness of an internal state that "monitors" a kind of contingency, and (iii) charity as a maxim for settling what is to count as monitoring a contingency.

So far, I am discussing only knowing by seeing with one's eyes. Perhaps, though, deep vindicability is required for *any* state of mind to count as knowledge, in a strict sense of the term. If so, that would yield a sense of *belief* in which not all judgments need be beliefs. To believe, we can say, is to take oneself to know. Or at least it is epistemologically incoherent to believe something and think one doesn't know it. Belief, then, *commits* one to the claim that one knows. If knowing, in the strictest sense, involves there being a deep vindication of the capacities one exercises—an account of why beings like us would tend to get that sort of thing right—then believing in this sense commits one to thinking there exists such a deep vindication. One need not claim to know what the vindication is, but it is incoherent fully to believe, in this strong sense of the term, and yet deny that any such deep vindication is to be had.[3]

A deep vindication, if it is to be had, speaks to the problem of varying mental constitutions. Plato trusts his own judgment, to a degree, because it would be incoherent not to do so. That in itself gives him no reason to trust Xanti's judgment. Suppose, though, he trusts his eyes and other senses for a further reason: he accepts a deep, Darwinian vindication of the senses.[4] This vindication applies to him as a product of natural selection. Xanti is equally a product of natural selection, and so the deep vindication applies equally to her. When it comes to sensory judgments, being a product of natural selection is an epistemic virtue because of the selective advantages of the contingency detection schema. And it is an epistemic virtue that isn't "cooked" to yield particular, preordained substantive judgments.

One urgent question to ask about such lines of thought is whether they apply just to the senses, or extend beyond sensory apprehension to other clear-cut cases of knowledge and belief. Mathematics offers a

---

3. True, it is natural in some contexts to say, "I believe it but I don't know it." One thereby claims a degree of belief that falls substantially short of certainty. One does still believe that one "more or less" knows it. To my ear, it would sound strange to say, "I'm certain, but I don't know it"; in avowing belief with certainty in something one doesn't know, one would be confessing to incoherent thinking, to a certainty that is inadequately based.

4. We are now, of course, far away from the historical Plato, who hasn't heard of Darwin and distrusts the senses.

prime test case. Is there an explanation of why beings like us would tend to get mathematics right? The question would demand vastly more than a cursory look; it is a major question in the philosophy of mathematics. Let me speak quickly, though: Simple counting and adding are needed for us to think about everyday experience. Our long-ago ancestors didn't balance checkbooks, but the capacities later used in banking were needed in that earlier day for other tasks. Perhaps these were capacities for simple counting, addition, or subtraction, or perhaps they were more general capacities to reason about objects and kin. We may not be able to reconstruct the correct story of why beings like us were shaped to have capacities to get simple arithmetic right, but it would be puzzling if no such account were correct. The rich consilience of our arithmetic views is no sheer fluke, we can be sure, and so there is a correct explanation for this consilience. What kind of explanation of the consilience would fail to be an explanation of a tendency to get the matter right?

Like remarks would apply to simple geometry: good spatial visualization must be important for hunters and warriors. Other parts of mathematics, though, involve exercising our capacities in ways that were invented far too recently to have affected our native capacities—axiomatic geometry, reasoning about wheels, calculus, and the like. Even settling what would count as a deep vindication of the capacities involved would require far excursions into the philosophy of mathematics. And if we knew what deep vindication requires, we couldn't provide the vindication, for we couldn't expect to recover enough of the psychic history of our coming to think as we do in these parts of mathematics. Still, it is reasonable to think that such a deep vindication exists—unless there is some way we could have achieved the complex coherence we find in mathematics and yet be massively in error. Engineers build bridges that don't fall; could the correct explanation of this fail to vindicate their capacities for mathematical reasoning? The right explanation presumably involves capacities that were reproduction-enhancing among our ancestors, and a history of invention and correction that these capacities, in extended application, made possible. As for, say, the frontiers of set theory, what can be said about these baffles almost anyone who cannot accept a mysterious mathematical Platonism. We can't, then, reasonably use advanced set theory as a test case of what knowledge must be like.

The tie of knowledge to deep vindication requires far more investigation than I can give it. Suppose, though, investigation of clear, fairly uncontroversial cases of knowledge would confirm my suggestion that knowledge, in a strict sense, requires deep vindicability. Do our planning capacities likewise have a deep vindication—whether or not we can reconstruct it? The instrumental aspects of these capacities presumably do; abilities to order goals, balance them, and pursue them must always have been reproductively important for our ancestors leading complex social lives. The deep puzzle concerns our capacities to "track" the *right* ultimate ends rather than something else, our capacities to track, in our plans, the property that constitutes being okay to do. Planning that tracked perfectly an utterly misguided end would not be a matter of knowing what to do. We think that we are not hopeless judges of what to live for, and that by experiencing life, reflecting on experience, and pondering matters and discussing them, we can improve our judgments in these realms. Should we think that the capacities we use to do so can be given a deep vindication?

Judgment without Claims to Knowledge

Distinguish two questions we can ask about plans and deep vindication, about plans as beliefs in a strong sense of the term 'belief'. In this strong sense, recall, it is incoherent to *believe* something and deny that there exists any deep vindication—known or unknown, perhaps even unsuspected—of one's capacities to get such matters right. The first question is whether our plans *must* be beliefs. Does planning in itself, *ipso facto*, commit one to the claim that there exists a deep vindication of one's planning capacities? Or could one plan without, in this specially full sense, believing in one's plans? Second, suppose that logically, plans needn't be beliefs. We might nevertheless form judgments that constitute full-fledged beliefs as to what's okay; such a pattern of judgments might be logically optional. Our second question is whether to acquire full-fledged planning beliefs. Would such a pattern of plans and factual judgments be wise or warranted?

To the first question, I'll suggest an answer quickly: one might make one's plans with full coherence, and yet deny that any deep vindication of one's planning capacities is to be had. Why not, after all? Something parallel goes for factual judgments. My own factual judgments are beliefs: in making them, I commit myself not to deny that a deep vindication of my capacities for such judgments is somehow to be had. Suppose, though, I came to judge that no such deep vindication exists. I wouldn't then stop making judgments of fact, everyday and scientific. I cannot, after all, lead my life without making such judgments. Instead, I would go on making these judgments, but move to a modest assessment of their epistemic status. I would no longer claim fully to *know* whereof I judged, and so my judgments wouldn't fully be beliefs in this strict sense.

Planning too is indispensable in life, and so one cannot reasonably hold one's planning hostage to there being a deep vindication of one's planning capacities. I might perhaps form beliefs in the full sense as to what is okay to do and what is not. But I should be prepared to give up what makes these judgments fully beliefs, while keeping them as judgments.

Judgments do bring commitments, even when these judgments are not full beliefs: there are coherent and incoherent ways to judge, and so one judgment can rule out another on pain of incoherence. One important commitment is this: if I make a judgment, I commit myself to that judgment's being warranted. That is to say, it is incoherent to make the judgment and deny that it is warranted (even if, as it happens, the judgment and the denial are both true). This we can make sense of in terms of plans. To think judgment *P warranted*, we can say, is to plan to make that judgment. More precisely, it is to treat judgment *P* as okay in one's planning, to rule out ruling it out. A plan to make a judgment is not directly practical, but in a broad sense it is epistemic. That is to say, it is not a plan for action, a plan for what to do, but rather, a plan for what to judge. We plan judgments as well as acts. Think, for instance, of planning an experiment: I put litmus paper in a solution, and judge the solution acid if and only if the paper turns red. My plans for an experiment, explicit or implicit, include not only provisions for what to *do* given certain observations I might make, but also for what to *conclude*: I tell myself, in effect, "If the litmus paper turns red, judge the solution to be acid." Without a plan for what to conclude, the experiment would be pointless. (This allows, to be sure, that I may expect to "wing it", to cross certain bridges when I come to them, and just proceed in hopes that I'm somehow putting myself in a better position to judge. In this regard too, planning to judge is like planning to do: I can leave some of my actions unplanned, and expect to "wing it" when the time comes.)

In experiments, then, contingency plans for action and for belief go hand in hand, sharing much the same status: I can plan to judge a solution acid if litmus paper turns red, and plan then to use the solution to polish brass. I judge both what is the thing to do and what is the thing to believe.

Now in this case of an experiment, the contents of the judgments I plan for are purely factual; I plan, say, to judge the solution acid, alkaline, or neutral as I observe the paper to be red, blue, or gray. We can equally well plan, though, for judgments that are plan-laden: plans for what to do, or more complex judgments that include an element of what to do.

If we judge without forming full beliefs, a demand for coherence still applies. If I judge that cattle are on the hill, then I'm committed to the plan to judge, if in my present situation, that cattle are on the hill. It would be incoherent, after all, to make a judgment and yet, in my plans, rule out so judging in that very situation. In judging, then, I'm already committed to a plan: the plan so to judge in my situation. Not, to be sure, that I normally go out of my way to make such a plan; a requirement that I must would lead to a regress: must I plan so to judge, plan to plan so to judge, and so on? Still, I do *commit* myself to all these layers of plans: I rule out rejecting them.

We commit also, in the normal course of life and thought and planning, to a more extensive kind of planning for judgment: planning for further investigation. Often I'll want to think more, to ponder matters further than I have. I ponder what to believe, but even more, perhaps, I ponder what to do. Sometimes even in pondering what to do, the uncertainty I need to resolve is purely factual: I'm clear what to do once I ascertain certain facts. Many kinds of pondering what to do, though, don't take this clear form. I'm not sure what further facts I need, or if I think certain facts relevant, I haven't yet planned out what to do for each of the various ways the facts may turn out to be. To work toward a decision, I try, perhaps, to imagine the alternatives vividly. I talk with others whose judgment I give some weight, or I postpone a decision until I have had more experience with such matters. I do these things without having settled, in my mind, what discoveries of natural fact would support what decisions. In such cases, I haven't reduced my practical uncertainties to purely factual uncertainties. Neither have I factored my questions into purely factual ones, on the one hand, and purely practical ones on the other. I investigate further in hopes of settling what to do, and also in hopes of answering questions that are plan-laden but not *purely* practical. I plan for such investigation; I treat it as okay to pursue.

Coherent planning, then, requires a kind of trust in one's capacities to plan. I don't mean here a bullheaded overconfidence, but a trust that one has some capacity to judge how to live, and to judge how to ponder further how to live in a way that holds out hope of making better judgments. I have been treating such attitudes as having content, a content that mixes plan with fact, and exploring what such attitudes—crucial to living at all—commit us to. I have been asking, then, in effect, what the content might be of a coherent practical faith that we are not in a hopeless position to figure out what to do in life.

To live, I must trust my judgments to a degree, and think that certain kinds of investigation hold promise of better judgments. These views, I have been suggesting, can be put in the form of plans for accepting plans—along with more complex kinds of content that intertwine plan with fact. In the course of life, we may not have elaborate views of how all this goes. But my questions are these: what kinds of views *could* we have and be fully coherent? Do the attitudes we normally take toward life and figuring out how to live it, I ask, lie anywhere in the vicinity of a coherent set of views? Is there, in other words, a satisfactory and coherent hyperdecided view of ourselves and our lives that we *could* take, without radically changing our minds about life and how to live it?

These questions apply even to judgment without claims to knowledge, to judgment that does not commit one to claiming the existence of a deep vindication. If, as it turns out, our plan-laden judgments ought to have this status, they are still subject to a rich set of logical and pragmatic requirements. Demands for coherence still apply, and in living and making judgments at all, one manifests a kind of practical faith—a practical faith in one's capacities.

A deep internal vindication of one's plans would go beyond such a practical faith. With a coherent practical faith, I might say something like this: "I have to trust my powers of judgment and investigation, to some degree, or how else can I live? In order to pursue my life at all, I have to assume, if the question arises, that I am not hopeless at figuring out how to live. And so equivalently, I have to assume that I'm *a kind of being* who isn't hopeless at thinking how to live. I accept that I am such a being." My question has been whether we must say more. Must I not only trust that I am such a being, but think one could *see why* beings with our nature would be like this, why we wouldn't be hopeless at judging how to live? A deep vindication is more than a mere conjoining of practical faith with self-understanding.

We see, then, two senses in which we can attribute knowledge to ourselves and to each other, one less demanding than the other. In the preceding chapter, I explored knowledge as reliability: to attribute knowledge to someone is to plan, in certain ways, to defer to the judgments of such a person. Now I am speaking of knowledge in a more demanding sense: to attribute knowledge in this stronger sense is to attribute it in the weaker sense, and also to commit oneself to there being a deep vindication of one's plans to defer.

Human Designs and Human Design

Plans that are not full beliefs are possible, I have been arguing. Now to our second question: are these the kinds of plans to make? Or should we form beliefs all out as to what is okay to do and what is not? This question, as I am interpreting it, has become the following: Take our best factual account of our capacities for planning, along with our best planning judgments. Will these have us expecting a deep vindication of our capacities to plan?

Such a vindication, as I have said, would have to be internal to our ways of thinking and planning. We cannot step outside our factual and planning judgments as we work toward vindicating them. A deep vindication of our capacities that we ourselves accept, then, will be an *internal* vindication. On the other hand, it should be more than a trivial vindication of the form "J, and here's why we are the kinds of beings who would judge that J." For any judgment we make, there is presumably a correct causal explanation of our making it. A trivial vindication would just combine this causal story with an expression of the judgment it explains. Suppose, for instance, I think that what is ultimately to be sought—the *end*, let's say—is perfection (on some particular conception of what perfection consists in). I have, imagine, a causal story of why I would so judge. Then I can say, "Here is why I am the sort of being who would tend to judge the end correctly. Perfection is the end, and here is why I am the sort of being who would judge that perfection is the end." As a vindication, this lacks a prime virtue of the contingency detection schema: it does not explain why, in such matters, I would tend to be *correct as such*. It tells why I so judge, and just says that so to judge is to judge correctly. Full-fledged belief, let's say, commits one to there being a deeper kind of vindication than this. I have been vague about how a "deep internal vindication" of our powers of factual judgment would go—of our powers as human beings, and as modern, educated human beings with some training in scientific thinking. But the kinds of vindication that I have in mind when I use this phrase should be recognizable, however controversial it may be whether such vindications are to be had for commonsense facts, or for science. What I'll try to do is not to refine and sharpen the notion of such a vindication and argue that it can be had. These matters are widely explored, in one form or another; they are not ones on which anyone could expect to make quick progress or achieve quick changes of mind. They raise questions of whether common sense and science constitute knowledge in as deep a sense as some of us think.

Rather, I want to ask what we should think if we are *epistemic optimists:* if we do expect deep internal vindications of human factual common sense, and of core parts of modern science. What should epistemic optimists think about plans, about questions of what to do? In part, practical questions resolve into questions of how things are, but what about the rest of what is at stake? For this, should an epistemic optimist look for something parallel to knowledge? Should he hope for a deep internal vindication of practical judgment?

Or might there be beings much like us, who like us have complex views on what to do, but who are hopeless at judging what to do? We are products of natural selection, and when it comes to everyday facts, natural selection should make us somewhat reliable: that's what the contingency detection schema tells us. Can we say the same kind of thing, though, for knowing what, ultimately, to pursue in life? Why would being wrong about ultimate ends have stymied reproduction in ancestral populations? Why would getting this right have promoted the replication of one's genes in later generations?

Accomplishing a deep, Darwinian vindication of our planning capacities would depend on a crucial correlation: between reproductive success and what's to be sought in life. Now everyone will agree that there is such a rough correlation. That goes for adherents of many positions that are at odds with each other on what's ultimately to be sought in life. Everyone, after all, will agree that there are correlations between the various candidates, and that pleasure, staying alive, developing one's capacities, love and friendship, carrying out one's responsibilities, and the like all correlate with being the thing to do, and all correlate too with enhancing one's reproductive prospects.

Can we, though, offer any deep explanation of the correlation? If what's ultimately to be sought in life were one's genetic reproduction, *that* would explain the correlation—but such a view, I take it, would be ridiculous. For a man, it might place a premium, in modern conditions, on being a supplier of sperm banks.[5] It rejects sexual pleasure and intimacy as a goal—or any other kind of pleasure, fulfillment, or interpersonal bond—except as its pursuit works, indirectly at least, to promote one's genetic reproduction. (In calling such plans ridiculous, I express scorn for them and a determination not so to plan. I also press you, the reader, to join me in this.)

Now we can, to be sure, explain why we would *find* things to be worth seeking if they had correlated with reproduction in ancestral populations. That is what natural selection can be expected to accomplish in its shaping of our planning capacities. Our problem, though, is whether we can see why, for beings like us, finding things to be of value should go with their genuinely *being* of value. It's clear why we would *think* so—that, indeed, is trivial: when I find myself *judging* something to be worth seeking, I find that it *is* worth seeking. But that does not let us see why I would judge correctly as such, why my thinking a thing worth seeking would go with its being indeed worth seeking.

More slowly: three items are in play:

G: good, being worth seeking
P: preference, what we do value
R: reproduction of one's genes

G, more precisely, is being ultimately worth seeking, and R is having a reproduction-enhancing tendency in ancestral populations. We are asking why we tend to prefer things that are worth seeking—why, let us write it, $P \approx G$. As Darwinians, we can see why $P \approx R$, why we tend to prefer what enhanced reproduction among our ancestors. This last

5. See Nozick, *Nature of Rationality* (1993), p. 30.

helps us with our question, though, only if we already see why $R \approx G$, why things that enhanced reproduction among our ancestors tended to be worth seeking. I'm saying that we have no independent reason to think this. That $R \approx G$ is plausible enough, to be sure, but its plausibility depends entirely on the plausibility of $P \approx G$, of thinking that what we judge good tends to be good. We use $P \approx G$ to reason from $P \approx R$ to $R \approx G$. We can't, then, use the last to support the first: what's good does correlate with what reproduced ancestral genes, but we can't use this to support the conclusion that what we do in fact value is truly worth seeking.

Again, if we could convince ourselves, independently, that $G = R$, that one's genetic reproduction *is* what's ultimately to be sought, then we would have the argument we need. But to be convinced of this is to plan—and to plan bizarrely: it is to plan, for any circumstance whatsoever, to do what holds out best prospects of reproducing one's genes. Why do that? It's one thing to recognize a correlation between the two; it's another to set up reproduction as the *standard* of what's worth seeking. (And we can see why natural selection wouldn't shape us to think reproduction the one thing ultimately worth seeking. Our genes "use" more specific enthusiasms they "program" us for to get themselves reproduced: for sex, for prestige, for pleasures, for revenge, for jealousy, and the like.)

A deep internal vindication of our planning judgments, then, would have to show why beings like us would be good judges of ultimate worth, even in those cases where ultimate worth comes apart from maximizing the long-run reproduction of one's genes. Now it's hard to see how this could be accomplished. If we demanded that our plans constitute *beliefs*, in the strong sense, in what to do, and so demanded that a deep vindication be available, that would put strong, implausible constraints on what might make things worth seeking. We would have to think that one's genetic reproduction *is* what's ultimately to be sought. This we should take as a *modus tollens*, not a *modus ponens*: we have strong reason to reject the view that genetic reproduction is what's ultimately to be sought. On the other hand, it's no commonplace that planning is believing.

Could it be instead that although the human genetic plan is not *for* getting right the purely practical component of what to do, human invention has achieved this? Parallels exist: we aren't shaped by natural selection to be readers, but somewhat fortuitously, the capacities we were genetically "designed" to have make us trainable as readers. That's what made the invention of communication by writing possible. We get it right what words are on the page, and there is presumably some correct story of how this happened, a story that explains why the normal human infant can grow up to read. Likewise with science: no one is a scientist without a special kind of education, a kind that has been around at most for a dozen generations. Still, we can explain how human makeup and historical developments have by now made us somewhat reliable as scientists, somewhat reliable in our views on the hidden structure that underlies appearances. Our story of all this will not consist just of trivial self-congratulation by scientists; it won't just take the form "We think that there are atoms, and lo and behold, there are." Or if it does, then science fails to give us the kind of knowledge that many of us claim for it, and though we should nevertheless make the best scientific judgments we can, we should not strictly *believe* findings of science.

A parallel story of human progress in discerning ultimate ends, it seems to me, would have to start with humanity already as somewhat reliable judges of what's to be sought in life. Turn again to parallels: science refines common sense, and if we weren't as a species somewhat reliable judges of what's what, no part of our species could have developed modern science. As for reading, the written word is a matter of convention: correctness in reading and writing is conformity, near enough. There's no question of whether written English might somehow be massively mistaken, apart from whether it works for communication—and in judging whether it does, we refine capacities we have simply as human beings. Now what's ultimately to be sought in life isn't just a matter of convention. (To think it was, after all, would be to plan to go along, in every circumstance and whatever the consequences, with whatever convention might conceivably have arisen.) What's worth seeking in life is something a culture could get right or get wrong. It is plausible that histories of invention, refinement, and cultural transmission have improved human capacities to judge what's worth seeking in life. Perhaps—or perhaps agriculture, civilization, and modernity have worsened our capacities for discerning the worth of life. But in either case, whatever improvements there have been must be refinements of capacities we have as human beings.

If, then, our practical capacities can be deeply vindicated—if some correct, non-trivial account could be given of why we aren't hopeless judges of what's to be sought in life—the story must apply, to some degree, to normal human beings in normal conditions. It cannot just apply to a special, enlightened group. Such a story, to be plausible, must fit our best current, scientific understandings of the nature of humanity; it must also fit planning judgments we can find reasonable. I have been baffled in seeing how any such story could be told.

I mean all this not at all as a counsel of despair. To despair of *knowing*, in the strongest sense, what to do is in no way to despair of life or value. Plans needn't be beliefs in the strongest sense. We have every reason to plan, and some plans are warranted and others are not. We have reason to deliberate what to do, within limits, and requirements of coherence apply to plans and other plan-laden judgments, not just to beliefs. To plan is to judge, and we may be wrong in our judgments of what to do or what to seek. All these things I have been arguing in these chapters, and none of this is brought into question if plans aren't fully beliefs and can't fully be knowledge.

～ 14

Impasse and Dissent

$\mathcal{B}$ACK TO THE CASE of Plato and Xanti, the example introduced in Chapter 12. Ethical intuitionists must fear discursive impasse—a kind of impasse that anyone is forced to allow as conceivable. Intuitionism can offer no satisfactory account of ethical knowledge, it is widely thought, if such an impasse can arise. Suppose, after all, that two parties disagree fundamentally, and each is fully coherent in his own view. Each then must be reduced to accusing the other of something like "moral blindness"—or "moral hallucination", or both in some combination.[1] If they make these accusations, it is hard to say what could make one party right and the other wrong.

My own views face similar problems. Plato and Xanti, after all, seem to have reached such an impasse: Plato regards Xanti as prone both to a kind of planning blindness and to planning hallucination. She is "blind", he thinks, in that even in ideal conditions, her plans would be unresponsive to certain genuine considerations, or responsive to them but insufficiently so. She is blind to the immense planning weight that civic obligation adds to the scales. And she is prone to "hallucination" in that her plans would respond to certain bogus considerations, or overstress certain genuine considerations: family ties, intimacy, and

1. See Frankena, "Naturalistic Fallacy" (1939) for charges of "moral hallucination" and "moral blindness", and Strawson, "Ethical Intuitionism" (1949) for a classic critique of intuitions.

food on the table, for instance. This is Plato's view of Xanti—and Xanti takes a like view of Plato.

Such an impasse could take either of two pure forms. The first is the one I have pictured. Let two hyperdecided planners, Hera and Zeus, both be correct in all their factual judgments. Hera plans in a way that both regard as correct in its epistemic (or quasi-epistemic) qualities: either she herself possesses all the quasi-epistemic virtues, or she defers to the judgments she would make if she did possess them all. The same goes for Zeus. Nevertheless, imagine they form incompatible plans. Each, then, regards the other as blind or prone to hallucination (or both at once). Each thinks the other defective not in such epistemic credentials as being dispassionate, say, and vividly knowledgeable, but in the kind of mental constitution needed to "see" what the situation calls for even in the best of epistemic conditions. Since such a pure form of impasse is rooted in differing mental constitutions, we can call it a *constitutional impasse*.

A second, quite different pure form of impasse is also possible. Hera and Zeus have reached this second pure form of impasse if each regards the other as equipped with full planning capacities, but caught up in a web of self-reinforcing falsehoods. Each is in "reflective equilibrium", as we might say, but each disagrees with the equilibrium the other has reached. Hera accepts epistemic state I_H as ideal for planning, whereas Zeus accepts state I_Z as ideal for planning. They both know that each of them, if in state I_H, would plan, for Soc's situation, to take the hemlock. They both likewise know that in state I_Z, each would plan to flee. Each, then, thinks that in ideal conditions the other would judge correctly on the matter: in that sense, each credits the other with perfect *capacities* for planning. But neither credits the other with being in ideal conditions, and they disagree on what to do if in Soc's shoes. Each regards the other as competent but entangled in a false but coherent view of what to do and how to plan. Call this a *multi-equilibrium impasse*.

Hyperdecided disagreement might, of course, combine both kinds of impasse. As for actual disagreement among ordinary, somewhat agnostic judges, it will allow for more complexities still. If each party is fully coherent, their states of mind may well each allow for hyperdecided completions of diverse forms—some of which leave the parties at an impasse of one or both pure types, and some of which allow resolution.

Earlier I argued that the whole quasi-realistic logical structure I have constructed depends on the possibility of "disagreement in plan". I deferred, though, as prematurely deep, the question of why difference in plan should constitute disagreement. Stevenson, when he spoke of "disagreement in attitude", thought it crucial that "at least one of them has a motive for altering or calling into question the attitude of the other" (*Ethics and Language*, 1944, p. 4). The disagreements I am now considering, though, are not cases of Stevensonian disagreement in attitude: Xanti and Plato are not disagreeing about what is to happen; they are disagreeing over what to do if one is oneself placed in a certain kind of situation. Xanti plans if in Soc's shoes to flee, and Plato, to take the hemlock. Their problem is not how to act jointly, and it is not what is to happen; it is what to do if placed as a given person in a given plight.[2]

This is no disagreement at all, it might be objected. It is just a difference of personal characteristics, like having different hair colors. One person plans to do one thing, and the other to do something else. True, their plans are for exactly the same situation that one could be in—but why does this make their difference in plans a disagreement, a difference of opinion? They disagree, say I, on what to do if placed in Soc's shoes—but perhaps they only *differ* in this regard, without disagreeing. It's just, perhaps, that I've got my plans and you've got yours.

Judgment Individualism: Change of Plans

To investigate whether there can be such a thing as disagreement in plan, think first of an individual planner. Can young Plato, say, change his mind about what to do, coming to reject his earlier thoughts? Or is a change of plan like trimming a beard, a change of a personal characteristic from one time to another, but not something that *ipso facto* puts one in any disagreement with one's earlier self? First thing in the morning, just before he trims his beard, Plato plans to stay in Athens for the rest of his life. His beard now trimmed, he decides to leave the next day—and not because he has gained new information in the meantime. Trimming his beard doesn't *ipso facto* put him in disagreement with himself; he may have planned for days to trim it just when he does.

2. Michael Ridge has independently noted the contrast between what I'm now calling "disagreement in plan" and Stevensonian "disagreement in attitude".

Contrast this with a change of factual belief: just before Plato trims his beard, Xanti expects him to stay in Athens for the rest of his life; right afterward, she expects him to leave Athens the next day. She has not, then, merely changed a personal characteristic; she rejects what she earlier thought; she now disagrees with her previous state of mind. What, then, of Plato's change of plans? Is it like a change of beard, a change that needn't involve agreement or disagreement in one's earlier state. Or is it like a change of mind, coming to disagree with what one previously thought?[3]

Even brilliant young Plato can't settle everything in an instant. One minute, he decides to go into exile if Soc flees the city. That bears on his musings the next minute about setting up school in the Lyceum: in case Soc flees, doing so would require a change of mind about exile. Plato's plans may mature over the course of hours or days or even months. He can of course come to reject a plan that he has earlier made. He doesn't, though, at each instant treat his earlier thoughts on what to do as mere possibilities for what to think now. To do so would be to fragment his planning over time in a way that would be paralyzing.[4] And since he has to join earlier thoughts with later ones, he has to regard them as compatible or incompatible. He must regard himself as still accepting what he previously concluded, or as changing his mind.

For a single person over time, then, plans must act as judgments: one must be able to accept or disagree with determinations one has previously made. Various fragments of one's contingency plans for living will be compatible or incompatible, and these relations of compatibility or incompatibility will have many earmarks of being matters of logic. This by itself is enough to yield many of the quasi-realistic conclusions I derived in earlier chapters: whereas in those chapters I spoke often of hyperdecided observers, I sometimes spoke instead of hyperdecided states that the individual could move to without changing his mind.

All this allows, though, for a kind of individualism about planning

---

3. In changing plans, Plato changes his expectations for what he will do—just as Xanti does. But this change of plans, we can say, has two components which need not go together: a change in self-prediction, and a change of hypothetical decision as to what to do if in tomorrow's situation. I have been arguing that the two are separate, as in the case of the weekend binge alcoholic thinking ahead at midweek.

4. On planning and avoiding this kind of fragmentation, see Bratman, *Intention, Plans* (1987).

judgments, a position that runs like this: Plato's contingency plans at one time, we can agree, may be at odds with his plans at another time, or with the plans he would make in other circumstances. But Plato and Xanti are different individuals, and so in planning differently, they are not in disagreement. Plato plans, if in Soc's situation, to take the hemlock. If on trimming his beard he were to plan instead, for the same situation, to flee and live, he would be disagreeing with his earlier determination. Xanti plans, for being in Soc's situation, to flee and live; is she likewise disagreeing with Plato's hypothetical determination to take the hemlock? No, it's just that Plato has one plan for the situation and Xanti another. Plato can disagree with his prior determination of what to do if in Soc's plight; but Xanti, being another person, cannot. It's just that she has one plan for the situation and he has another. So maintains one kind of individualist.

Individualism, in one of the many senses of the term that are too often lumped together, would be the following view: In the first place, an individual human organism is to have full unity and integrity; a person is to enjoy continuity in thought, insofar as she is free from a pathology of personal disintegration. Each individual, though, is autonomous in thought: no one is to continue the thought of another. I can, of course, take your thought as a datum or as a prod to thinking matters through on my own. I can also use your thinking as a time-saver, but only as I can suppose you are thinking what I would think anyway, given information and epistemic virtues that don't include being prone to your influence. This, to be sure, is not the way we always are in fact, but that only demonstrates another kind of pathology to which the spirit is vulnerable, a pathology of non-differentiation. Call this view *judgment individualism*; it is the plan-laden view that each individual is to form a separate, integrated unit of judgment.

On this individualist picture, Plato and Xanti may still profit from sharing their plans with each other. Each stands as an island of judgment as to what to do, but each can use the other in limited ways: as a source of testimony, as a proposer of thought experiments, and as a sourcebook of arguments to contemplate and accept or reject. Neither, though, is to treat the other's judgments as his own.

My talk of changes of mind from time to time points to an even more extreme form that an insular view of planning could take. As I swing from mood to mood, I could reach impasses with myself. We could even imagine Hera as hyperdecided and factually correct at each moment, but going from mood to mood in her planning, at odds today with her views of yesterday—but always coherent at any single time. Hera could then take no judgment of hers at one time as tentatively settling the matter at another. At one moment, to be sure, she can record facts for later notice, propose thought experiments for her later contemplation, and invent arguments for her later scrutiny. None of this, though, would be because she places trust in her future self. She can treat her future self manipulatively or with respect, but not as continuing her present train of thought.

This seems a strange state to be in from day to day or hour to hour—though we can be forced into milder forms of it when we find we need multiple alarm clocks, or seek a way out of procrastination, or work to cope with addictions and milder temptations. A person's internal life may be an uneasy tangle of continuing inquiry, on the one hand, and the internal politics of the soul on the other. Perhaps human life must inevitably be like this, to some greater or lesser degree; happy is the one whose well-considered enthusiasms, compromises, and schedulings animate all of life or almost all.

Even, then, if a flesh-and-blood human organism is bound to be temporally fragmented to some degree, this can't be a credible ideal. We must count a change of plan as not only a change, like a shave or a haircut, but as coming to disagree with one's earlier planning. I can disagree in plan with my self of another time, and likewise with you, who can disagree in plan with yourself over time. Shall we be judgment individualists, then? Can I disagree in plan with myself only, and not with you?

One way it might be tempting to support judgment individualism would be to appeal to the possibility of impasse. If there is not even the seed of settling a dispute between two people, then the dispute is not genuine, the claim might be: it is not a real difference of opinion. But this kind of argument, if it works, would refute the other half of individualism: that the individual constitutes a single mind, so that different plans of the same individual *can* be compatible or incompatible. Any kind of impasse that is possible between individuals will be conceivable for a single individual across different times.

Individualism in another sense would be the view that my reasonable goals may conflict with yours, that my pursuit of the things to pursue in my life may be at odds with your pursuit of the things to pursue in your life. We might label this view *goal individualism*. Hedonistic egoists are individualists in this sense, though they need not be judgment individualists. One's own pleasure ultimately is the thing to pursue in life, Hedda maintains, but maximal pleasure for one person may preclude maximal pleasure for another. This, she thinks, is a view to come to in common inquiry. There are sure to be tensions in acting on both views at once, treating goals as distinct but judging as common endeavor.[5] Common inquiry may not, after all, be sufficiently maintained by a mere confluence of interests; it may break down into a contest of sales-manship and propaganda. Logically, however, the two sets of issues are distinct: the theses of goal individualism cut across those of judgment individualism.

Putting Our Heads Together

We each find some choices obvious and others troubling. We each have some views of what is important in life—if not explicit doctrines, tacit views manifested in our reactions to the choices that we and others face. We each, though, have our uncertainties to cope with as well. I may turn to you, then, to help me with my planning for life, and ask you for advice. The advice I ask from you may be limited: I may have fully settled for myself what to pursue and what is worth giving up for what, and simply want advice on how most effectively to pursue this schedule of goals. Often, though, my uncertainties will be more funda-mental. I may be unclear, say, how to balance the demands of ambition against the appeal of tranquillity and enjoyment. I can ask your advice on a question like this, on a question of ultimate ends; we could call this *fundamental advice*. Or I may ask for advice for what to do now, in a spe-cific situation, but without presupposing some particular weighting of ultimate ends. My question, say, is whether to take a job offer; the ques-tion is not one of ultimate ends purely, but it might hinge, among other things, on questions of ultimate ends that I have not settled for myself. I am then asking you for advice that is, if not purely fundamental, at least tinged with fundamental questions. I am asking you, we can say, for *fundamentally tinged advice*.

5. Stephen Darwall has stressed these tensions to me.

What, then, am I requesting when I ask your "advice"? We could, if we wanted, simply take the notion of what's *advisable* as understood, and say that to *advise* me is just to tell me what it's advisable to do. Suppose, though, we try not to take advice or advisability as an unexplained notion. When I ask you for advice, we can say, I try to get you to help me with my thinking, to join with me in thinking what to do. My request might be limited: I want you, say, to take on a certain weighting of ultimate goals—the one that's the weighting to use in decisions, on my view of things—and to think for me how to achieve the greatest balance of these ends. Usually, though, in thinking what to do, I don't have my ultimate ends and their weights all worked out. When I ask you to put your thoughts together with mine and help me with my planning, my request is not limited to pure questions of means. I am then, in effect, asking you for fundamentally tinged advice. Your advice may not be highly analytical; it will probably not take the form of working out the goals to have, the weights for them to carry, and the implementation of that weighting of ends. Ordinary, fundamentally tinged advice will not separate these elements out, and as my adviser, you may well have no view as to how they separate out. Still, the advice you give me is fundamentally tinged in that it could not be derived from your views of natural fact alone.

Suppose, then, I do seek your fundamentally tinged advice. I may find you helpful as an adviser, and I may not. One extreme stance I might take is to treat you as a guru who is to have my complete deference. This, however, goes far beyond the ordinary case of just asking you to help me with my thinking. Toward my own thinking, after all, my stance is not to take each thing I think as settled beyond any challenge and rethinking. On the one hand, I don't take my planning conclusions of a minute ago simply as posing suggestions for what to think now; I take them as tentatively settling matters. Only tentatively, though: I can rethink and come to disagree with what I myself have thought earlier. I can conduct internal debates as to what to do or what to seek. When I ask you and others to put your heads together with mine and help me think what to do, this is a stance I might take to what you say. I'll take not a stance of complete deference to you, but take instead the same stance I take to my own thoughts when I find they don't yet speak with one voice. I may then find yours a helpful voice to add to my internal dialogue. (Or, to be sure, I may find your thoughts an in-trusive nuisance.)

Whether I find your words helpful or not, if I hear you joining me in my thinking, I then regard you as voicing thoughts that I can reject or come to accept. Yours is a voice like my own inner voice, and just as I can accept or reject my own thoughts of a few moments ago, so I can accept or reject yours. I can even argue, and you my advisers can argue back, or argue with each other. I treat your planning thoughts, then, as thoughts I might have and accept or reject. I interpret you as having thoughts that are apt for agreement and disagreement—and you re-spond similarly to my own voicings. If we converse on these terms, we have a socially established practice of mutual interpretation, which car-ries with it standards for what constitutes disagreement.

You and I can also converse as advisers to someone else, thinking with her what to do in her situation. We can do this in make-believe mode as well, working out advice that we don't expect really to offer—advice, say, to Socrates who is long dead, and whom we wouldn't pre-sume to advise to his face if he were among us. We can think together about situations that are hypothetical, working out advice together for what to do in those situations. Engaging in such thought experiments rehearses us for living. Hypothetical questions may be relevant to the question of what I myself am to do now, but also to decisions you or I may face later on. The chief reason, then, to adopt the stance of an ad-viser, a giver of fundamentally tinged advice for what to do in a situa-tion, may not be actually to advise the person who is in that situation, but to put our heads together in working out more generally how to live.

We may, then, become partners in a joint inquiry on how to live, en-gaging in a common enterprise of working out what to do and why in possible situations. I then treat your thoughts somewhat as my own: your thoughts and mine are both open to scrutiny, and our points of view differ in much the same way as my own point of view can change from time to time as I swing from one set of enthusiasms and cautions to another. When two points of view yield conflicting judgments, then on this picture there is something to resolve.

Contrast, though, two different respects in which we can disagree. You and I think together for me and think together for you, we are imagining. What we decide to promote if in your situation may then conflict with what we decide to promote if in mine. Suppose, for instance, we conclude that one's own pleasure is the thing ultimately to pursue. Your long-run pleasure may trade off against mine—if, say, we are rivals in love. Such rivalry, of course, would strain our roles as genuine advisers to each other: I might advise you to display your defects and do so boastfully—not because that is my genuine plan for what to do if in your shoes, but because your doing so would play into my hands. Rivalry can strain even the appearance of genuine advice, making proferred advice incredible. Sincere advice, though, as I am picturing it, expresses my plans for what to do if in your shoes—and that may differ from what, in my own shoes, I *want* you to do.

This contrasts with a different kind of conversation: joint planning, where you and I converse on what shall happen, devising a joint scheme for what you shall do and what I shall do. In joint planning, we don't count as agreeing until we are both set to promote the same goals, as identified from a common standpoint. If you plan to win away my lover, I agree with you in joint plan only if I too plan to promote your winning her away. This needs some qualifications: my plan need mesh with yours only for contingencies where what I do would make a difference to whether you win her away. Then too, I needn't plan to get her to love you at all costs: I might, for instance, rule out being cruel to her and still agree with you in joint plan—so long as you rule out getting me to be cruel to her. We must agree, in effect, on what to treat as gains and what as costs from a common point of view.

If you and I plan for what I am to do, it follows, your planning thoughts and mine may agree in one sense and disagree in another. We can discuss what to do if in my shoes, or alternatively, we can discuss what jointly to favor. I would be happier with her than without her, we are both convinced, and she would be happier with you than with me. I think that the thing to promote is the happiness of those one loves; you think that the thing to promote is one's own happiness. We then agree in what we favor: we both favor my resigning my suit in favor of yours. We disagree on what to do in my place: you think the thing to do is to pursue her; I think the thing to do is to get out of her life. The same preferences, then, will constitute agreement in one sense, as views on what is advisable, and disagreement in another sense—the Stevensonian sense.

When we discuss what I am to do, it may be unclear which way we are treating each other's thoughts. We may simply not be facing any question of possible conflicts between what I'm to promote and what you are to promote. It won't always be clear, then, whether we are arguing as adviser and advisee, or as joint planners; there may be no fact of the matter.

Exclusion and Interpretation

Quasi-realism for contingency plans requires that there be a relation of compatibility and incompatibility in plans, that one piece of a plan can logically exclude another—as planning not to take the hemlock logically excludes planning to take it in the same situation. If only we can say what constitutes this exclusion, then we achieve a logic of planning judgments that mimics the logic of prosaically factual judgments. That gives us a logic of judgments that range from pure planning to pure naturalistic belief, with all kinds of mixed judgments lying in between, judgments that are both fact-laden and plan-laden.

All this yields at least a notion of the content of judgments that is relative: *given* a relation E of exclusion among fragments of plans, we can speak of the logic of plans *with respect to* this relation. Such a logic, I have shown in earlier chapters, generates judgments that mix plan with fact. We see now, though, that your view of what to promote may be compatible with mine in one sense, and incompatible with mine in another. We may agree on what to do in every possible situation, and still disagree on what jointly to promote. I may agree with you on what to promote jointly, and yet disagree on what to do in my situation. The same pairs of plans, yours and mine, may constitute agreement in one sense and disagreement in another. Is there any reality, then, to whether you and I are agreeing or disagreeing in our plan-laden judgments? Or is there only agreement with respect to one exclusion relation or another?

If the same pair of contingency plans can be in agreement with respect to one exclusion relation and in disagreement with respect to another, then they have *content* only with respect to an exclusion relation E. Let E_A be the exclusion relation pertinent to advice, and E_J the one pertinent to joint planning. With respect to E_A, my plans constitute views on what is the thing to do in one situation or another; with respect to E_J, they are views on what it would be good for one to do, good or desirable from a common standpoint. Which kind of question am I thinking about as I form my contingency plans?

That, we should respond, is a matter of interpretation. There are different spirits in which we can put our heads together and discuss what I am to do—different stances we can take as we share our planning thoughts. I have named two crucial ones: the stance of fundamentally tinged advice, and the stance of joint planning. On a given occasion, then, am I voicing advice or am I voicing my favorings? Is there a fact of which of the two I am doing? There clearly is a fact as to what I can sincerely advise: what I think advisable is a matter of my plans for being in your shoes. There clearly is a fact as to what I favor: that is a matter of my plan for being in my own shoes, taking account of you in whatever way I do. There may be no clear fact, though, of which of these aspects of my planning I am purporting to voice when I tell you what to do. In that case, with respect to one interpretation of my words, I am proffering advice, whereas with respect to another, I am speaking on my own behalf, demanding perhaps or requesting perhaps, and in any case voicing my own goals.

Often, though, it will be plain enough from the way the conversation proceeds which of these I am purporting to do. What considerations do I adduce? What ripostes from you do I treat as relevant? In what conversational circumstances do I evince disagreement? In the case of discussions of natural fact, which factual subject I am pursuing is open to interpretation, and there are normally grounds that favor some interpretations over others. Just so with planning discussions: advisability and desirability are two different subject matters, and which of them is under discussion, in a particular conversation, can be settled by well-grounded interpretation.

A crucial ground favoring one interpretation or another, as I have said, will be what discussants treat as disagreements—or more precisely, what they appear to treat as disagreements. What one treats as a disagreement determines what the subject matter is. Consider crude preferences in food, expressed with "Yum!" and "Yech!" You say "Yum!" to asparagus, suppose, and I say "Yech!" We may treat these voicings as working toward a joint plan for distributing food. Then there is no disagreement; clearly the asparagus goes to you. Or we may treat it as a critique of food, so that there is something to be resolved as we work toward a joint standard of taste in food. The same reactions can figure in logically different ways.

Often too, a conversation will have no one clearly best interpretation. When we disagree, it will often be unclear what the logical crux of the disagreement might be. We do pursue our uncertainties and our disagreements, but not as purified issues that philosophical analysis has revealed. Nothing in a conversant's current state might determine how to respond to new factual information, new thought experiments, and newly proposed considerations and arguments.

Engagement: Point and Coherence

I may find your fundamentally tinged advice helpful, or I may not. I may find certain aspects of what you say not to be worth heeding; I may want to get your voice out of my head. Or at least, I may want to distinguish your voice clearly from my own: I may find it a hindrance to let your voice join with mine and so give things you say the weight of claims in my thoughts, but still find what you say helpful as a source of possibilities for what to think. On the other hand, I can treat the thoughts you voice as I treat my own recent thoughts, as settling matters temporarily, or claiming to settle them but competing with other claims or reservations. There will be a whole range of attitudes I can take, from treating you uncritically as my guru, to letting your voice join mine in thoughts we can criticize, to guardedly taking you as a source of ideas, to wanting no exposure to your thoughts.

Suppose, though, I just find you unhelpful and hindering. Then I can respond in at least two different ways. I can simply disagree with much of what you say, rejecting it and trying not to let it influence my thoughts. Alternatively, I may not treat you as even voicing thoughts that I can accept or reject. You have your plans and I have mine, and difference in plans is no kind of disagreement. If you say to take the hemlock if faced with Soc's plight, that's your contingency plan; mine is to escape—and that is all we have to say to each other. I can, in short, take either of two stances: when a difference in plan between us is a genuine difference, when it pertains to exactly the same circumstance that a person might be in, I can regard the difference either as a disagreement or as a mere personal difference that doesn't constitute a disagreement. How shall we choose between these two stances?

A promising way to approach the problem is suggested by Wittgenstein's treatment of mathematics. Wittgenstein stressed the logical possibility of an impasse in mathematics, a kind of impasse more extreme than any I have been picturing, an impasse in two people's reactions, or in two groups' reactions, to mathematical questions as they arise. Another community, imagine, is so foreign to us in their mathematical judgments that we cannot converse with them. We contemplate them, and cannot even interpret what they do as reasoning—and yet they give every sign of being able to manage complex matters. Our practice of mathematics, Wittgenstein suggested, depends on the contingent fact that we are not like that with each other: our reactions to new questions do roughly coincide.[6]

Now questions of how to live, I have been suggesting, we can treat as genuine questions, as questions on which we can agree and disagree. I have sung the advantages of being able to join together in thinking about how to live. Like the practice of mathematics, though, the practice of thinking and discussing how to live will be hostage to our having sufficiently congruent reactions to issues that arise. Our reactions may be congruent enough in some areas and not in others. In that case, treating how to live as a subject matter, as a topic for agreement and disagreement, may have sufficient point in some realms and not in others.

Wittgenstein's question of point, though, is not the only one to ask of a practice. We can ask too whether the practice coheres, or whether instead, following it leads to pitfalls and self-contradictions. Much of philosophy consists in exploring the coherence of practices of thought. The practice of mathematics is remarkable for its intricate coherence—questions of ontology and epistemology aside, which remain vexed topics in the philosophy of mathematics. I have focused my efforts in this book—and in large parts of my earlier book *Wise Choices, Apt Feelings*—on such questions of coherence.

Treating how to live as a topic for agreement and disagreement, I have maintained, depends on according us all a kind of fundamental

6. *Philosophical Investigations* (1953), I:§§240–242 and elsewhere.

epistemic symmetry. Not that we are all equally good judges of how to live, but if we aren't, some explanation is to be had. The explanation must be non-indexical; it must not depend, at base, on picking out my judgments as mine or yours as yours. This symmetry requirement is both plan-laden and fact-laden: it depends both on what constitutes being an ideal judge on questions of how to live, and on what we are like as judges. What constitutes being ideal is a matter of plan, of whom to rely on in questions of how to live. What we are like is a matter of fact, of the psychology and sociology of human planning. Meeting the symmetry requirement, then, is hostage to the facts of what we human beings are like. It could be that we so disagree on these facts that for no plausible account of what makes a person ideal as a judge of how to live would we agree if we were ideal.

We might, then, need to draw back from presenting our plan-laden judgments as claims, to draw back on pain of incoherence in light of the facts. Perhaps, that is to say, we must forgo regarding each other's plans for living, in all their aspects, as subject to accord or dissent. In *Wise Choices* I explored what some coherent stratagems of retrenchment might be, how we could have those kinds of conversation that are helpful and coherent while setting aside those that are not. We can treat a conversation as parochial to a community or to a group of fellow spirits. We can restrict the subject matter of our discussion, addressing, say, hypothetical questions of what to do given certain goals and commitments, or questions of practical consistency.[7] These are forms that our disengagement could reach even if, ideally, we had each individually come to a reflective equilibrium, finding no defects in his own thinking and giving the judgments of the other what he regards as due weight.

All this pertains to questions of coherence: the coherence of making claims to each other about how to live or of renouncing making such claims. Coherence and point are different questions; coherence won't guarantee point. This we can see from the two pure kinds of planners' impasse with which I started this chapter—two ways we might each be factually informed and each, by his own lights, an ideal judge of how to live, and yet disagree with each other. If we were at such an impasse, then neither of us would have anything to say to the other that the other was prone to heed. For if I know all, and if I am, by my own

7. See my *Wise Choices* (1990), chap. 10.

lights, an ideal judge of matters, then I have already been exposed to all ideas and influences of yours that I think would improve my judgment. Faced with such an impasse, with no ways left to work toward accord, we could find no point to treating questions of how to live as topics for agreement and disagreement. Neither of these kinds of pure impasse, though, makes it incoherent to treat these questions as real questions, subject to agreement and disagreement. Neither case, after all, forces us to reject our fundamental symmetry as judges: in each case, you accept a story of why I am defective as a judge and I accept a story of why you are; neither of us disqualifies the other as a judge just because I am not you. In short, even when each of us is ideally informed and coherent, questions of point and coherence can come apart. To treat us as agreeing and disagreeing may be coherent but without point.

Our real-life frustrations engaging each other, of course, won't take such a purified form; we won't each singly be ideally coherent and informed. The stories I have told in this book of ideal coherence, of gods and goddesses, were not about us; they provided useful thought experiments, useful ways to explore the logic of thoughts that we ourselves can have. Even in our partial confusion, though, we can ask two distinct questions. First, is there *point* in treating questions of how to live as real questions, subject to agreement and disagreement? Second, is it *coherent* to do so? Would our ideal judgments of how to live accord with each other? These questions are heavily plan-laden, and also heavily laden with issues of natural fact. Answering them depends both on thinking how to judge and learning how human beings do judge. These will not be questions that we can answer with great justified confidence, but they are questions for a broadly anthropological and philosophical ethics to pursue.

Hopes for a Common Inquiry

Should Socrates have taken the hemlock or should he have fled into exile? That, I have been proposing, is a question of what to do—of whether, if faced with his plight, to take the hemlock. This is a question, it seems, on which I, individually, can change my mind. Is it, I have been asking, a matter also on which you and I can agree or disagree with each other? To ask what Socrates "should" have done is to treat the question as open to discussion, as subject to accord and dispute by those in the conversation. Whether to do this, I have been proposing, is an issue of what discursive practices to enter into. Insofar as we find it helpful to join in thinking such questions through, taking each other's voices into our streams of thought, we have impetus to enter into such a practice. Insofar as we find each other's voices intrusive, as voices to be ejected from one's own thoughts, we each will find reason to retreat from such a practice. Retreat consists in forgoing those responses that constitute taking oneself to agree or disagree with what others are saying, by refusing to converse or think on that basis.

When we stop conversing on certain topics, it will normally be without settling the precise logical status of what we are doing, the possibilities of engagement and their limits. "I just can't talk to him and reason with him," our rough thoughts can go; "there's something perverse in his thinking—or is it me? He's in a different world; the things I find relevant he just doesn't!" My own way of trying to address such frustration and bafflement has been to ask what precise truths these expressions of frustration could be getting at. "Different people live in different worlds and have their different truths," we may be told. Someone else admires steadfastly the courage of his own convictions, dismissing all others as blind to the truth. Neither of these is the lesson to draw.

In successful realms of science, communities of inquiry develop a stance far more healthy and plausible than either of these, a stance toward knowledge and reliance on each other's judgments. Humanity has progressed far in constructing accounts of what puts a person in a good position to judge; conceptual coherence and a critical responsiveness to evidence loom large in this account. Not that scientists and scientifically informed outsiders have reached any high degree of precision in our epistemologies of science; not that science lacks deep-rooted controversies; not that there aren't branches of science and purported science that are pervaded by identifiable epistemic perversities. Still, highly sophisticated methods, for instance, of assessing medical data allow for a critical reliance both on one's own informed judgment and the informed judgments of others. Neither epistemic despair nor smug dogmatism belongs in these inquiries. Rather, the good scientist's implicit story fosters both a degree of self-assurance and a degree of modesty: it requires critical self-scrutiny, as well as critical heed to judgments of others.

Might we hope for the same kind of critical reliance on ourselves and on each other in questions of how to live? In Chapter 13 I claimed one real difference between the two areas of inquiry: in important realms of science, a deep vindication of our powers of correct judgment seems to be in the offing, whereas there is no such plausible prospect for questions of how to live. Why are we equipped to know what the world is like—or are we? Compare this question with the parallel one for how to live: why, we might ask, are we equipped to know how to live—or are we? About the world we can hope for an answer that is not trivially self-commending. About how to live we cannot, if I was right.

Apart from this major difference, however, questions of how things stand and questions of how to live run parallel in many dimensions. What we can say of the one kind of question we can, in many cases, say of the other. True, good science responds to evidence, and what evidence is to be had depends on reality, on what the world truly is like. An intricate network of pathways, though, leads from evidence to scientific judgments, and what to conclude depends not only on the evidence but on which modes of relying on it are valid, on plan-laden issues of how to respond to the evidence. How to live must of course also rest on evidence, and a plan-laden, epistemological gap likewise divides conclusions on how to live from their evidence. At this grossly abstract and unspecific level of analysis, the prospects for a self-critical reliance on ourselves and each other don't differ between scientific questions and questions of how to live. Of course, it in no way follows that a rigorous science of how to live is at hand. Even medicine is an art and not a science, as the lawyer's boilerplate runs, and the same goes all the more vastly for that most general art of all, the art of how to live. The prospects on which I am musing are not for a science-like rigor in thinking how best to live. Important facets of the question can perhaps be imparted rigor, but surely not all the issues that most vex us. We might still, though, emulate the virtues of good science in other regards in our inquiries on how to live. If we treat these questions as forming a genuine subject matter, open to agreement and disagreement, to better and worse ways of judging, then we will heed ourselves and heed each other, but with careful scrutiny of whether we have done what is needed to achieve good judgment.

How extensive a subject of how to live could there be? No deep vindication will be found for our claims to know how to live—and this, I admit, makes prospects for common inquiry more dicey for living than for scientific understanding. Nevertheless, I urge us to proceed with some tentative faith in each other's powers of judgment, with hope that we can engage one another on questions of how to live, that agreement and disagreement are possible on these matters, and that through joint inquiry we can progress from disagreement toward more agreement, and be the better for it. That is the faith built into our normative language. Many will urge the drawbacks of such a tentative faith—and if the predominant view favored it, I might myself be urging the drawbacks. Here, though, I'll extol.

We depend on intimate circles of friends with whom we can explore questions of how to live; none of us is good at thinking such questions through in isolation. Why, though, engage the thoughts of anyone remote in place, time, and outlook? Partly, of course, because we need urgently to think how unlike people from different traditions can live together in one world. Joint planning for living together hasn't been the topic of this book, since agreement on how to live if in each person's shoes might not, for anything I have shown, mean agreement on how to accommodate each other. In working our way to joint goals, though, it may help if we at least appreciate our diverse goals as worthy and reasonable, when we can. I want especially to stress, though, another reward that joint thinking on how to live can bring, the kind of insight and fellowship that discussing how to live in our different circumstances can foster. To gain these rewards, we must first distinguish clearly the question of what to do if like you from what to do if like me; we must fathom, both of us, the rich array of differences between your life with its problems and mine. If you and I succeed in this, we both can then learn about your life and about my own, and draw gain from exploring together how to lead your life and how to lead mine. Considerations that, as I learn, matter in your life may turn out to matter also in mine. Exploring these questions together, we can deepen our insights into differences between one person and another, and the ways these can bear on questions of what to pursue and what to value in life.

How best to live as you or as me might still be a pseudo-question, in that thinking jointly how to live has insufficient point. Nothing I know assures us that this is a question to treat as genuine. It may also, though, be a question we can coherently treat as open to inquiry together. I am urging we proceed with the hope that these are questions humanity can enrich itself by discussing.

That we should proceed with this hope is a plan-laden judgment, a judgment open to inquiry. My own word on this cannot be either the first or the last.

References

Aaquvist, L. 1973. "Modal Logic with Subjunctive Conditionals and Dispositional Predicates." *Journal of Philosophical Logic* 2: 1–76.

Adams, Ernest. 1975. *The Logic of Conditionals: An Application of Probability to Deductive Logic.* Dordrecht: D. Reidel.

Ayer, A. J. 1936. *Language, Truth and Logic* London: Victor Gollancz.

Baier, Kurt. 1958. *The Moral Point of View: A Rational Basis for Ethics.* Ithaca: Cornell University Press.

Barkow, Jerome H., L. Cosmides, and J. Tooby. 1992. *The Adapted Mind: Evolutionary Psychology and the Generation of Culture.* New York: Oxford University Press.

Blackburn, Simon. 1981. "Reply: Rule-Following and Moral Realism." In Steven H. Holtzman and Christopher M. Leich, eds., *Wittgenstein: To Follow a Rule,* 163–187. London: Routledge & Kegan Paul.

—— 1984. "Knowledge, Truth, and Reliability." *The Henrietta Hertz Lecture of the British Academy.* Cited as in Blackburn, *Essays* (1993), 35–51.

—— 1984. *Spreading the Word: Groundings in the Philosophy of Language.* Oxford: Clarendon Press.

—— 1985. "Errors and the Phenomenology of Value." In Ted Honderich, ed., *Morality and Objectivity: A Tribute to J. L. Mackie,* 1–22. London: Routledge & Kegan Paul.

—— 1988. "Attitudes and Contents." *Ethics* 98: 501–517. Cited as in Blackburn, *Essays* (1993), 182–197.

—— 1991. "Just Causes." *Philosophical Studies* 61: 3–17. Cited as in Blackburn, *Essays* (1993), 198–209.

—— 1991. "Reply to Sturgeon." *Philosophical Studies* 61: 39–42.

—— 1993. *Essays in Quasi-Realism.* Oxford: Oxford University Press.

—— 1993. "Gibbard on Normative Logic." In Enrique Villanueva, ed., *Philosophical Issues* 4: *Naturalism and Normativity,* 60–66. Atascadero, Calif.: Ridgeview.

———— 1993. "Realism: Quasi or Queasy." In Haldane and Wright, *Reality* (1993), 365–383.

———— 1996. "Blackburn Reviews Dworkin." James Dreier and David Estlund, eds. Brown Electronic Article Review Service. World Wide Web, *http://www.brown.edu/Departments/Philosophy/bears/homepage.html*, posted Nov. 11, 1996.

———— 1998. *Ruling Passions: A Theory of Practical Reason*. Oxford: Clarendon Press.

Boghossian, Paul. 1989. "The Rule-Following Considerations." *Mind* 98: 507–549.

Boyd, Richard N. 1988. "How to Be a Moral Realist." In Geoffrey Sayre-McCord, ed., *Essays on Moral Realism*, 187–228. Ithaca: Cornell University Press.

Brandom, Robert. 1994. *Making It Explicit*. Cambridge, Mass.: Harvard University Press.

Brandt, Richard. 1959. *Ethical Theory*. Englewood Cliffs, N.J.: Prentice Hall.

———— 1979. *A Theory of the Good and the Right*. Oxford: Clarendon Press.

Bratman, Michael. 1987. *Intention, Plans, and Practical Reason*. Cambridge, Mass.: Harvard University Press.

Brink, David. 1989. *Moral Realism and the Foundations of Ethics*. Cambridge, England: Cambridge University Press.

Chalmers, David. 1996. *The Conscious Mind*. New York: Oxford University Press.

Cohen, Joshua. 1997. "The Arc of the Moral Universe." *Philosophy and Public Affairs* 26(2): 91–134.

Darwall, Stephen L. 1997. "Reasons, Motives, and the Demands of Morality: An Introduction." In Darwall et al., *Moral Discourse* (1997), 305–312.

Darwall, S., A. Gibbard, and P. Railton, eds. 1997. *Moral Discourse and Practice: Some Philosophical Approaches*. New York: Oxford University Press.

Davidson, Donald. 1974. "On the Very Idea of a Conceptual Scheme." In *Inquiries into Truth and Interpretation*, 183–198. Oxford: Clarendon Press, 1984.

Davies, Martin, and Lloyd Humberstone. 1980. "Two Notions of Necessity." *Philosophical Studies* 38: 1–30.

Divers, John, and Alexander Miller. 1995. "Platitudes and Attitudes: A Minimalist Conception of Belief." *Analysis* 55(1): 37–44.

Dreier, James. 1996. "Expressivist Embeddings and Minimalist Truth." *Philosophical Studies* 83: 29–51.

———— 1999. "Transforming Expressivism." *Noûs* 33(4): 558–572.

Dworkin, Ronald. 1996. "Objectivity and Truth: You'd Better Believe It." *Philosophy and Public Affairs* 25: 87–139.

Ewing, A. C. 1939. "A Suggested Non-Naturalistic Analysis of Good." *Mind* 48: 1–22.

Field, Hartrey. 1994. "Disquotational Truth and Factually Defective Discourse." *Philosophical Review* 103: 405–452.

Firth, Roderick. 1952. "Ethical Absolutism and the Ideal Observer." *Philosophy and Phenomenological Research* 12: 317–45.

Foot, Philippa. 1959. "Moral Beliefs." *Proceedings of the Aristotelian Society* new ser. 59: 83–104.

Frankena, William. 1939. "The Naturalistic Fallacy." *Mind* 48: 464–477.

Frege, Gotlob. 1918. "Thought." In Michael Beaney, ed., *The Frege Reader*, 325–345. Oxford: Blackwell Publishers, 1997.

Geach, Peter. 1965. "Assertion." *Philosophical Review* 74: 449–465.

Gibbard, Allan. 1981. "Two Recent Theories of Conditionals." In W. L. Harper, R. Stalnaker, and G. Pearce, eds., *Ifs: Conditionals, Beliefs, Decision, Chance, and Time*, 211–247. Dordrecht, Holland: D. Reidel.

—— 1982. "Human Evolution and the Sense of Justice." *Midwest Studies in Philosophy* 7: 31–46.

—— 1986. "An Expressivistic Theory of Normative Discourse." *Ethics* 96: 472–485.

—— 1988. "Hare's Analysis of 'Ought' and Its Implications." In D. Seanor and N. Fotion, eds., *Hare and Critics*, 57–72. Oxford: Oxford University Press.

—— 1990. *Wise Choices, Apt Feelings: A Theory of Normative Judgment*. Cambridge, Mass.: Harvard University Press.

—— 1992. "Moral Concepts: Substance and Sentiment." In James E. Tomberlin, ed., *Philosophical Perspectives* 6: *Ethics*, 199–221. Atascadero, Calif.: Ridgeview.

—— 1992. "Thick Concepts and Warrant for Feelings." *Proceedings of the Aristotelian Society*, suppl. vol. 66: 267–283.

—— 1993. "Moral Concepts and Justified Feelings." In Brad Hooker, ed., *Rationality, Rules, and Utility: New Essays on the Moral Philosophy of Richard B. Brandt*, 81–95. Boulder: Westview Press.

—— 1993. "Reply to Blackburn." In Enrique Villanueva, ed., *Philosophical Issues* 4: *Naturalism and Normativity*, 67–73. Atascadero, Calif.: Ridgeview.

—— 1993. "Reply to Sinnott-Armstrong." *Philosophical Studies* 69: 315–327.

—— 1994. "Meaning and Normativity." In Enrique Villanueva, ed., *Philosophical Issues* 5: *Truth and Rationality*, 95–115. Atascadereo, Calif.: Ridgeview.

—— 1996. "Thought, Norms, and Discursive Practice: Commentary on Robert Brandom, *Making It Explicit*." *Philosophy and Phenomenological Research* 56: 699–717.

—— 1998. "Preference and Preferability." In C. Fehige, G. Meggle, and U. Wessels, eds., *Preferences*, 239–259. Berlin: de Gruyter.

—— 1999. "Morality as Consistency in Living: Korsgaard's Kantian Lectures." *Ethics* 110: 140–164.

—— 2003. "Reasons Thin and Thick." *Journal of Philosophy* 100: 288–304.

Gibbard, Allan, and William L. Harper. 1978. "Counterfactuals and Two Kinds of Expected Utility." In C. A. Hooker, J. J. Leach, and E. F. McClennen, eds., *Foundations and Applications of Decision Theory*, vol. 1, 125–162. Boston: D. Reidel.

Haldane, John, and Crispin Wright, eds. 1993. *Reality, Representation, and Projection*. Oxford: Oxford University Press.

Hale, Bob. 1993. "Can There Be a Logic of Attitudes?" In Haldane and Wright, *Reality* (1993), 337–363.

—— 1993. "Postscript." In Haldane and Wright, *Reality* (1993), 385–388.

Hare, R. M. 1970. "Meaning and Speech Acts." *Philosophical Review* 79: 3–24.

—— 1971. "Wanting: Some Pitfalls." *Practical Inferences*. London: Macmillan.

—— 1981. *Moral Thinking: Its Levels, Method, and Point*. Oxford: Clarendon Press.

—— 1988. "Comments." In D. Seanor and N. Fotion, eds., *Hare and Critics*, 199–293. Oxford: Oxford University Press.

Harman, Gilbert. 1977. *The Nature of Morality*. New York: Oxford University Press.

——— 1986. "Moral Explanations of Natural Facts—Can Moral Claims Be Tested against Reality?" *Southern Journal of Philosophy* 24, supp.: 57–68.

Hawthorne, John. 2002. "Practical Realism?" *Philosophy and Phenomenological Research* 64(1): 169–178.

Horwich, Paul. 1990, 1998. *Truth*. Oxford: Oxford University Press. (2d ed., 1998.)

——— 1993. "Gibbard's Theory of Norms." *Philosophy and Public Affairs* 22: 67–78.

——— 1994. "The Essence of Expressivism." *Analysis* 54: 19–20.

——— 1998. *Meaning*. Oxford: Clarendon Press.

Jackson, Frank. 1998. *From Metaphysics to Ethics: A Defense of Conceptual Analysis*. Oxford: Clarendon Press.

Jackson, Frank, Graham Oppy, and Michael Smith. 1994. "Minimalism and Truth Aptness." *Mind* 103: 287–302.

Jackson, Frank, and Philip Pettit. 1998. "A Problem for Expressivism." *Analysis* 58(4): 239–251.

Jeffrey, Richard. 1991. *Formal Logic: Its Scope and Limits*, 3d ed. New York: McGraw Hill.

Kamp, J. A. W. 1971. "Formal Properties of 'Now'." *Theoria* 37: 227–273.

Kim, Jaegwon. 1993. *Supervenience and Mind: Selected Philosophical Essays*. Cambridge, England: Cambridge University Press.

Korsgaard, Christine M. 1996. *The Sources of Normativity*. Cambridge, England: Cambridge University Press.

Kripke, Saul. 1972. "Naming and Necessity." In Donald Davidson and Gilbert Harman, eds., *Semantics of Natural Language*, 253–355. Dordrecht, Holland: Reidel. Also as *Naming and Necessity*. Cambridge, Mass.: Harvard University Press, 1980.

——— 1982. *Wittgenstein on Rules and Private Language*. Cambridge, Mass: Harvard University Press.

Lance, Mark, and John O'Leary-Hawthorne. 1997. *The Grammar of Meaning: Normativity and Semantic Discourse*. Cambridge, England: Cambridge University Press.

Lenman, James. 1999. "The Externalist and the Amoralist." *Philosophia* 27: 441–457.

Lewis, David. 1969. *Convention*. Cambridge, Mass.: Harvard University Press.

——— 1973. *Counterfactuals*. Cambridge, Mass.: Harvard University Press.

——— 1979. "Attitudes *De Dicto* and *De Se*." *Philosophical Review* 87: 513–543.

Mackie, J. L. 1977. *Ethics: Inventing Right and Wrong*. New York: Penguin.

McDowell, John. 1978. "Are Moral Judgments Hypothetical Imperatives?" *Proceedings of the Aristotelian Society*, supp. vol. 52: 13–29.

——— 1984. "Wittgenstein on Following a Rule." *Synthese* 58: 325–363.

Millar, Alan. 2002. "The Normativity of Meaning." In Anthony O'Hear, ed., *Logic, Thought and Language*, 57–73. Cambridge, England: Cambridge University Press.

Miller, Alexander, and John Divers. 1994. "Why Expressivists about Value Should Not Love Minimalism about Truth." *Analysis* 54: 12–19.

Moore, G. E. 1903. *Principia Ethica*. Cambridge, England: Cambridge University Press.

Nagel, Thomas. 1970. *The Possibility of Altruism*. Princeton: Princeton University Press.

——— 1986. *The View from Nowhere*. Oxford: Oxford University Press.

Nakhnikian, George. 1963. "On the Naturalistic Fallacy." In Hector-Neri Castañeda and George Nakhnikian, *Morality and the Language of Conduct*, 145–158. Detroit: Wayne State University Press.

Nozick, Robert. 1981. *Philosophical Explanations*. Cambridge, Mass.: Harvard University Press.

——— 1993. *The Nature of Rationality*. Princeton: Princeton University Press.

O'Leary-Hawthorne, John, and Huw Price. 1996. "How to Stand Up for Non-Cognitivists." *Australasian Journal of Philosophy* 74: 275–292.

Peacocke, Christopher. 1992. *A Study of Concepts*. Cambridge, Mass.: MIT Press.

Putnam, Hilary. 1975. "The Meaning of Meaning." In Keith Gunderson, ed., *Language, Mind and Knowledge: Minnesota Studies in the Philosophy of Science*, vol. 7, 131–193. Minneapolis: University of Minnesota Press.

Railton, Peter. 1986. "Moral Realism." *Philosophical Review* 95: 163–207.

——— 1993. "Non-Cognitivism about Rationality: Benefits, Costs, and an Alternative." In Enrique Villanueva, ed., *Philosophical Issues* 4: *Naturalism and Normativity*, 36–52. Atascadero, Calif.: Ridgeview.

Rosen, Gideon. 1998. "Blackburn's *Essays in Quasi-Realism*." *Noûs* 32(3): 386–405.

Savage, Leonard J. 1954. *The Foundations of Statistics*. New York: Wiley.

Sayre-McCord, Geoffrey. 1997. "'Good' on Twin Earth." *Philosophical Issues* 8: 267–292.

Scanlon, T. M. 1998. *What We Owe to Each Other*. Cambridge, Mass.: Harvard University Press.

Scheuler, G. F. 1988. "Modus Ponens and Moral Realism." *Ethics* 98: 492–500.

Searle, John. 1962. "Meaning and Speech Acts." *Philosophical Review* 71: 423–432.

Segerberg, K. 1973. "Two-Dimensional Modal Logic." *Journal of Philosophical Logic* 2: 77–96.

Sidgwick, Henry. 1907. *The Methods of Ethics*. 7th ed. London: Macmillan.

Smith, Michael. 1994. *The Moral Problem*. Oxford: Blackwell.

——— 1994. "Why Expressivists about Value Should Love Minimalism about Truth." *Analysis* 54: 12–19.

Sperber, Dan, and Dierdre Wilson. 1986, 1995. *Relevance: Communication and Cognition*. Oxford: Oxford University Press.

Stalnaker, Robert C. 1968. "A Theory of Conditionals." *Studies in Logical Theory*, *American Philosophical Quaterly* Monograph Series 2.

——— 1978. "Assertion." In Peter Cole, ed., *Syntax and Semantics: Pragmatics*, 315–332. New York: Academic Press. Also in Stalnaker, *Context and Content*. Oxford: Oxford University Press, 1999.

Stevenson, Charles L. 1937. "The Emotive Theory of Ethical Terms." *Mind* 46: 14–31.

——— 1944. *Ethics and Language*. New Haven: Yale University Press.

——— 1963. *Facts and Values*. New Haven: Yale University Press.

Stratton-Lake, Philip, ed. 2002. *Ethical Intuitionism: Re-evaluations*. Oxford: Clarendon Press.

Strawson, P. F. 1949. "Ethical Intuitionism." *Philosophy* 24: 23–33.

——— 1950. "On Referring." *Mind* 59: 320–344.

Sturgeon, Nicholas L. 1985. "Moral Explanations." In David Copp and David

Zimmerman, eds., *Morality, Reason, and Truth*, 49–78. Totowa, N.J.: Rowman & Allanheld.

——— 1986. "Harman on Moral Explanations of Natural Facts." *Southern Journal of Philosophy* 24, supp.: 69–78.

——— 1986. "What Difference Does It Make Whether Moral Realism Is True?" *Southern Journal of Philosophy* 24, supp.: 115–141.

——— 1991. "Contents and Causes: A Reply to Blackburn." *Philosophical Studies* 61: 19–37.

——— 1992. "Nonmoral Explanations." In James E. Tomberlin, ed., *Philosophical Perspectives* 6: *Ethics*, 97–117. Atascadero, Calif.: Ridgeview.

Svavarsdóttir, Sigrún. 1999. "Moral Cognitivism and Motivation." *Philosophical Review* 108: 161–219.

Tooby, John, and Leda Cosmides. 1992. "The Psychological Foundations of Culture." In Barkow et al., *The Adapted Mind* (1992), 19–136.

Unwin, Nicholas. 2001. "Norms and Negation: A Problem for Gibbard's Logic." *Philosophical Quarterly* 51, no. 202 (January): 60–75.

Van Fraassen, B. A. C. 1977. "The Only Necessity Is Verbal Necessity." *Journal of Philosophy* 74: 71–85.

Van Roojen, Mark. 1996. "Expressivism and Irrationality." *Philosophical Review* 105: 311–335.

Walton, Kendall L. 1990. *Mimesis as Make-Believe: On the Foundations of the Representational Arts*. Cambridge, Mass.: Harvard University Press.

Williams, Bernard. 1985. *Ethics and the Limits of Philosophy*. Cambridge, Mass.: Harvard University Press.

Wittgenstein, Ludwig. 1953. *Philosophical Investigations (Philosophische Untersuchungen)*. New York: Macmillan.

Wright, Crispin. 1986. *Realism, Meaning and Truth*. Oxford: Blackwell.

——— 1992. *Truth and Objectivity*. Cambridge, Mass.: Harvard University Press.

Zajonc, R. B. 1980. "Feeling and Thinking: Preferences Need No Inferences." *American Psychologist* 35: 151–175.

Index